W9-AJL-978

Fle
pb

THE THREE
STOOGES™

AMALGAMATED MORONS
TO
AMERICAN iCONS

Broadway Books
New York

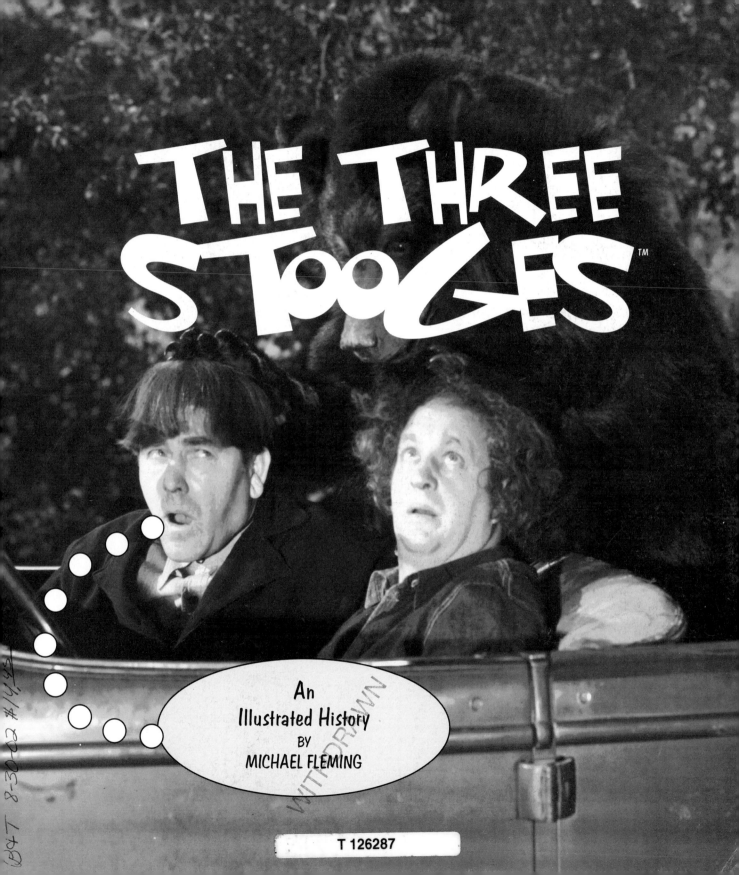

THE THREE STOOGES™

An
Illustrated History
BY
MICHAEL FLEMING

A hardcover edition of this book was originally published in 1999
by Doubleday, a division of Random House, Inc. It is here reprinted
by arrangement with Doubleday.

Broadway Books titles may be purchased for business or promotional use or for special sales. For information, please
write to: Special Markets Department, Random House, Inc., 280 Park Avenue, New York, NY 10017.

PRINTED IN THE UNITED STATES OF AMERICA

BROADWAY BOOKS and its logo, a letter B bisected on the diagonal, are trademarks of Broadway Books,
a division of Random House, Inc.

Visit our website at www.broadwaybooks.com

First Broadway Books trade paperback edition published 2002

Designed by Terry Karydes
Illustration (part three) by Christian Engel
Interior photographs courtesy of C3 Entertainment, Inc.

The Library of Congress has cataloged the Doubleday hardcover as follows:

Fleming, Michael, 1960–
The Three Stooges: an illustrated history: Amalgamated
Morons to American icons / by Michael Fleming. — 1st ed.
p.   cm.
Includes index.
1. Three Stooges (Comedy team) 2. Comedians—United States Biography.
3. Motion picture actors and actresses—United States Biography.   I. Title.
PN1995.9.T5 F585 1999
791.43′028′092273—dc21
[B]   99-31113   CIP

ISBN 0-7679-0556-3

1   3   5   7   9   10   8   6   4   2

This book is dedicated to my children,
Stephanie, Ryan, and Jamie;
to my wife, Anna, who lights my way;
and to my mother, Mary, for convincing me early on
that nothing is impossible if you are willing to work hard enough to achieve it.

CONTENTS

FOREWORD BY
MEL GIBSON

ACCORDING TO THE WRITER OF THIS BOOK, i SEEM TO HAVE BECOME AN UNWITTING TORCH CARRIER FOR THE MEMORY OF THE THREE STOOGES. iN TRUTH, AND LiKE THE MiNDSET THE STOOGES DiSPLAYED iN THEiR SHORTS, THERE WASN'T A LOT OF THOUGHT PUT iNTO THiS. iT'S NOT LiKE i SET OUT TO TURN A FEW OF MY MOViES iNTO STOOGES HOMAGES. iT'S JUST THAT SOME OF THE FiLMS i'VE MADE OVER THE YEARS, FROM THE MAD MAX TO THE LETHAL WEAPON SERiES, HAD WELL-ORCHESTRATED, OVER-THE-TOP SCENES WHERE THERE WAS HEAVY EQUIPMENT AND SOMEBODY GETTiNG BRAiNED PRETTY GOOD.

Inevitably, they always made me think of the Three Stooges.

In *Lethal Weapon,* there's the scene in which my character, Martin Riggs, goes undercover, and, unarmed, has to appear insane in order to arrest three guys who *are* armed. Now, we're about to shoot the scene and I see these three guys standing there and I think of Moe, Larry, and Curly. One of them's cute and chubby, like Curly;

another guy's kind of dumb, like Larry; and then there's the Moe character, who speaks to me and is a bit meaner.

I figure if my character's supposed to be crazy and anything goes, why not take them down with some eye poking and face slaps? I asked the director, Dick Donner, if I could do it. Donner's a TV junkie who was also a Stooges fan, and he says yes. It was something we just worked out on the set on the spur of the moment. It worked, and the Stooges became part of the fabric of Riggs, this haunted insomniac who'd certainly find the Stooges on some station in his all-night channel surfing. It became one of the things that stamped Riggs as fun-loving, though a bit combustible, out of his mind, and capable of Stoogelike mayhem. Riggs would love the Stooges.

I had the same instinct on the *Mad Max* films, which reminded me most of all of the Stooges. That's because George Miller, who directed the trilogy, is a real specialist in setting up Rube Goldberg–type sequences that involve heavy equipment and have a domino effect that usually ends in tragedy. I was just commenting on what was there and telling him that these felt like Stooges routines. But George surprised me. He told me that as a little kid he had nightmares about Moe, that Moe represented everything he was afraid of. The thought of this director being haunted as a child by this Stooge who was barely five feet on his tip-toes was absolutely hilarious to me. But what I felt was actually frightening about the Stooges was the thought of the guys who actually wrote these shorts and motivated those three idiots. Those guys who sat around and came up with these cruel punishments, thinking they would be funny.

People have very different feelings about the Stooges. Women, well, it's practically a gender distinction. Along with "capable of bearing children," a general characterization of a woman is that she must hate the Stooges and be absolutely baffled why her husband laughs like an idiot while watching Curly strip the teeth off a tree saw when it's run across his nubby cranium; or Larry wince as Moe tears chunks of the little hair he has left from Larry's head; or Moe crash through the table he's standing on until Curly saws it straight through.

For me, there has never been any mixed feeling about the Stooges. I've always loved them. I first remember watching them when I was five or six years old in New York, before my dad moved us to Australia. There was this guy with the cop's outfit, Joe Bolton, who introduced them, and I remember being completely fascinated by the whole thing. These guys bonking each other with a crowbar. My brothers and I laughed our asses off, and when we'd hear that ridiculous theme song that sounded like birds chirping, we'd run like it was the ice cream truck. I don't know quite why we liked it so much. It's your basic lowbrow humor, and yet I find it immensely pleasing in some primal way.

As a parent, I'm careful to remind my kids not to try those moves at home. When I was a kid, my brother Donal, who was two years younger than I, wasn't as lucky. I actually did the Stooges things to him. Once, I said, "Hey, look at me and don't close your eyes, no matter what I do." He does it, Donal standing there with that childlike trust and reverence for his older brother.

And I poked him right in the eyes. I mean, really a good one, fingers right in there, one that would make Moe proud. And he's just in shock, moaning "Owww, owww," holding his eyes. By now, I'm trying to quiet him, saying shut up, shut up, it'll be okay. Soon, my mother picks up on what happened, and I get a nice whap under the jaw. It was one of those Pavlovian experiences where I learned that if you poke out your brother's eyes, you are going to experience immediate pain yourself. And also, naturally, you can hurt your brother.

The Stooges inspired many clever ways to dispense punishment, some of the best involving heavy, lethal-looking plumbing equipment. That was a disciplinary staple of the shorts that starred Curly, who was easily my favorite Stooge. To me, Curly was magnetic, having something that none of the others had—an instinctive ability to make you laugh on command. Maybe it was his innocent, childlike appearance, the way he looked and sounded.

Whatever it was, he was the most watchable and funny. My kids love the Curly shorts, and my son Milo, who's eight, just thinks they're the greatest. We watch them all the time.

It's hard to figure out why the Stooges have lasted so long. They are certainly different from the Marx Brothers, whose movies I enjoy just as much or more. You had to be thinking a little harder when watching the Marx Brothers; the dialogue was just so much sharper.

The Stooges, on the other hand, had this raw immediacy, this primal humor that hits you right in the gut. And what's wrong with that, letting your IQ take a holiday every now and then?

Perhaps the secret of understanding the humor of the Stooges is the almost universal understanding of what it's like to get hit in the head. I know what it's like to step on a rake and get nailed in the face because I've done that.

As a kid I can distinctly remember being in the kitchen, looking for cookies. After opening the low cupboard and not finding them, I hopped up on the top counter to look in those cabinets, then jumped back down to the floor. Trouble was, I had forgotten to shut the bottom cabinet door, and my legs weren't long enough to hit the floor. I landed right on top of the door, right on my unmentionables. It was a real Stooge moment. We all have them, where we're in so much pain that we can't scream or cry. We can just walk around, clutching our damaged goods.

As for the writer of this book, the first time I met him was for a cup of coffee while I was in Manhattan to open *Braveheart*, the film about the Scottish folk hero William Wallace, which I directed a few years ago. When he showed up, telling me how much he liked the film, it was hard not to notice the rather large gauze bandage on his forehead, or that blood had pooled under the skin in the area around his eyes. Two days prior, he confessed, he'd had a workout mishap on a roman chair, a contraption where you hook your legs under an adjustable piece of metal held fast by a pin. All your body weight is concentrated on that piece of metal as you lean back. The author forgot to insert the pin and fell back onto the floor. That was nothing, because the cast-iron metal foot pad went flying in the air in a perfect arc and came to rest dead center on his forehead. Twenty-five stitches later, he was that rarity, an Irish guy with a facial scar. Suffice it to say, he's got the battle scars that prove an innate understanding of stoogery.

PROLOGUE

MANY TIMES IN STOOGE SHORTS, CURLY HOWARD WAS FACED WITH EXECUTION AND GIVEN A CHOICE BETWEEN BEING BURNED AT THE STAKE OR BEHEADED. HE'D CHOOSE THE FORMER, REASONING THAT "A HOT STAKE IS BETTER THAN A COLD CHOP." WELL, THE STOOGE STORY PROVED TO BE A HOT ONE, BUT IT LEFT AN INCREDIBLY COLD TRAIL. AFTER ALL, THE STOOGE STORY BEGINS ONSTAGE NEARLY EIGHTY YEARS AGO, AND THE TROUPE MEMBERS ARE LONG DEAD.

Several resources were used to bring Moe Howard, Larry Fine, and Shemp Howard to life in this book through quoted material. Some of this material was derived from testimony that Moe Howard gave during a 1961 lawsuit with the heirs of his brother Jerome, which reads like a Stooge history. Other quotations were taken from notes the Stooges furnished about their lives for studio biographies, and some observations from Fine were gleaned from *Stroke of Luck,* the memoirs he wrote after his stroke. C3 Entertainment, Inc., a partner in this venture, owns all rights.

Other quotes are from newspaper accounts of the period.

Several books from the period also proved helpful in bringing to life otherwise long-forgotten moments in Hollywood history. Those include *King Cohn*, written by Bob Thomas about Columbia Pictures chairman Harry Cohn; *The Great Movie Shorts*, by Leonard Maltin; *When the Stars Went to War: Hollywood and World War II*, by Roy Hoopes; and *Being the Three Stooges: The White Brothers*, by David Bruskin.

Numerous people who were intimately familiar with the Stooges and their history were generous beyond the call of duty. They include director Edward Bernds, Jules White's brother Sam White, Joe DeRita's widow, Jean DeRita, actress Diana Darrin, and film historian Leonard Maltin. A special debt of gratitude goes to Moe's daughter, Joan Howard Maurer. Aside from her collection of original scripts, Stooge memorabilia, and a complete scrapbook of news clippings, Maurer is easily the most knowledgeable Stooge historian alive, as evidenced by her own literary efforts that include writing *The Three Stooges Scrapbook* with Jeff and Greg Lenburg. Maurer was generous in sharing that knowledge and her own reminiscences for this book.

A special thank-you to the folks at Doubleday, namely Patricia Mulcahy, Siobhan Adcock, Jennifer Griffin, and Denell Downum, for making this book a reality. And thanks to Colleen Columbia for clerical assistance and Linda Lee for research.

THE THREE
STOOGES™

PART ONE

CHAPTER ONE

A STOOGE IS BORN IN BROOKLYN

Jennie and Solomon Gorovitz, parents of Moe, Curly, and Shemp.
The pair were second cousins, which Moe once blamed for
their sons' nuttiness.

THE PATH THAT WOULD LEAD THE THREE STOOGES TO A TWENTY-FOUR-YEAR STAY ON THE COLUMBIA LOT TRACES BACK TO THE TURN-OF-THE-CENTURY BROOKLYN NEIGHBORHOOD WHERE MOE, SHEMP, AND JEROME HORWITZ GREW UP—NOT MUCH MORE THAN A PIE THROW AWAY FROM A NEIGHBORHOOD RAPSCALLION NAMED CHARLES ERNEST LEE NASH, THE TRANSPLANTED TEXAN WHO WOULD CHANGE HIS NAME TO TED HEALY AND CHANGE THE FACE OF SHOW BUSINESS BY TRANSFORMING THE HORWITZ BOYS INTO MOVIEDOM'S MOST FAMOUS MORONS.

The story begins with Solomon and Jennie Gorovitz, second cousins who fell in love, married, and fled Lithuania because of an influx of Russian troops who did not take kindly to Jews. They immigrated to the United States eager for a new life. They wound up with a new name as well. Not an uncommon occurrence in the processing of immigrants during the rush to emigrate, a mistake was made in their naturalization papers. By the time they settled in a poor section of Brooklyn, the name on their mailbox was Horwitz.

Jennie became a real estate agent and developed a real flair for selling properties even though she could barely speak English. Solomon was a very religious man who worked part-time as a fabric cutter but was often unemployed. Living sparingly in a working-class neighborhood, Jennie bore five sons.

Their first son, Irving, arrived in 1891, followed by Benjamin. Both would eventually go into insurance. Then Solomon and Jennie got on a creative hot streak. First came Samuel, who became known as Shemp right from childhood, a nickname resulting from his mother's inability to pronounce his real name. Shemp arrived in 1895, and Moses (Moe) came two years later. Jerome arrived in 1903. The man who would come to fame as Curly was called Babe during his child-hood, a family nickname that stuck with him until he died. Moe used the moniker in conversation and even in business letters he wrote his brother.

Though Curly would go on to make the most fetching femme during the not uncommon Stooge drag forays, Moses was the child who bore the brunt of Jennie's desperation for a girl.

"From the time I was able to go to school or, in fact, walk, my mother used my head—hair, rather that is—to make these cigar curls, which I had hanging down on my head from the time I was four years of age until I was eleven," Moe later recalled. "And I went to school that way and fought my way to school, fought in school and fought my way home, until a buddy of mine said, 'I'm sick and tired of fighting with you on account of your hair. I think we ought to do something about it.' I went to this boy's home, used his mother's scissors, cut the whole thing off." The result, he said, was a close cousin to the upside-down-soup-bowl cut he'd sport through-out his career.

Thanks mainly to Jennie's burgeoning success in brokering and later buying and selling proper-ties, the Horwitz family began to prosper. They moved to the more upscale Bath Beach section of Brooklyn (now Bensonhurst). Jennie allowed herself to dream the ultimate dream of an immi-grant: that her sons would go on to be well-edu-cated professionals. The first two achieved that success, but as for the others, she'd have to settle for children who sometimes masqueraded as well-educated professionals.

Any hopes she had that the three younger sons would become doctors or lawyers were quickly dispelled as Moses and Shemp developed disdain for the classroom and fell in love with show business. Babe, who tagged along with his brothers and was happy doing whatever they did, followed suit.

Moe was by all accounts an intelligent lad but had major problems with attendance and dedica-tion. Moe recalled "attending several schools and being tossed out of them regularly. I attended P.S. 128 in Bath Beach, P.S. 101, and P.S. 163. I went to Erasmus Hall High School for two months, and they asked me if I wouldn't leave the premises and make it easier for the rest of the children, as I was a very disturbing influence."

The very behavior that would earn him a liv-ing caused nothing but trouble in school. "Fri-days, we'd have written tests, and I was quite bright and finished tests much earlier than the others, and during the scratching of the other children's pens, I would release an Indian war whoop the likes of which no school had ever heard," Moe once wrote. "I'd spend half of my school days in cloak rooms, under a teacher's desk, and in the principal's office. My grades were excellent, my deportment was atrocious."

This kind of irresponsibility seems highly uncharacteristic for the man who would become the leader of the Three Stooges, handling all of its finances, setting up the live stage tours, and accounting for every penny the act made. But he picked up those accounting skills later out of necessity, and for the most part, school held little for him. He stayed just long enough to find his calling when he was introduced to drama. Once focused on that, the boy became a dedicated student, single-minded in his pursuit to become an actor. He credited his sixth- through eighth-grade teacher, Miss Lillian Duffy, for prodding him into theater.

"I dramatized, directed, and worked in *The Story of Nathan Hale,* after which I constantly played in school productions," Moe recalled. After playing a Hessian general in the play, acting became his obsession. "I worked in *Pinafore,* I put on and played in a Pinero play called *The Matrimonial Agency,* and put on and directed plays in grade schools and in high grades." He also directed "mock fights," dances that featured comic choreographed bouts, a good introduction for his later comedy. All the while, he was encouraged by his mentoring teacher. But even she couldn't curb his wild side.

"My attendance record was more atrocious than my deportment," Moe admitted. Too many days were spent playing hooky in the dime-seat sections of live theater, then called the 10-20-30 melodramas for the price of seats in the theater. But Moe was hardly a screwup. Indeed, he was riveted by the process of acting, and while Shemp and Curly became far more animated comic presences, Moe was always the best-trained and most skilled actor in the family.

Watching such obscure plays as *Milkie the Sewing Machine Girl, St. Elmo, 10 Nights in a Barroom, The Old Homestead,* and *The Two Orphans,* he adopted theater as his classroom. And his attention never wavered. "I would select a character from the first act and follow him through the entire play, oblivious to all others," Moe recalled. "I had a tremendous desire to play these parts which, in later years, I did. I played every one of these parts for two seasons on a showboat up and down the Mississippi."

He left home in 1914 at the age of fifteen and would never return to school. His dream took him to the banks of the Mississippi River, where he scammed his way into the theater company of a showboat called the *Sunflower.* He began by doing odd jobs but got the baptism-by-fire training given by the live theater. Soon he was playing all kinds of roles, even sixty- and seventy-year-old characters. Shakespeare, blackface, Moe Horwitz took any role he could get.

Shemp, like his younger brother Moe, was much better at creating mischief than getting good grades. A chronic complainer and prankster who later became famous for his hypochondria and fear of, well, everything, Shemp caught the acting bug from his brother. He'd team with Moe to put on plays and comedy routines. They dragged along their little brother, Babe, who would inevitably wind up the butt of their jokes.

Shemp and Moe were very close, and Moe's older brother was shocked that he was running away to Mississippi, though there's little sign that Moe's parents shared his concern.

"It began during the summer," said Moe's daughter, Joan. "Having parents who were brought up in Europe, they were a different animal. His mother was bright but couldn't speak English well, and his father was into his religion. I think that with five kids to look after—and my dad next to youngest—that at that point they probably didn't pay much attention. Not that she didn't love her sons. The only one nervous about him leaving for Mississippi was Shemp, and maybe he was jealous because he didn't have the courage to go himself. Shemp was a worrywart."

After a couple of seasons on the boat, Moe

Healy and the boys. They were his foils—meaning he slapped them around the stage and underpaid them. But he also taught them how to be stooges.

rejoined his brothers, and they worked on their routines around the neighborhood and became fixtures on the Coney Island boardwalk, hamming it up for their pals and passersby. It was there that they became friendly with a mischievous lad named Charles Ernest Lee Nash, who was later to take the stage name of Ted Healy. The Horwitz boys often camped out in a tent owned by Nash, who later acknowledged they would use the lack of parental authority to terrorize the neighborhood by stealing bread and milk deliveries.

Nash set the tone for the subsequent relationship between himself and the Horwitzes when he left Moe to be collared by a cop while Nash himself dashed off to safety—even though it was Nash who pulled the prank Moe would pay for.

"I knew, at that moment, I was destined to become a Ted Healy stooge," Moe said in the March 1934 issue of *Shadowplay* magazine. "For it was then I learned to take it."

CHAPTER TWO

MOE AND SHEMP BECOME ACCIDENTAL STOOGES

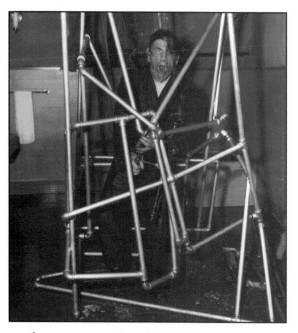

Shemp re-creates a classic Curly plumbing mishap in the
1949 short Vagabond Loafers.

MOE HAD GOTTEN A COMPLETE EDUCATION IN MISSIS-
SIPPI, PLAYING COMEDY AND STRAIGHT ROLES IN
EQUAL DOSES. BY 1921 HE'D BLOOMED PHYSICALLY TO
THE PROPORTIONS OF FIVE FEET FOUR INCHES TALL AND
146 POUNDS, AND MOVED TO PENNSYLVANIA, WHERE HE
TOOK UP WITH THE MARGUERITE BRYANT PLAYERS, A
DRAMATIC STOCK COMPANY. HE ACTED IN TWO PLAYS
PER WEEK, WITH SUMMER PERFORMANCES AT OAKFORD
PARK IN JEANNETTE, PENNSYLVANIA. THERE, MOE'S DRA-
MATIC FORAYS INCLUDED SHAKESPEARE.

It was a repeat of all the plays I had seen as a boy and had the delight of playing the very characters I had selected as a boy," he recalled. "The names of a lot of these plays meant nothing, because they were pirated and played under different titles, to escape paying royalties. For instance, the wonderful play *The Misleading Lady* was called *The Nutmeg Match*. Others that were public domain such as *The Two Orphans, Ten Nights in a Barroom*, held their original titles."

That culminated in a run for more than a year of Margaret Mayo's *Baby Mine,* in which Moe played the comic foil through 1921.

Shemp, meanwhile, set about to find honest work after leaving school. He operated a novelty shop. He became an apprentice plumber. That career ended when he burned himself with hot solder while joining pipe fittings. While plumbing stoogery would be commonplace later on, Shemp had had enough.

"I guess I was tender at that age," Shemp said later. "Since then, I've taken worse punishment as a slapstick comedian."

While Moe pursued stage drama, Shemp veered into vaudeville.

"Many years ago he did a vaudeville act for a short period of time, where he played straight to a fellow who played what we termed then 'Jew comedian,'" Moe later recalled. "We used to call him a 'Hebrew comedian.' I don't like to use that word because I think it is not nice. In those days that's what was used."

Aside from his goofy looks, Shemp was a talented comic, and he dragged his more serious brother into the laugh racket. Together they worked up a blackface act and even got to do some silent-film work. The brothers starred with Hall of Fame baseball player Honus Wagner in a series of twelve two-reel silent sports comedies, which they filmed outside Pittsburgh. The result: it's a good thing Wagner could hit a curveball. He won five batting titles for Pittsburgh but was not Oscar material.

"I think," said Moe, "that perhaps they made banjo picks out of the film."

Moe and Shemp began working together on the vaudeville circuit in 1923, though that turned out about as well as had their film work. Legend has it that in their first foray, they appeared at the end of a bill, got not a single laugh, and suffered the indignity of watching the crowd walk out during their routine. It grew worse when they found out that's why they were hired—to clear the room of stragglers to make way for the next group of paying customers.

But they were learning. They'd changed their last name to the less ethnic Howard. Moe himself described that early work as "not good but loud. We held the record of that period because in those early days of vaudeville, the manager in the contract had the right to cancel any act after the first performance. And we played seven theaters in one week, which means we were thrown out after the first performance each time at each theater. Due to that clause in the contract, there came a very well known saying from superstitious actors—and weren't we all—never to send your laundry out until after the first show." It was a tradition Moe would adhere to throughout his entire career.

The Howard brothers' fortunes soon changed for the better. It began when they noticed that

their old pal Healy was top-lining a stage act of his own. The family is still divided over whether it was Shemp or Moe who first became a member of Healy's troupe, but they are consistent about the circumstances.

It happened one fateful night at a Brooklyn vaudeville house.

Healy was in a jam because the second in his act, an acrobat, had tired of having cold water poured on him and quit in a huff. Moe, who apparently was playing in a stock company directly across the street at the time and was between acts, was persuaded by Healy to go AWOL from his show and replace the defector. Moe took the dousing, his baptism into stoogery. Moe claimed several times that he was the first to join Healy, followed by Shemp. But even Moe's daughter, Joan, feels that the order could have been reversed or that the two could have joined Healy during the same performance.

In any case, Shemp became part of the act when Healy spied him in the audience and coaxed him to participate. Shemp heckled him, then came onstage, much to the amusement of the crowd. The improvisation between the heckling Shemp and the slapping Healy left the audience in stitches.

They knew they were onto something, and Healy immediately made Shemp and Moe members of his team.

Healy, the roguishly charming Irishman, had grown to more than six feet tall, and by the time Moe and Shemp saw him again, had gotten married and had become an established stage presence. Healy began his stage career doing burlesque, then performed a single in blackface, doing passable imitations of Eddie Cantor, Ed Wynn, and Al Jol-

Healy's first wife, Betty Braun, who was part of the early Stooge stage act. Though divorced, she never stopped loving Healy, and when he was killed after a bar fight, it was she who pressed for police investigation.

son. He married dancer Betty Braun in 1922, and they became partners in an act that caught on with the Keith Theater in Jersey City, landing a contract for forty-six weeks. Shortly after that, Healy had the idea to add four people to the act, for the purpose of being his stooges.

Joining Healy was an easy choice at the time. The boys were still finding their way. And their pal seemed to know what he was doing. So they didn't mind the fact that they were trading an unsuccessful partnership for an arrangement where they were suddenly employees of their old friend.

The term "stooge" at that time was condescending parlance for Healy's foils. His comedy was a mix of vaudeville song and dance, but the highlight came when Healy orchestrated mayhem between himself and his stooges. He'd play straight man, and when his lackeys delivered dumb answers, he'd dish out a beating consisting of slaps and eye pokes. For instance, the question "Do you know Abraham Lincoln?" would be met with

"Nice to meet you" and a crisp slap from Healy. The slaps outweighed the jokes, and Healy hit them hard, the theory being that you wanted the person sitting in the back row to hear the blows.

"I defy anyone to describe the performance in words," said Moe. "This is something that would have to be seen, because it was mostly sight comedy. Here and there there was a joke. Well, it is not so much a joke as it is an incident. When we stepped onto the stage, we handed Ted a note which he read. 'This will introduce three charming gentlemen. They are very talented. They sing, dance, female impersonations, acrobats; in fact, they are the best act of this kind in the nation. Very truly yours.' And he said, 'Who wrote this?' And I would say, 'I did.' And that caused a complete smack right across the three faces, a sweeping smack."

When Moe joined Healy in 1924, he was forced to put his dramatic aspirations on hold. There were other concerns involved in being a stooge. Like hairstyle. Moe needed a funny one, and recalled the bowl cut he'd given himself in front of his friends at the age of eleven.

"I went to this boy's home, used his mother's scissors, cut the whole thing off. When I looked into the mirror, the next time I saw myself like that was with Ted Healy," said Moe. "I recalled what I looked like, and that's the way I wore my hair."

Shemp's was a greasy middle-of-the-road hair part which was a funnier comic tool than that of his brother. The hair was long and would fly forward over his face after a particularly spirited beating.

Hitching their wagon to Healy's burgeoning career, the Howard brothers were on their way.

CHAPTER THREE

A FINE FIND

Healy and his Stooges: bad hair, big dreams.

WORKING FOR HEALY WAS HARDLY AN E-TICKET TO THE BIG TIME. THE WORK WAS CATCH-AS-CATCH-CAN. HEALY PAID LOUSY AND SLAPPED HARD. BUT AT THE TIME, THE HOWARDS WERE GRATEFUL TO BE WORKING. AND LEARNING.

On its first incarnation, the act was billed "Ted and Betty Healy." Also on the card was a trio of dancers. And the stooges.

"Ted Healy at the time did two acts on the same vaudeville bill," said Moe. "He would do the act with his wife and the dancers, and then he would proceed to call an assistant from the audience, and we would go up and do the remaining portion." Though the ensuing comedy seemed impromptu, much of it was scripted.

"Ted Healy developed the dialogue, but as to gestures and personalities, that was left to ourselves. We would decide that we were going to use a joke, which Ted Healy would start, and answers would come from either I or Shemp or both. As long as we had the body of the joke itself, the terminology used or the words used made no difference, as long as the punch line was there."

Healy owned the act, which at the time seemed to be fine with the Howards. They were treated like employees, and when Healy would get paid $1,000 or more for a week's work, he'd give Moe and Shemp $100 each.

A year later, a third stooge was added to the act. His name was Moody Braun, and he was Betty Healy's brother. Healy finally relented to her urging that her brother be given a job. Brotherly love didn't last long.

"I don't mean this detrimentally to the person himself, but he was extremely incompetent as a performer," Moe recalled.

Braun did show Healy and the Howards that there was strength in numbers. Though they were still experimenting with material, it was clear the act benefited from the presence of a third stooge. The act moved around the country and might be called anything from Ted Healy and the Lost Soles, to Ted Healy and His Racketeers, to Ted Healy and His Gang, to Ted Healy and His Three Southern Gentlemen. The formula was so herky-jerky, Moe recalled, that at one appearance at the Palace Theatre, Healy used nine stooges onstage at the same time.

All that changed during a performance in 1925 at Chicago's Marigold Gardens when Healy and the Howards watched a nutty and wild-haired performer doing a Russian dance in tails and high hat while playing a fiddle. Healy and the Howards rushed backstage to meet him, knowing they'd found the final missing piece to their act.

His name was Larry Fine, a likable, easygoing Philadelphian. Follically challenged even then, his

Young Stooges sing, likely off-key.

proximity to the crib, Feinberg was testing the gold qualities of jewelry with a chemical called oxalic acid, a powerful mixture that turns phony gold green or eats through it. It has the latter effect on human skin.

Larry awoke, reached through the crib, and grabbed the bottle. His father pulled it away at the same time, not noticing that some of the liquid had splashed onto his son's arm. When his mother returned, she undressed the boy. By that time, the acid had eaten away part of his arm. It was so serious that the hospital wanted to amputate. His father would have none of it and found a doctor who grafted skin from the child's leg over the wound.

As part of his therapy, Larry was given violin lessons to strengthen his arm, and he became an accomplished musician. He also took up boxing during his formative years, primarily to further strengthen his arm.

As was the case with the violin, Feinberg was a quick study. After training alongside such fighters as featherweight champion Benny Bass, he began taking amateur fights as a teen, showing promise. Until his father found out.

Clearly feeling that his son's future was in music, the elder Feinberg tracked him down to a gym. After watching his son win by early knockout, Feinberg cornered the youth and threatened to clean his clock. The boxing career was over, though learning to take a punch would certainly come in handy when he became a human punching bag for Healy and later Moe.

Despite playing violin in school bands and

scalp situation lent itself to his trademark hairstyle which would later be ripped off by Bozo the Clown. It was a look decided upon during their very first meeting.

"When we came into his dressing room, he was at the point where he had wet his hair, prepared for combing, and when he saw us, he neglected to comb his hair back, and as it kept drying, it started standing up in curls all over the top of his head," Moe recalled. "So Ted Healy said, 'If you will wear your hair that way, forget the tails and fiddle, you can join with us at $100 per week.' Larry said, 'For a hundred, I'll forget everything.' "

Born October 5, 1906, in Philadelphia, Lawrence Feinberg was the son of jeweler Joseph Feinberg and his wife, Fanny Lieberman. His prowess as a violinist was the result of a terrible accident that scarred the youngster for many years. One night, while his mother was out at the movies, his father baby-sat the toddler. In close

Early Stoogery.

Nixon's Grand, Allegheny, and other theaters in Philadelphia. He met Gus Edwards, who with his brother, Ben, needed a replacement for an act called the Newsboy Sextette. Larry played violin, danced, and did Jewish dialect. He played twelve weeks in Philadelphia, twenty weeks in New York, and fifteen in Boston, joining Eddie Cantor, Walter Winchell, George Jessel, Georgie Price, Herman Timberg, and Billy Gould in the act.

Feinberg's father was as unconvinced of his son's career choice as he had been when Larry boxed. He coaxed Larry into the jewelry business. Like Shemp Howard's attempt at honest work, Larry's foray into jewelry was short-lived.

"I lasted three months," Larry later recalled. "The boss came to me one day and gave me two weeks notice and salary and an extra bonus of $100 to go on the stage, because I kept everyone laughing in his place and they were getting no work done."

It didn't take Larry long to find his true calling, or true love, for that matter. On the strength of his stint with the Newsboy Sextette, he was given a job by theatrical agents Jules Black and Jolly Joyce. They were organizing a school-age act being readied to tour for hospitals and entertain military troops. By his own account, Larry played "the sissy in Lord Fauntleroy clothes," alongside a group called the Haney Sisters and the husband and wife team of Marty and Nancy Bohn.

even conducting the orchestra, Feinberg was already rebelling. Touted as a potential concert violinist, he became more interested in jazz than the classical music he was being taught. At thirteen and all of four feet two inches (he'd eventually reach the same diminutive five feet four inches as Moe), he'd play hooky to seek out music publishers for jazz sheet music, teaching his fellow grammar school students the numbers. A combination of events kept Feinberg from realizing his parents' dream. His teacher wanted Feinberg to be sent to Europe to seriously study the violin, but the onset of World War One prompted his mother to refuse to send him overseas.

Stuck at home, Feinberg caught the vaudeville bug. He got a job that paid two dollars a performance, in which he'd sing in movie houses, and appeared at the Keystone, Alhambra, Broadway,

Early Stooges, when Larry had most of his hair.

Shortly after, Larry was involved with a talented singer named Nancy Decker. Unfortunately for Larry, the Haney Sisters—led by Mabel Haney—lobbied for her to drop him and she did. Mabel might have had ulterior motives, because soon after, she and Larry were an item. She was a beautiful blue-eyed blonde with a singing voice she'd been honing since she began performing at the age of four. They carried on an affair in secret, because he was Jewish, she Roman Catholic. They dropped the secrecy and married on June 22, 1926, when Mabel converted to Judaism. They remained wed until their deaths, and Mabel became a colorful fixture when the Stooges toured in later years.

After they were married, they left the act to form a trio, the Haney Sisters and Fine. Together, they performed an act called "At the Crossroads."

"It was an act consisting of the two sisters as traffic cops on the road to music land," said Larry. "My wife directed traffic toward the jazz section, and their sister Loretta toward the classical. I came in the middle of the road and they each tried to convince me which road to take, so my wife did a jazz dance, which I played for her, and then my sister-in-law, a beautiful dancer, did a classical dance while I played that on the violin for her. I wrote this act myself, including the music. Then we joined and did a combination jazz and classical singing and dancing. We introduced the Charleston in vaudeville in Charleston, South Carolina. That was quite a coincidence and we got a lot of write-up on it." They worked together until 1928, starting in the Broadway show *Good News* and touring all over the country.

The trio was riding high, and after playing the Paramount Theatre in Toronto on a bill that included a popular emcee and future Stooge straight man, Eddie Laughton, a booker named Sol Berns offered them fifteen weeks touring Canada. But Larry's sister-in-law Loretta had had enough.

She was engaged to a man in Philadelphia and wanted to go home. She did, and it proved a fortuitous move for Fine. Mabel and Larry, trying to figure out what to do after losing their partner, stayed on a few extra days in Canada with Laughton and his wife and were taking in a performance on amateur night.

Because several of the acts were snowbound and couldn't make it, Larry was asked to fill in. "I was embarrassed and I had just played the theater and I said they'll recognize me as a professional," said Larry. Eddie Norton, the man who'd booked Larry as a pro and who was in a bind, convinced him to don blackface and do a routine of a comedian named Mel Klee, who was part of the Haney Sisters and Fine bill. Larry was called Joe Roberts.

"My wife was sitting with Eddie Laughton's wife in the box, and when she saw me come out, she ran down the aisle because she didn't want to watch," said Larry. "But she never got out, because I started to get laughs right away and she came back. Naturally, doing this professional's act, I was a riot." The contest was rigged so that Feinberg didn't win, even though he drew the loudest applause from the audience.

Later that night at a party, the booker, Sol Berns, tried desperately to find the blackface comic who'd brought down the house. "He was questioning Eddie about how he could get in touch with the blackface comedian, and he said to me, 'If I didn't know you were part of the Haneys' act, I'd swear it was you,'" Larry recalled. "Never having done blackface before, I left a little bit of the black

Larry and Mabel Haney. She went from his stage partner to his life partner.

in my ears, and he finally noticed it and knew it was I who had done the act, and he said to me, 'I'll give you the fifteen weeks I was going to give the trio, and for the same money, as a single.'"

Mabel agreed that her husband should go it alone, and she decided to retire. But Loretta called her sister and said that after a vicious argument with her beau, she was ready to rejoin the act. Already locked into the fifteen-week deal, Larry was stuck in Canada while his wife and her sister headed back to the States to continue as a duo. But Larry and Mabel missed each other so badly that they couldn't bear to be apart.

"It's two weeks before Christmas and they are working for Mike Fritzel, who owned the Chez Paris in Chicago, and my wife called me," said Larry. "I was in the St. Catherine's in Canada, and she said, 'This is going to be our first Christmas and we'll be apart, why don't you quit and come to Chicago? I'm sure you can get a lot of work around here.'"

Berns, whom Fine considered a friend, allowed him to leave and head for Chicago, where he'd first be glimpsed by Healy and the Howard brothers.

CHAPTER FOUR

FROM VAUDEVILLE TO HOLLYWOOD

A typically colorful vaudeville marquee.

ONCE IT BECAME CLEAR THAT HEALY AND THE HOWARDS WANTED LARRY FINE TO BE PART OF THEIR ACT, THE TRICKY PART WAS GETTING HIM OUT OF A CONTRACT HE'D SIGNED TO EMCEE A REVUE AT MANN'S RAINBOW GARDENS. GETTING THAT JOB HAD SEEMED A STROKE OF LUCK FOR FINE, WHO WAS ADRIFT AS HE TRIED TO FIND A USE FOR HIS UNUSUAL TALENTS.

Fine had gotten the Rainbow Gardens job during a card game with Fred Mann, owner of the club, the revue producer LeRoy Prinz, and its publicist, Mort Hyman. During a hand that afternoon, Mann was interrupted with a phone call saying that his emcee, the comedian Ray Evans, had abruptly left the revue because he wasn't getting top billing above the emerging songstress Ruth Etting. Calmly puffing a cigar, Fine attempted the ultimate bluff. He told his cardmates he could not only do the job, but could do it better, since he danced and played violin. And he pulled it off.

"I went on that night, and was quite a hit, and Mr. Mann signed me to a three-year contract," said Fine. He'd play the Rainbow Gardens in Chicago, as well as another in Havana.

That was great until Fine met Healy, who at the time was in a bind of his own. After hitting Chicago with the touring company of a Shubert-produced show called *A Night in Spain,* Healy was suddenly given two weeks' notice by Shemp, his

chief foil in the show. It was a popular show—Al Jolson was on the card—but Shemp had gotten a better money offer to do a double act. It was also clear that Shemp, who shrank from confrontation, had tired of Healy's offstage antics. He was drinking much of the time, and by all accounts he was not a pleasant drunk. Shemp had been battered by Healy in the Broadway shows *Earl Carroll Vanities of 1925* and *Passing Show of 1927,* and he was ready for a break. At a party while Healy mulled over his dilemma, Larry met up with them.

"Healy and Shemp took one look at me, and Shemp, who was anxious to leave, suggested to Healy that he could use me, and they yelled me to the table and offered me the show," said Larry. It was a much higher profile opportunity, and Fine was thrilled. Trouble was, Mann, who held his contract, wasn't.

"When I mentioned it to Mr. Mann, he refused to let me out of the contract," said Larry. "The next day was a Wednesday matinee at the theater and Healy invited me over anyway, and when I saw Shemp in the show I went backstage and told Healy I didn't think I could do it. Shemp was so great, and I explained to him I couldn't get out of my contract anyhow." They had dinner that evening. Just when it looked like Fine would be stuck, fate intervened again.

When he returned to the Rainbow Gardens, it was padlocked by the Internal Revenue Service, which had cracked down because Mann's café had been caught serving liquor, which was illegal under the prohibition of the day. Fine said it was a scheme involving the café's managers and waiters. Though Mann apparently knew nothing about the illegal liquor sales, he took the crackdown as hard as any man could.

"I immediately called LeRoy Prinz and asked him how I stood with this contract, since the place was closed," said Fine. "Was I still on salary or not? He told me very sadly that Mr. Mann committed suicide from the shame. I immediately took another cab back to the theater and told Mr. Healy the situation. He let me stand in the wings and watch the show again, and hired me."

Shemp left, and Fine took his place for more than fifty weeks of the show's run. He followed that with another Healy-led revue, *A Night in Venice,* which held the billing "Ted Healy and His Three Southern Gentlemen." The show was a smash, playing the prestigious Palace Theatre in New York. It ran through 1929 and closed in Boston shortly after the stock market crash, when live theater business began drying up along with the disposable income used for entertainment.

The acts themselves changed from time to time. In his memoirs, *Stroke of Luck,* Fine recalled the time Healy conjured up an act in which their costar was a bear—a real bear.

The act began with Moe wrestling the bear, a fairly harmless animal which would chase Moe off the stage. When Moe returned, he'd drag out a dummy bear that had a rope attached to it.

"Moe would throw the dummy out to the audience, and Shemp would pull it back with the rope. It always went over well, frightening and making the audience laugh at the same time."

Once, Moe fell, knocking the rope loose from Shemp's grasp. When Moe jumped up and flung the bear, it kept going, braining a man in the audience and causing the woman behind him to faint. The guy eventually sued, and the first show ended. The second show didn't go much better because as Moe got ready to grapple with the bear again, the creature employed a move most unorthodox for wrestling—it defecated all over the stage. "They turn off the spotlight and darken the stage," Fine wrote. "An attendant runs out with a broom and shovel to clean up the mess. While cleaning, the spotlight accidentally is turned on and spotted right on the attendant that was cleaning up the mess. The audience roared with laughter, and the attendant just turned around and took a bow. Now the audience went berserk with laughter and wouldn't stop. Finally, Ted Healy raised his hands at the audience to stop, and when they quieted down a little, hollered out at them, 'If that's the kinda crap you want . . . we'll shovel it to you.' "

According to Fine, that set the audience laughing even harder. Unfortunately, the manager of the D.C. Loew's Theater was not amused. He fired them immediately and got Loew's to cancel the rest of a contract that was supposed to run ninety weeks.

Moe had problems of his own at the time. He

had fallen in love with and married Helen Schon-berger, a cousin of the magician Harry Houdini, the same year that Shemp married his wife, Gertrude. Moe temporarily left acting around the time his daughter, Joan, was born, mostly because an aunt who helped raise his wife railed about the prospects of a woman raising a daughter when her husband was busy cavorting in show business. His wife's concerns led him to bow out of *A Night in Spain* and take a short leave of the business.

As it turned out, there was actually little cause for the beefing aunt to complain. She was getting her ammo from a most curious and beefy source.

"There was a group called the Beef Trust, which was essentially a bunch of fat ladies doing dances," said Joan Maurer, Moe's daughter. "My mother was practically an orphan and this one aunt was a relative of someone in that group and had heard that show business personalities could not live a normal life."

But a normal life and Moe just did not mix. He tried his hand at real estate, taking cues from his mother and buying and restoring properties. He did not have her touch and promptly lost his shirt. He began getting involved in the theater again. In 1927, while he was still concentrating on real estate, he directed for the Bensonhurst Theater Guild a musical called *Stepping Along*, which he wrote with a friend, Dr. Sam Cohen. Before long, he was back taking slaps from Healy.

Working for Healy had its pros and cons. The grizzled Irishman with the

bulbous nose and bald pate was one of the great characters of the day and molded the slaphappy style that was to become the Stooge signature during their run at Columbia. The Healy regimen was largely based on spontaneity, as were most of the events in his life. His singing ability was never hailed for anything more than its volume, but sing and dance he did. Partway through his act he'd be interrupted by a heckler or a messenger, who'd be brought onstage and become the butt of his merriment.

There was not much glory and plenty of indignity in being a Healy stooge. Healy cast a long shadow, was clearly the star. His antics were quickly establishing him as one of the best-paid entertainers on the vaudeville circuit. While he was quick to dispense a slap, he wasn't slapping huge sums on his partners. Reports filed during

Moe and wife Helen. For a screen and stage couple, they provided a remarkably stable homelife for their children, Joan and Jeffrey.

the period of Healy's heyday had him pulling down salaries that were generally in the neighborhood of $1,750 a week, and he once made a record $6,500 top-lining the New York Palace. Very little of it found its way into the pockets of his sparring partners. In fact, they generally received around $100 to $150 a week.

Healy's eccentric style also made him a high-maintenance employer, because he was so diametrically opposed to the demeanor of the Stooges offstage. Both Moe and Larry had gotten married early, and, though there were reports that Larry developed a taste for the ladies while he drank and toiled on the road, both were by most accounts devoted husbands. They were teetotalers compared to Healy. He lived for the nightlife, a hard drinker whose demeanor grew uglier as the bar tab grew higher. Confrontation was not uncommon.

"Healy started out in the business slapping them around, which became quite a staple for the Stooges," said Edward Bernds, who became close to the Stooges when he was directing them in shorts and, later, features. "The boys hated him. Moe hated him for two reasons. One was that while he did not exactly cheat them on money, he took all the money and paid them an absolute minimum. He hogged it all, and when he later negotiated with MGM, he made deals where he got a lot of money and they didn't get very much of it at all.

"And the other thing Moe said was that there are ways of hitting and slapping that don't hurt so much. But he said that onstage during vaudeville, Healy would really belt them. And of course, the boys had to go right ahead. They couldn't stop the act and complain. So Moe hated him for that. He deliberately hurt them and cheated them out of money. And the other thing the boys said about Healy was that the drunker he got, the nastier he got."

But it was a necessary apprenticeship for the Stooges, who by this time got Shemp back into the fold and were developing timing and routines, sometimes by accident. There's a legendary and perhaps apocryphal story that Moe's signature move, the two-finger eye poke, came when Shemp executed it for real on Larry as they argued during a card game. As Fine sat in shock while his eyes welled up with water, Moe laughed so hard he fell through a glass door, according to his daughter. From that moment on, it became a staple of the act. That kind of trial by error was common in those days. In a laudatory *Shadowplay* magazine feature on Healy in March 1934, a reporter observed the rough byplay between the young Stooges.

"They beat one another into pulps. One day, Moe socked Curly till he staggered through the rest of the show simply stupefied. More stupefied than usual, that is. The minute they were offstage, Curly was at him. 'What do you mean, hitting me like that?' he screamed. 'Why, the audience could hardly hear the slap. Next time, I'll make it good and hard.' And he meant it. Only Moe missed Curly the next time and caught Larry a pipperino on the jaw. Larry staggered and would have fallen, if the boys hadn't grabbed him and immediately gone into that football huddle of theirs, which the audience thought planned and simply went crazy over. Had they only known it, it was done to keep Larry off the floor. Started as an accident, it is now the hit of their act."

To give an idea of how ribald and full-contact

their act became, a review of their Shubert show *A Night in Venice* gave a blow-by-blow which made the event sound more like a night at the fights.

"The crowd laughed last night often and heartily," wrote the reviewer. "Ted Healy drew four paid spectators from the audience, inviting them to wrestle with a bear. The four unsightly fellows spent some 15 long minutes slapping each other's faces. That was perhaps the highest point in the evening's humor. Following which one of the slappers wrestled with the bear and had his clothes ripped off. When that was done, two sailors appeared and pretended to put his head in the other's mouth. Thereafter the two threw themselves about. Ted Healy had a habit which he indulged throughout the evening of leaping on the neck of those who displeased him and bearing them to the floor. Good robust humor, you see."

Despite the seemingly crude comedy, reviewers ate it up. Another thumbs-up came from the *Evening World News,* whose reviewer concluded, "I don't know the names of the three comics in Ted Healy's gang, but I'm guessing they are Shemp Howard, Harry Howard (Moe) and Larry Fine. They made me forget all my woes. This is a show to see if you want genuine entertainment."

Such physical contact is a lot more fun to observe than to receive. But despite the hard hits and low wages, Healy offered a wealth of potential, and in 1930 the stooges rode his tattered coattails right into Hollywood.

Healy got the lead in a Fox film called *Soup to Nuts.* The comedy, written by the famed cartoonist and inventor Rube Goldberg, gave the act billing as "Ted Healy and His Racketeers" and included the stooges as well as a xylophone player named Freddie Sanborn and a magician named Ralph Elmer.

Variety's review of their first film was as bracing as a Healy backhand. Called a film that could play "the Class C and minor grinds," the reviewer declared unkindly that "it might have been better judgment for Fox prestige to have left this on the shelf. For what the Fox studio turned out in *Soup to Nuts* is a two-reel Keystone of the silent days, padded into over six reels with dialog."

Though the stooges are singled out for faint praise, Healy is not. "Not only is Healy, a comedian whom the New York Palace pays $6,000 a week for headlining in that ace vaude house, made into a straight man, but he is turned into a flip romantic juvenile with a girl as unfunny as he is here, hanging onto his neck all the while."

The reviewer ends by reminding that a Keystoner harkens back to the early days of two-reelers "when a 12% average in a picture house actually was a fact, where the act was slapstick, the most ludicrous and tiresome of all low comedy."

While *Soup to Nuts* might have missed the mark, the reviewer missed its significance. The film was the event that reassembled the group and gave them their first taste of Hollywood. And they were getting ready to preserve the Keystoner spirit for the next thirty years.

More than that, while critics did not respond well to Healy in the role of a romantic lead, his formerly anonymous stooges were suddenly being singled out for praise on their own, for the very first time in their career. This did not go unnoticed by the boss. It would help drive a wedge between the stooges and the man who made them.

CHAPTER FIVE

THE TED OFFENSIVE

Healy and his Stooges, after Jerome replaced Shemp and shortly before the boys
broke with their mentor for good.

SHORTLY AFTER THE BOYS WENT TO HOLLYWOOD, iT WAS BECOMING CLEAR TO THEM THAT THEY WERE READY TO GRADUATE THE CLASSROOM OF TED HEALY. iT WAS TIME TO START ON CAREERS OF THEIR OWN, WHERE THEY COULD FINALLY EXPECT AT LEAST AN EQUITABLE CUT OF THE PAY.

The talking picture was here to stay. Compared to the foul-smelling vaudeville houses and cold winters back east, Hollywood, with its warm climate and endless sunshine, was where Howard, Fine, and Howard wanted to be. Especially after filming their first feature on Fox's Western Avenue lot.

Larry recalled the excitement of working on the lot.

"The Cafe de Paris, the studio commissary, was just opened, and while here we met some wonderful people who were getting started just as we were," said Larry. One was John Wayne, who had just gotten out of college and worked in the props department.

The boys were teamed with a xylophonist named Freddie Sanborn and billed as "Ted Healy's Racketeers," appearing in *Soup to Nuts* as firemen who assist Healy in breaking up a party. They also played a Mexican army of revolutionists.

Each knew the possibilities of making it in talking pictures, and they were aware that Healy realized he might lose his employees.

"When we left for the coast to make this pic-ture, Ted Healy said, 'Now, one or more or all of us are liable to get somewhere in the picture industry,' " said Moe. " 'Good luck to the best man or all of us.' This is what he said."

The film, directed by Benjamin Stoloff, was expected to be a solid hit. And Healy, who fancied himself stepping up into leading-man roles, hadn't seen the possibility that his mates and not he would be the beneficiaries of the film. But that's exactly what happened. Fox topper Winnie Sheehan cornered the trio at the film's premiere and offered a seven-year contract. Trouble was, Sheehan had no interest in their leader.

At first, Healy reacted with good spirit. Moe recalled: "When we told him that [Fox] would like to sign us up at the studio, Ted said, 'Well, more power to you, boys. I told you something like this would happen.' And he went on to New York."

Actually, once he had time to reflect on the snub, Healy got hopping mad. Practically before the ink had dried on the contract, Healy set about to sabotage it.

"Mr. Sheehan ran the picture and decided he

wanted us and not Healy, which aggravated Mr. Healy no end," Larry recalled. "Healy left for New York that same day, but before he did he went in to see Mr. Sheehan and told him he thought it wasn't cricket to take his boys away from his act," Larry recalled. "So Mr. Sheehan canceled our contract. Meantime, Healy went to New York and so we were left out here."

The boys were booked by their William Morris agents into the Paramount Theatre in L.A. for a lengthy run under the name Three Lost Souls for $900 a week. But they got a lot more than that from Fox, if Larry Fine is to be believed in his memoirs.

Fine claimed that his own threat to take the matter of their canceled contract to a lawyer coaxed out a much larger settlement—$30,000, plus passage back to New York.

During this time, Moe began asserting himself as the leader of the suddenly rudderless trio.

"I would get the salary from the front office," said Moe. "From the money, we would pay the railroad man for the transportation. If anyone spent money for clothing, it came out of his own pocket, because each one had his own idea of what he would like to wear to make himself funny. Then the salary was split three ways."

Sabotaging the Fox deal wasn't all Healy did to his former charges, who vowed not to work with him again. Healy was downright hostile.

"From the Paramount we worked in theaters in San Francisco and Seattle," said Larry. "Mr. Healy got an injunction against us claiming we were using his material. We had to go back to New York for an arbitration case, which we won. Then Shemp, Moe, and I, we worked quite a lot, but Healy kept hounding the theaters, threatening

lawsuits and injunctions against the theaters, which didn't make it easy for us."

Healy aired charges in the press that his former foils were using material that belonged to him. Healy's rep, Paul Dempsey, brought two complaints to the Joint Complaint Bureau. There were reports of Healy threatening to bomb a theater they performed in.

Healy also sent his wife, Betty, to spy on their shows. But Healy had little to back up his charges. The live shows given by the trio consisted mainly of recycled routines from a Broadway show and a film over which Healy had no control. The boys were smart enough to appeal to J. J. Shubert. The showman was no fan of Healy and gave them contractual blessing to use any routines they wanted from shows they had performed in for him.

"Most of the material we were using, we did use out of Shubert's *A Night in Venice,* which was material and sketches that the Shuberts owned," said Moe. "And some of the material was out of the film, *Soup to Nuts,* which Fox owned. So we got permission from both. And any other material that we used with Healy, we deleted from the act."

Working solo, the Howards and Fine finally realized just how underpaid they had been. Solo, they weren't pulling down near the wages earned by their boss, a top vaudeville headliner, but it didn't matter. Splitting their earnings evenly, they instantly doubled their previous salaries.

Healy continued right along, replacing his charges with three other stooges, the team of Mousie Garner, Jack Wolfe, and Dick Hakins.

It was an exciting period, Garner recalled, because Healy was eminently bookable but entirely unpredictable. Even in the way he auditioned the new team.

"Hakins had already worked with him and I just went up there and he just gave me a bang to the head," said Garner. "I never saw that type of comedy before. So I jumped on him, bit his ear, and hit him back. Ted looks at me and says, 'Get in the corner, you're hired.' I didn't know what was happening. I guess he was trying to get a little reaction out of me. Wolfe came over to me and he says, 'Mr. Healy, what you did to him goes for me too.'"

The new Healy foils were game, but they were no match for the seasoned stooges they were replacing. Garner recalls that Healy was completely bitter that his former charges had gone on their own.

"Oh, yeah, was he ever," Garner said. "He didn't get over that. I have no idea what he paid them, it wasn't my business. I know what he paid me and it wasn't great but it was satisfactory. Instead of getting a big salary, because he was making big money, I got $150 a week, which was pretty good in those days. I never complained about my salary and we never gave him a hard time. But all in all, he wanted them back."

The stooges were proving a hard act to follow. And the replacement stooges knew it.

"They were the originals," said Garner. "I know we didn't do the job they did because they knew him so well and Ted knew them. Ted never bothered to help us or show us what to do—we had to figure it out ourselves. I had to figure out my own style. They all were hitting pretty hard, and I wasn't too crazy about that kind of comedy. My favorite kind of comedy was the Marx Brothers or Laurel and Hardy, a bit more intelligent. It wasn't easy, because you could just tell when Ted worked with us, he wasn't happy. But we went out there and got as big a laughs as they did, I can tell you that."

The bitterness between the stooges and their former boss was taking its toll, especially on the sensitive Shemp. When Healy threatened to bomb a theater the boys were playing in, the stooge grew so unnerved that he wet the bed while the trio traveled by train to another city. Unfortunately for Larry, he was sharing a bunk with Shemp. By his own account, he woke up soaked. Worse, Shemp had quietly told the porters that Fine was the bed wetter, not he.

Despite the two-year rift and lots of bad blood, Healy called his old partners when he landed another Broadway show with the Shuberts, this one called The Passing Show of 1932. Surprisingly, the trio returned for the opportunity to go back on Broadway. Garner, Wolfe, and Hakins were summarily dumped.

The reconfigured stooges suffered an immediate setback, as Healy's bull-in-a-china-shop methods derailed their big Broadway bow.

"We started rehearsing with the show, and rehearsals went on past the four-week limit, when Ted Healy found that his contract didn't contain a starting date of the show," said Moe. "He immediately stopped rehearsing, and we went back in and played vaudeville."

Larry later attributed part of the delay to one of the cast members taking sick, but he also put most of it on Healy's own motives. Basically, he was always broke and leveraged the loophole for a better deal elsewhere.

"While waiting, Mr. Healy booked some theaters in Chicago and he was paid $6,300 net for the four of us," said Larry. "He had signed a contract with Shubert for $3,000 for the four of us. When he realized how much more money he could get out of the show, he then found a loophole in his Shubert contract and he broke it."

Mind you, while Healy was pulling down those big numbers, Moe recalls being paid only $140 per week at the time—which was less than the $150 Garner recalled earning. Healy was sued by J. J. Shubert for breaking the contract but prevailed in court. But Shubert exacted a measure of revenge. He walked away with 25 percent of Healy's act.

"During the litigation, Mr. Shubert saw that he couldn't win the case," said Larry. "So he offered Shemp the star part in the show at quite a lot of money. So Shemp promptly gave Healy his notice. And that's when Jerry, known as 'Curly,' Moe's younger brother, replaced Shemp."

The Shubert move was a big blow to Healy; though Shemp had little problem saying good-bye to Healy and his drinking, Mousie Garner said the rubber-faced comic was Healy's favorite stooge. "Shemp was the best. He understood Ted the best and what he wanted," said Garner.

But Shemp saw better opportunities on the horizon. After the Shubert stint, he went into the motion pictures, playing the character Knobby the cornerman in the short-lived series *Joe Palooka*, which filmed at the Warner Bros. studio in Brooklyn. He would appear in numerous films, including playing a bartender in the critically acclaimed 1940 W. C. Fields comedy *The Bank Dick*.

Ever the worrier, Shemp had to be reassured by his brother before leaving, fearful his exit would break up the act.

"He was reluctant to go, saying, 'Well, what are you going to do for a third man?' " Moe later recalled. "And I said, 'Don't worry, Shemp. We'll take Curly, we'll break him in, and we'll take him along.' "

That decision was to be one of the defining moments in Stooge history.

CHAPTER SIX

A CURLY CONVERGENCE

Jerome shed his waxed mustache and long locks to become Curly,
the most physically gifted member of the slapstick troupe.

JEROME HOWARD WAS THE YOUNGEST OF THE HOWARD CLAN, BY ALL ACCOUNTS A MAMA'S BOY. BUT HE ALSO IDOLIZED HIS BROTHERS AND WAS ALREADY TRYING TO FOLLOW IN THEIR FOOTSTEPS. WHILE THEY WERE BARNSTORMING THE VAUDEVILLE CIRCUIT, JEROME WAS SLOWLY DEVELOPING HIS TALENTS. HE CUT A DASHING AND GRACEFUL FIGURE ON THE DANCE FLOOR, WITH A FULL HEAD OF WAVY HAIR AND A CAREFULLY WAXED MUSTACHE. JEROME HAD GOTTEN HIS FIRST TASTE OF THE BUSINESS PLAYING A HUMOROUS CONDUCTOR FOR THE ORVILLE KNAPP BAND IN A ROUTINE THAT INVOLVED A TEAR-AWAY TUX WHICH HE'D LOSE BY THE END OF A SONG, CLAD ONLY IN HIS KNICKERS. WHEN THE CALL CAME FROM MOE, JEROME WAS MORE THAN READY.

Though shy and a bit heavyset, Jerome was considered very handsome. But he was more than willing to give that up for the chance to join in the circus life his brothers were leading. If Moe, Larry, and Shemp sported bizarre hairdos, Healy told Moe that something would have to be done with Moe's younger brother.

"I had my hair out in bangs, Larry had his hair in the wild fireboy fashion, and Shemp wore his hair very long, parted in the middle, with the ends flipped over each ear," Moe recalled. "Curly allayed our fears by saying, 'You wait here twenty minutes, and I'll be back with a hairdo that will be very becoming with the rest of the boys.' He returned in twenty minutes, took off his cap. The revelation was astounding because his hair was clipped so close that he looked like a billiard ball. It was then, actually, that we named him Curly."

Curly was self-conscious about the loss of his hair and mustache, at first keeping his cap on in public to hide it. In his very first performances he was also nervous, which raised his normally low voice a few octaves. Healy loved that as much as his haircut and signed him on for $75 a week.

"What he did for the first three weeks was just run across the stage in a bathing suit and a little pail of water," Moe recalled. "That's all he did, run across and back, for some time."

The youngest Howard proved a quick study, and it wasn't long before he was on his way toward becoming the most animated of the Stooges.

Quartet once again complete, in 1933 Healy and the stooges headed back to Hollywood, where their first attempt at movie stardom had been derailed. They played their vaudeville act at the New Yorker Cafe, a speakeasy in the basement of the Christy Hotel on Hollywood Boulevard. As luck would have it, the combination of the Depression and a major earthquake stranded the comedy team.

"In the middle of the engagement at the New Yorker Cafe, our president of the U.S. Franklin Delano Roosevelt closed all the banks," Moe later recalled. "At which time, customers were paying their tabs with checks that could have been deposited only with a tennis racket. Our salaries were paid in the same type of checks, uncashable. It was difficult to stay on the diet we assumed for the following few weeks, but we made it. Some of us became thinner, the thin ones became a shadow, but we lived through it."

Ironically, their willingness to work for free cemented their screen careers once and for all.

Byron Foy, an old friend of Healy's, and Ben Stoloff, who'd directed Healy and the stooges in *Soup to Nuts,* had completed an independent film called *Are These Our Children* and were planning to show the film to Hollywood executives in the form of a benefit. Though tired of unpaid work, Healy and the boys reluctantly agreed to perform. It might have been the best career move they ever made.

That's because the attendees included such studio toppers as Jack Warner, Harry Cohn, Louis B. Mayer, and Carl Laemmle. Their routines bowled over the executives. Suddenly, Healy and his stooges had several movie contract offers before them.

"At the end of the act . . . we were swamped by Jack Warner, Louis B. Mayer, Harry Cohn of Columbia, all the majors offering us jobs and contracts," Larry recalled. "We went home, talked it over and decided on MGM."

They pacted with Mayer to do six two-reel comedies, an arrangement that quickly fell on the rocks.

"The first picture we made, it was so bad I think they burned it up without ever releasing it, and fired the director and us," said Larry. They played four aviators flying a plane around the world upside down and backward, and if that sounds funny, it wasn't. Upon viewing the dailies, director Nick Grinde was fired on the spot by Mayer, along with the film's stars.

But once again the ever-resourceful Healy turned a sow's ear into silk.

"Healy and his stooges proceeded to Louis B.

Mayer's office and with the interesting plea to let us continue with the rest of the series, we made the offer that we would do the next comedy gratis," said Moe. "If he liked it, we would finish the contract, and if he didn't, we would graciously but reluctantly leave the studio."

The shrewd Mayer knew a good deal when he saw one.

"He accepted the proposition, and that this time we wrote the story."

Even better for Mayer, Healy and his stooges took existing MGM stock footage and used it, making the group even more cost-efficient.

While brainstorming, they viewed two dance numbers filmed but not released by the Dodge Twins, a couple of dancers.

"We wrote a story around these two dance numbers, thereby getting approximately $120,000 worth of production for practically nothing, all done in color, and very successful," said Moe.

The film was called *Nertsery Rhymes,* and the stooges played Healy's children. "He was telling us bedtime stories to get us to go to sleep, so that he could go out to a party, and in telling us the fairy tale of the Dodge Twins and pointing to a photograph of the Dodge Twins, which was a single frame clip out of the dance number, this picture came to life and went on with the number," Moe explained.

That salvaged the MGM deal, and they went on to make several pictures using other discarded studio footage that would otherwise have never been seen. So, lavishly staged musical numbers might show up in shorts such as *The Big Idea,* which Healy did with the stooges and Bonnie Bonnell. Even though they had very little corre-

lation to the plot, using them was a cost-efficient excuse to burn off footage that was rotting on shelves.

They made several features for MGM, including *Dancing Lady,* Hollywood's first million-dollar musical, which starred Joan Crawford, Clark Gable, Fred Astaire, Robert Benchley, and Nelson Eddy. They were quickly becoming the toast of the town.

MGM put the boys to work together, but they also worked separately when the need arose. Larry scored a bit part in *Stage Mother,* and Jerome top-lined a Stooge-like comedy called *Roast-Beef and Movies,* one of the first films done in Technicolor. Moe and Curly appeared in clown makeup in one scene of *Broadway to Hollywood.* Healy did a serious role in *Operator 13.*

But the work they did together was drawing notice, and not just for Healy, as evidenced from reviews of the period. The boys got a solid shot to show their stuff in the David O. Selznick–produced *Meet the Baron,* a film that was supposed to showcase the talents of radio comic Jack Pearl as Baron Munchausen. Not quite. One Gotham tabloid critic, Thornton Delehanty, pronounced Pearl barren of comedic talent ("Jack Pearl is one of the least funny persons we have ever seen, and the only thing less funny is his Baron Munchausen characterization"). That doesn't mean Delehanty completely panned the picture; in his estimation, Jimmy Durante and Healy and his stooges were its saving graces. "The happy part, for us, is that Jimmy Durante, Ted Healy and his stooges and Edna May Oliver intercept all [Pearl's] passes and score heavily in their own favor."

The signature scene for Healy shows Oliver as

an uptight dean of Cuddle College, with Healy and the boys janitors. During a musical number featuring fetching coeds singing in the shower, the water turns off. It gives Healy and the boys several minutes of uninterrupted screen time, playing cards, slapping each other silly, and doing a clumsy job of fixing the shower while trying to catch an eyeful of the scantily clad lovelies. There's even a few lines that would show up in later Columbia Stooge shorts. "Get the tools," says Healy after taking the call to fix the showers. "What tools?" asks Moe. "The tools we been using the last ten years." "Oh, those tools," the stooges say in chorus.

"Even though the Healy gang has a tendency to imitate the Marx Brothers in their rowdy comedy style, it is nevertheless refreshing to see how expertly they put over their material; and the material itself is in the best slapstick vein," wrote Delehanty. The *New York Times* also singled out Healy and his stooges for praise.

The raves were not universal, however. Healy's all-too-realistic slapping had an adverse effect on Jennie Horwitz, mother of Moe, Curly, and Shemp. Intrigued by the successes her boys were becoming, she caught a show. She was not amused.

"She's sitting there and sees them beating each other onscreen, and she proceeded to get up. She had an umbrella and she began waving the umbrella at the screen and screaming in Yiddish, cussing and cursing Ted Healy for hurting her kids," said Joan Maurer. "Finally, one of the ushers had to go down the aisle, take her by the arm, and bring her out of there. She couldn't understand what was going on. It looked so real to her."

Mothers aside, the act was working as well

onscreen as it did onstage. But the success began to go to Healy's head, as well as his wallet. Healy signed the contract for all of them, but once again the boys were on the short end of the cut. The first time they left him, Healy haunted them in what became a low point in their personal lives. Said Larry: "When Healy was making all the trouble for us, and we couldn't get work for a while because he was suing and threatening to sue, and I had my wife and child to take care of and was too proud to ask my folks for help, we missed a lot of meals. A man can stand that for himself, but not for his wife and children."

This time was different. Whereas Healy had been angry because the big break was coming to the boys and not him, here, Healy was feeling like the moment was right for him. Suddenly, the stooges were the liability holding him back. MGM was parting company with Jimmy Durante, a studio staple who'd appeared with Healy and the boys in *Meet the Baron*. Healy was convinced he'd take his place—solo. If only he could ditch his stooges.

"Ted's manager, Paul Dempsey, said to us that Healy was going to sign up with MGM to play in features," said Moe. "He didn't think that Ted ought to continue with the boys. He was doing very well on his own in features, which he was doing in between the shorts that we made there. And we were agreeable. And right there we shook hands and decided to part company."

Even though Healy would no longer have to pay them, the move proved disastrous, and this time Healy couldn't be angry with the stooges' pursuit of their own screen fortunes. They, in turn, would not miss Healy's arithmetic.

But the man who belted Moe, Larry, and Curly for years was about to suffer the ultimate slap in the face.

Just as happened at Fox with *Soup to Nuts,* Healy would be outshined by his costars. This time he linked up with the Ritz Brothers in *One in a Million*.

The Ritz Brothers became stars. Healy was hardly mentioned.

And Moe, Larry, and Curly, who in billing behind Healy were usually referred to as stooges with the lowercase spelling, were about to make the transition to uppercase.

CHAPTER SEVEN

A LONG RELATIONSHIP BEGINS

One of many methods of Stooge abuse: the ear pull, from
Three Little Beers, 1935.

ONCE THEY'D FINISHED THEIR SIX-PICTURE COMMIT-
MENT AT MGM AND PARTED FROM HEALY FOR GOOD,
THE HOWARDS AND FINE DIDN'T TAKE LONG TO FIND
ANOTHER HOME. IN FACT, IT HAPPENED MOMENTS AFTER
THE HEALY SPLIT.

Said Moe: "As I was leaving the front of MGM studio to get my car, an agent by the name of Walter Kane—and how he found out I don't know—said to me, 'I hear that you boys are now on your own. I think I can get you a deal at Columbia. Would you care to come over with me?' "

Hours later, Moe had signed a deal at Columbia to do two-reelers and raced back to tell his mates the good news. It was he who was left the most surprised.

Said Moe: "As Larry went out of the back end of the studio, where his car was parked, an agent by the name of Joe Rivkin approached Larry with the same thing. 'I hear you boys are on your own. I'm pretty sure I can get you a deal at Universal.' Larry agreed to go, and later told me with the same feeling of perhaps coming back to us with a great surprise. Therein, fate, which had been our constant companion along with Lady Luck, worked in devious ways. I signed a contract at Columbia Pictures for a series of six comedies while Larry was signing a contract at Universal for feature pictures."

Since they were regarded as a team with potential, neither studio wanted to let go. Finally,

it came down to the simple fact that the drive from MGM to Columbia was shorter than the route through the canyon to Universal.

"In the argument that ensued between the two studios, Columbia won out because I had signed by more than an hour before Larry did at Universal," said Moe. "Larry, to this day, says that if he had won out at Universal, with the contract he signed, there would never have been an Abbott and Costello at Universal Pictures."

Part of that comment might have been the longtime suspicions of the Stooges and their supporters that Lou Costello used to watch the boys perform as he was developing the character he'd make famous opposite Bud Abbott. The similarities between Curly's and Costello's mannerisms like the high-pitched voice were not coincidental, they felt.

Moe christened the group "The Three Stooges," and the boys were in business with Columbia on a contract that called for them to make one short, with an option for a whole season's worth should they prove themselves worthy. The very first documentable contract signed between the trio and Columbia came on March 19, 1934. The short-form deal memo called for a

Larry, in his first and only role as leading man, woos Marjorie White in Woman Haters. White was being groomed for stardom at Columbia but died in an accident not long after the short was filmed.

Curly, playing the fighter known as KO, appears about to be KO'd in *Punch Drunks*.

single two-reel comedy and paid the trio the collective sum of $1,000, with an option for an additional eight two-reelers at the same price. That arrangement was cemented with a long-form pact dated April 9, 1934, with the studio agreeing to pay the trio $1,000 for a short with the working title "A Symphony in Punches" (the actual first short would be called *Woman Haters*). "Symphony" would be their second short, called *Punch Drunks*.

Thankfully, the first short was unlike any future Stooge short. Directed by Archie Gottler from a story by Jerome S. Gottler, the short is an odd adventure in which the boys join a club that requires them to swear off women—even though Larry's gotten engaged to be married. The entire short is delivered in rhyming couplets. The

One-sheet for 1934 short Punch Drunks with Dorothy Granger. The short was the first to tap the comic potential of Curly, who turns into a fighting machine when he hears "Pop Goes the Weasel."

Stooges arrive in club headquarters with a slapstick frenzy the likes of which had never been seen before—a manic display of slapping, eye gouging, and wrestling—and it became clear exactly what they had to offer. The short wasn't specifically written for the trio, who, for the first and very last time, go under different names.

Oddly, Larry had the lead role in that first short, playing a guy named Jim. Curly (billed as "Curley" in the early shorts) is Jackie, and Moe is Tommy. Though the rhyming is awkward, the trio shows its stuff, delivering precision blows to one another with impeccable vaudeville-honed timing. Partway through the short, Larry begins to be shown up by Curly, who delivers his first "Nyuk, nyuk, nyuk" and even the first "Woop, woop,

woop, woop, woop, woop, woop" when Moe bites his toe in a sleeping car as Curly tries to sneak out to make time with Larry's girl.

The Columbia brass liked what it saw. The studio was formed in the mid-1920s by Harry Cohn, his brother Jack, and Joe Brandt as an upstart shingle which grew from producing two-reeler to feature product. While Jack Cohn and Brandt ran the business from New York, Harry was their West Coast emissary, a storied Hollywood figure. Cohn was an intimidating tough guy who cursed a blue streak and ruthlessly chewed out staffers and filmmakers. At least the ones who didn't stand up to him.

By the time the Stooges got to Columbia, Cohn was well on his way to elevating the studio above its origins on Poverty Row, a nickname given a concentration of producers and hustlers who put together movies on a shoestring. One of the ways he resolved to do this was by subsidizing feature productions with a strong short subjects department. The strategy was shrewd; several major producers of shorts such as Mack Sennett were getting out of the business, and that left a lot of talented writers, directors, and actors looking for work and willing to work cheaply. If Cohn could turn a short-subject act into an enduring hit, the films would not only be profitable, they

would provide tangible leverage for theater owners to book his Columbia features, no matter how
lousy they were.

Indeed, the Stooges arrived at a most fortuitous time: right before the studio established itself
on the map after Cohn recruited a brilliant Sicil-
ian director named Frank Capra, who would
direct Clark Gable and Claudette Colbert in *It
Happened One Night,* a film that made Columbia
respectable in one night, the evening it swept the
Oscars.

The film would become, aside from the
Stooges themselves, the best-remembered product
the studio ever produced. And the Stooges found
themselves right in the center of it.

In Larry Fine's memoirs, he recalled that
Cohn wasn't at all pleased with Capra's cut of *It
Happened One Night,* and grabbed the Stooges to
see the film and venture an opinion. This was just
after the Stooges got to the lot, before they'd even
made a short. When the boys gave the film a
thumbs-up, an aggravated Cohn told them to get
off the lot and never come back. Luckily, a pre-
view screening was held the same evening, and by
the next morning, the Stooges not only had jobs,
they became Cohn's good-luck charm.

And Cohn's determination to build a strong
two-reeler department as others were cutting
back allowed him to quickly establish a monopoly
on top talent for little money in what was considered a second-class genre. Soon Columbia
boasted such discarded talent as Buster Keaton,
Tom Kennedy, and Monty Collins. But the fresh-
faced Stooges quickly established themselves as
Columbia's signature shorts stars.

"Timing was on their side," said film historian
Leonard Maltin, who is one of a handful of people still alive who have viewed most of the two-
reelers of the 1930s, in his case for his book *The
Great Movie Shorts.*

"The Stooges started in 1934, and it was one
year later that Laurel and Hardy did their last two-
reeler before they moved on to features," said
Maltin. "In 1937 Hal Roach stopped making
two-reelers altogether, so part of their success was
the simple fact that the competition started to
dwindle away. Plus, it was during that period that
they started hitting their stride. It was that fortuitous combination, them getting better and the
competition falling away."

Stooge lore has always held that the Stooges
served twenty-four years without getting a raise.
That doesn't appear to be true, at least judging
from an examination of the contracts that were
signed by the boys. Following the success of
Woman Haters, Columbia picked up the option in
a May 1, 1934, contract that bettered their salary.
According to the documents, instead of eight at
$1,000, as originally stipulated, the contract called
for the boys to be paid $1,000 for their second
short, the Lou Breslow–directed *Punch Drunks,*
move up to $1,250 by the third short, the Oscar-
nominated *Men in Black,* and by short number
seven, they'd make $1,500.

They were paid as a group and divided the
money evenly. And they were free to work in features for other studios or scrape up stage work
when they weren't filming shorts. It was the blue-
print for one of the best contracts ever tendered
by Columbia Pictures. While their wages were
considered good for a period in which the country was still plunged into a depression, the Three
Stooges never earned another penny for any of
the 190 Columbia shorts they made. The shorts

went on to turn the Stooges into arguably the most memorable franchise Columbia ever produced, and the studio continues to make millions of dollars in syndication revenues for the shorts. But neither the Stooges nor their heirs got a dime.

The $10,000 sum for a year's worth of shorts was hardly a lot of money—Claudette Colbert got paid $40,000 just for starring with Gable in *It Happened One Night.* But to the Stooges, high school dropouts who'd lived the vagabond life of stage performing, the contract was an indication that they had finally reached the big time and maybe had a chance to become feature stars themselves.

The Stooges warmed to the two-reeler format quickly. While the first couple of shorts seem scattershot in style, all of them are considerably better than the MGM shorts they did in which Healy belted them all over the stage. Curly established himself as a standout in the second short, *Punch Drunks,* in which he plays a boxer who flies into a frenzy when Larry plays "Pop Goes the Weasel" on his fiddle. Moe, a fight manager, books his crazed fighter for a title match, only to have Larry's instrument crushed. That leads to a frenzied search to pipe the song to Curly, who's getting brained in the ring. The story credit went to the boys, the last time they'd have such a say in the material.

The Stooges fared even better on their third short, *Men in Black,* which got its title as a play on words from the

Clark Gable feature *Men in White.* The short, which featured the boys as manic physicians at the Los Arms Hospital, was the first and only Stooge short nominated for an Oscar as Best Short Subject film.

Memorable for the now trademark Stooge line "Calling Dr. Howard, Dr. Fine, Dr. Howard," it featured the newly minted medical school grads

A hallmark effort in establishing the Stooges as a powerhouse in Columbia's short subjects department, Men in Black was the only Stooge short nominated for an Oscar.

treating patients with sharp one-liners and a running gag in which they'd crash through the glass-paned door of the hospital administrator, who finally broke the door when he felt sure the Stooges were about to crash through it for the umpteenth time—when, of course, they missed the door completely.

That became a time-honored gag in Stooge and other shorts, also used in the variation of a sidewalk paver who, tired of having his cement tracked through, flings himself into the soup as the Stooges approach again—this time missing the mix.

Though *Men in Black* lost the Oscar to a cartoon called *La Cucaracha,* it mattered little. Columbia wasn't exactly dominating the dais in those days, and the nomination cemented the stature of the boys with studio brass and paved the way for their continued improvement.

The next dozen shorts were really the ones that forged the hard-and-fast style that would sustain the boys for more than two decades. Much of the credit goes to Jules White, a strapping film editor whom Cohn found to run the short subjects department. Quickly, the Stooges became his passion.

White, the younger brother of director/producer Jack White, cut his teeth on comedy, and by the time he hooked up with Cohn, White was ready to run his department. White knew comedy, but like Cohn, he was a no-nonsense executive. He succinctly described himself, said his younger brother, Sam, as a "technocrap. As in 'I take no crap from nobody.' "

In later years the Stooges would have a falling-out with White. He felt he deserved a lion's share of credit for molding the Stooge style in the formative years of two-reelers, an influence largely ignored by Stooge historians. Still others feel that the boys themselves deserve the credit, particularly Moe, a disciplined practitioner who kept his partners in line. Moe was so diligent, said his son, Paul Howard, that he knew not only his own lines by heart but everyone else's as well. Others feel Healy should get the most credit for pioneering the stooge style of comedy.

To Leonard Maltin, the credit must be spread around. "I don't think any single person gets a lion's share because it's a little of everybody," he said. "If they hadn't developed some style of their own with Healy, there wouldn't have been a starting point. And if Jules White hadn't had the experience he had in silent and visual comedy, then he wouldn't have known what to do with them in the first place. If Jules hadn't hired the right people to staff the department, they couldn't have gone anywhere with the potential that they had. That's for starters.

"I tend to favor Del Lord in this equation more than some of the others," said Maltin. "If you go by the results of the specific films, you can see the difference when he's behind the camera."

Lord was a veteran of the Mack Sennett shorts and was considered an expert in the madcap car chase scenes that were a Sennett staple. Ironically, when White found Lord he wasn't choreographing cars, he was selling them. On a used car lot.

To Sam White, his older brother Jules deserves more credit than he's been given. Jules directed more Stooge shorts than anyone else and, according to his brother, was the guiding influ-

Between takes of The Ghost Talks in 1949. Larry appears to be assaulting the family jewels of Jules White, who helped forge the Stooges' manic slapstick style.

ence behind the scripts, the pacing, even the physical slapstick that transformed the Stooges from a vaudeville stage act into screen stars: "In the earlier years when Jules changed the format into slapstick, Moe didn't know that much about slapstick and he was learning. From the way the scripts were constructed, they had considerable disagreements, but Jules was very tough and adamant and he said you either do it my way or you get the hell out of here."

Edward Bernds, who directed about twenty-five of the Stooge films, including several of the later features, feels differently. "Del Lord, the Mack Sennett veteran, did an awful lot of the Stooges' pictures, and I credit him with putting the Stooges on the right track," he said. "They had made several pictures before and were doing all right, but when Jules White hired Del Lord to do some Stooge comedy, he brought the Mack Sennett slapstick theme. Now, they had their slapping routine, but Del incorporated things like sight gags, fast action, special effects, the things that made the Stooges so successful."

Another veteran who contributed greatly to the Stooges' work, Clyde Bruckman, came aboard as writer. Leo McCarey, whose shorts included *Three Little Pigskins,* was a director whom Moe Howard prized. Ace gag writer Felix Adler came aboard to become a Stooge fixture, penning most of the shorts with the best verbal gags. Charley Chase, another fine comic, came to Columbia to act in and later direct Stooge shorts. White also employed his brother Jack as a writer and director, who first worked under the pseudonym Preston Black.

Though they were in a short subjects department that featured such talent as an aging Buster Keaton and Andy Clyde, the Three Stooges were soon turning out the most memorable and in-demand shorts of any of the roster of stars.

And it was reflected in their salaries. According to the contract they signed dated April 1, 1935, the Stooges reupped for another eight shorts. This time, the pay scale called for $2,000 for each of the first four and $2,250 for the remaining four.

CHAPTER EIGHT

HEALY AFTER THE STOOGES

Ted Healy, founder of the Three Stooges.

Once he was away from the boys for good, Healy continued to work, briefly reteaming with his cohorts Garner, Wolfe, and Hakins.

"It was 1936 and I figured the boat had already sailed, but I said I'd go to California and sit in the hot sun and see what happens," Garner recalled. "It didn't go too good."

On his own, Healy had little luck onscreen. He didn't have leading-man looks. Balding, with a large Irish potato of a nose, mouth set in a perpetually sour sneer. The Healy face had a lot of character, but he was no Gable. And his great gift for spontaneity and ad-lib made him much better suited to the stage than the screen.

Not surprisingly, he flourished onstage and on radio broadcasts. But one of the main reasons the Stooges wanted to be free of him was his inability to control his drinking. His penchant for nightclubbing was getting him into the kind of misadventures that the Stooges limited to the plots of their shorts. And it was taking a hard toll on the man.

As Stooge stature in showbiz history has elevated, Healy's legacy has been downgraded. Nowadays he's more commonly vilified for oppressing them than for hatching them and forging a style they maintained through their long careers. But Healy was much more than either of those.

In fact, such comic legends as Red Skelton, Milton Berle, and Bob Hope found their way early on by emulating Healy.

"He was one of the greatest comedians who ever lived," said Mousie Garner. "He didn't need anybody at all to be funny. He started the Stooges, and he was the one who showed them how to do it. I don't know if he gave them all their material, but he was certainly responsible for discovering them and showing them that style."

Healy was the Tom Sawyer of vaudeville. While Mark Twain's Sawyer could fast-talk his friends into painting a fence, Healy did him one better. He put together an act in which he'd take three stooges, slap them silly, and then keep most of the money for himself.

When he brought them together, Moe Howard, Larry Fine, and Shemp Howard were no-names. Healy, on the other hand, was among the most famous faces to come out of vaudeville.

Broadway impresario Billy Rose once wrote that "most of the natural comics I have known were a nickel phone call away from the loony bin." His favorite? Ted Healy. Rose met Healy when he'd put together his first show, *Crazy Quilt*.

"I remember when he first exploded into my office," Rose later wrote. "He looked like a cartoon from Disney. His baldy knob with its jug-handle ears loomed above a tie you could hear a block away. He wore a beat-up Skippy hat, carpet slippers (in December) and a camel hair coat big enough for a camel. In a well-modulated shriek, he started to sell me an act where he sang 'Old Man River' while a chimpanzee acted it out. I got dead stuck on him. He was as Irish as the whiskey on his breath. Funny? He could get belly laughs from a British diplomat." Rose included him in the show and said he got bigger laughs than headliners Fanny Brice and Phil Baker.

One of Healy's *Crazy Quilt* costars was David Bryan, whose wife, Adrian Booth Bryan, starred in numerous early Stooge shorts. She remembered Healy as a true original.

"My husband worked as a straight man for Ted Healy in *Crazy Quilt,* and David said Ted was a madman, but an adorable one. He had this monkey, and he would get a room at the top of a hotel and keep the monkey up there until somebody found out and kicked Healy out," said Bryan. "Then he wouldn't pay his hotel bill and he'd take the monkey and find another place for it."

While he certainly didn't pay the help well, Healy had a generous side, said Bryan. Her husband found that out one day, but had to go through a predictable Healy adventure to get there. "Ted was crazy about diamonds, and one night after a show, he told David, 'Come on, let's go out.' They went to a couple of bars, and it's three o'clock in the morning, nobody has had a shave and they're in these beat-up clothes. Ted takes them to this pawnshop and he's got all these diamonds and he wants the man to appraise them. He'd been picking them up along the way.

"They ended up getting taken to jail. The man called the cops, thinking they'd stolen the diamonds. One of those diamonds is still on my finger. It's a canary diamond, perfectly beautiful, and one of the first things David ever gave me.

"Ted was an erratic personality, but he was basically very good-hearted," said Bryan. "But he was crazy and would do crazy things. And he was always broke, he never knew how to handle his money. What kind of person collects unset diamonds and keeps a monkey in a hotel?"

The unpredictable Healy was born in Houston, Texas, on October 1, 1896, and moved with his family to New York as a youngster, where he first met the Howard brothers. After studying for a few years at De LaSalle Institute, Healy quit and sought to find fame, fortune, and adventure on the stage. He began in burlesque houses, doing blackface imitations.

He developed an act in which he'd play the straight man and his stooges would take a beating. The act worked this way: Healy would start a routine and pluck a "random" person or two from the audience. A few questions would break into a full-scale, orchestrated brawl. The formula was birthed after four castmates pulled no-shows and Healy brought out real audience members he drew humor from. It went over so well he realized he was onto something. The costars didn't need to be talented, they didn't even need to be in on the joke. Healy just needed them to bounce off. And abuse.

Healy is credited with pioneering the use of stooges as comic foils. Scripted lines weren't a problem, since Healy made it up as he went along. An example of his quick wit could be gleaned from an article in the *New York Evening Journal* from June 11, 1935, which described how Healy found a dollar on the sidewalk, with the man who dropped it quickly asking for it to be returned. "[Healy] said, 'Why, don't be silly, of course it's mine and I can prove it's mine. My name's on it,' and with that he reeled off E Pluribus Unum. And what's more, he got away with it." While that tale sounds too far-fetched to be true, it wouldn't be beyond Healy to try it.

Still, being around such an unpredictable, even unstable employer couldn't help but take its toll. And it was inevitable that the Howards and Fine would outgrow playing foil to Healy. Shemp exited the act because he hated confrontation, and Healy was a confronter—especially when he drank.

Indeed, Healy's after-hours exploits were regularly chronicled in newspapers. He married dancer Betty Braun, his partner in his stage act, but he wasn't exactly faithful.

On January 26, 1932, his wife aimed a $250,000 lawsuit at wealthy socialite Mary Brown Warburton, who, Betty claimed, was having an affair with her husband in Atlantic City hotels and theatrical dressing rooms. Betty claimed that Warburton's car and driver awaited Healy's exit from whatever venue he was playing, and that he had been given a diamond ring, walking stick with a gold head, wristwatch, and diamond-studded cigarette case by the woman. She even claimed that an agent had called her on Warburton's behalf, urging her to give up her husband so the socialite could marry him. Warburton denied the claims, but the embarrassment was substantial.

Betty divorced him shortly thereafter, but Healy's exploits got even more bizarre. On Christmas Eve, 1935, he was arrested for breaking up twenty-six-year-old dancer Marian Bonnell's furniture and then starting a fire that left Healy in hot water for attempted arson.

The incident, which took place in Santa Monica, became more bizarre because Bonnell had a loaded gun which she discharged to scare Healy off. She shot him in the hand.

"I'm too old to play with matches," Healy said in one report. "She must have got cold during the night. I went to call on Bonnie, and she fired on me." The woman claimed Healy had cut his hand punching it through her glass door.

Though Healy's sister, Marcia, called her brother's hijinks "just a Christmas impulse," Healy's drinking seemed bound to get him into serious trouble.

It did, almost exactly two years later.

By this time, Healy had gotten married again, to actress Betty Hickman. She'd just given birth to their first son, a ten-pound boy named John Jacob. His wife recuperated at University Hospital in Culver City with plans to return home on Christmas Day. By the time she was discharged from the hospital, she was a widow, and though the circumstances seem suspect even to this day, Healy's drinking had a lot to do with his demise.

After visiting his wife and baby, Healy headed out to several Hollywood hot spots to celebrate the birth. According to reports, he hit the Trocadero, the Brown Derby, and Clara Bow's, all popular Hollywood watering holes, where he got progressively drunker as he boasted about his son. Here the details get fuzzy, but it appears that Healy got into at least two separate knock-down-drag-out brawls. In one, dished out by an anonymous trio, Healy was beaten so badly that a cut over his eye had to be closed with surgical clips.

Healy went into convulsions the next day and died shortly after. Because of the condition of his face, foul play was suspected. Sidney Weinberg, house doctor at the Hollywood Plaza Hotel, became involved because Healy had shown up there, bruised and bloody, looking for Man Mountain Dean. Dean was a burly professional wrestler with whom Healy had acted, and Healy wanted Dean, a comedian named Joe Frisco, and a local sporting figure named Doc Stone to accompany him back to the bar for retribution. There's no indication that happened, and the doctor closed the cut with surgical clips and sent Healy home.

A Long Island man named Albert Broccoli came forward to claim that he'd been attacked by Healy that fateful night, but denied being the one who opened up a huge gash above Healy's eye.

"I was standing in the Trocadero Sunday night when Healy entered," said Broccoli. "I knew he had become a father a few days before, so I asked him to have a drink. He seemed quite unsteady, turned to an attendant and asked: Who is this fellow? I laughed that off and extended my congratulations. He staggered toward me and struck me on the nose. My nose began to bleed. The next thing I knew, he had hit me in the mouth, and followed this with a blow to the chin that almost floored me. I shoved him away, because I didn't want to hurt him, and attendants took him to an ante-room."

Broccoli denied he returned fire: "Later, the attendants came back and told me Healy wanted to see me. I went in and we shook hands. He got into a taxicab and that's the last I saw of him." Police investigators cast doubt on the man's version of events, particularly because Broccoli waited for the case to be closed before coming forward.

While Healy's widow kept quiet about the circumstances, his first wife refused to let his death go unchallenged, even after police couldn't find the two or three patrons who were believed to have taken Healy outside the Trocadero and beaten him to a pulp.

"I cannot sit by and see the man I loved and my partner of many years in vaudeville beaten and battered without asking the why of things that others seem willing to pass over without questions," she said. "Why didn't police question the witnesses who have come to me with their stories, and why can't the police say who it was that beat Ted so severely that he sobbed with pain when treated by a doctor?"

Despite the headlines in Gotham tabloids, an autopsy proved that Healy had actually died of a heart attack; his death was attributed to natural causes.

Perhaps not surprisingly, the man who'd made as much as $6,000 per week headlining vaudeville died penniless. A benefit featuring the likes of James Cagney was held to raise some money for the widow and her child.

"I enjoyed Ted as much as anybody while I was with him for about four years," said Garner. "He was a nice man, but when he got drunk I stayed away from him. But he was something. As good as Bob Hope or Al Jolson. He was one of the best there ever was."

Ted Healy, Jr., who was five days old when his father died, has spent years trying to remind Stooges fans that his father deserves a better legacy than that of an oppressive boss.

"Unfortunately, he's remembered not for his talent, but rather because he didn't pay the Stooges enough, and because he died in that altercation," said Healy Jr. "That's ludicrous, because he was a first-class vaudevillian. My father thought of the Stooges as his employees, and they were certainly unhappy in what they were paid. But they would also be unhappy with what they were paid later by Columbia, on their own. It concerns me that history hasn't treated him fairly"

CHAPTER NINE

AND A SCOWLiNG STOOGE SHALL LEAD THEM

As a Stooge, Moe sported an infamous bowl cut,
but offscreen he was meticulous about his appearance—he's
fairly debonair in this photo, for example.

AS THEY BEGAN TO FLOURISH BEYOND THEIR FORMER
MENTOR/TORMENTOR HEALY, MOE HOWARD CONTINUED TO
ESTABLISH HIMSELF AS THE CONTROLLING PRESENCE IN
THE GROUP. IT WAS A NATURAL TRANSFORMATION,
AND MOE SEEMED TO HAVE LITTLE CHOICE IN THE MAT-
TER BUT TO TAKE CHARGE.

Larry Fine, though an amiable guy who was a gifted musician and a skilled vaudevillian, all but boasted that he had an almost nonexistent attention span. He'd often forget lines and would have had zero interest in running the business of the Stooges or setting up the live stage appearances that the Stooges did twelve weeks a year to supplement their income. Larry was hard-pressed even to make it to the train on time. It's Stooge lore that Larry was never late for a train; but he was never early either, and would show up just as the conductor was shouting "all aboard," with Larry, his children and wife in tow, running and trying to balance luggage as they hurried to make the train. Moe, on the other hand, was the kind of guy who customarily was two hours early to the airport, just in case. Larry's fly-by-the-seat style drove him crazy.

Curly wasn't much different, and Moe's relationship with Jerome was closer to father-son than that of siblings. So it fell to Moe to attend to the business of the Stooges. He split their salaries—always in equal thirds.

The Stooges during one of their live appearances.

Moe, despite his earlier debacle in real estate, also proved an adept investor and would help his brother buy several houses.

And despite the seeming stability of the act at Columbia, Moe always kept his eye on Healy, with the memory of his earlier sabotage efforts fresh in his head. Before his death, Healy brought back Garner, Wolfe, and Hakins one last time, an act that continued even after Healy died.

Even though it left Healy's stooges and the Three Stooges battling over a name most people would consider an insult, Garner admits they were little competition for Moe, Larry, and Curly.

"Jack Wolfe didn't join because he was back home and ill, and we got another replacement," Garner recalled. "I can't even remember his name. We went out as the stooges, but it wasn't good. We were calling ourselves the Ted Healy Stooges, but by then they were so well known and such big stars that it just didn't go well. I wasn't happy doing it."

One press clip of the day had the dueling stooges meeting up at a Broadway eatery called McGinnis' restaurant and nearly engaging in a fistfight. Instead, the Howards and Fine hit their rivals with a cease and desist order.

More than sixty years later, Garner denies the rivalry was all that heated: "I was never jealous of them, there was nothing to be jealous about. They were the Stooges."

And the Stooges, while they weren't exactly pulling down movie star wages, were doing well. They didn't live lavishly, with Moe, always the leader, settling into a nice home in Toluca Lake with wife Helen, daughter Joan, and son Paul. Curly bought a home nearby.

Larry and his wife, Mabel, lived a more care-

The Howard clan: Joan, Jeffrey, Moe, and Helen.

A Fine family photo: Larry, Mabel, and daughter Phyllis. The group traveled together on most of Larry's stage tours.

Curly with two of his adopted dogs.

free existence, spending their money as they took it in. Though they, too, lived for a time in a house near Moe, they usually lived in hotels. They loved gambling and were always laying bets on some fleet-footed four-legged animal, whether horse or dog.

Curly was also interested in dogs, only his passion was accumulating them. He'd find them on the road and take them in. He was basically a loner, who, despite being the most popular Stooge because of his obvious natural talent, was quiet and self-conscious offscreen.

As the popularity of the Stooges grew, and they were top-lining eight two-reelers each year,

Moe tried to create a more structured existence for their enterprise. He and his mates formalized their first-ever arrangement together, and in the process, officially established Moe as the successor to Healy in steering Stooge fortunes. In a handwritten letter dated June 2, 1934, Moe wrote out a letter of agreement he presented for signature to the boys. In it, Moe appointed himself owner of the Stooges name:

It is hereby understood and agreed that the name "The 3 Stooges" is owned by Moe Howard solely and on this date comprises Moe Howard, Larry Fine and Curly Howard. It is further understood and agreed that if for any reason other than illness or accident, Curly Howard, Larry Fine or both should leave the 3 Stooges organization, then in that case Moe Howard has the right to replace either or both at his discretion and it is further understood that either Curly Howard, Larry Fine or both would have to pay to Moe Howard the sum of Two Thousand Five Hundred each as a penalty for disruption of the organization if as stated they should leave for a reason other than illness or accident. It is further understood and agreed that all salaries and monies earned by the 3 Stooges shall be split evenly three ways, between Larry Fine, Curly (Jerome) Howard and Moe Howard. Moe Howard is to sign all contracts.

The letter was purportedly signed by all three of the Stooges. Though it seemed a bizarre contract in that there was no penalty for Moe leaving the group and Curly and Larry were essentially giving up the control they had craved all those years they toiled under Healy, Moe later defended it during a deposition in a lawsuit filed by the heirs of Curly, who found themselves nonparticipants in the Stooge dynasty.

During that lawsuit, Moe argued the letter was a necessary precaution should Healy strike again.

"It was signed in anticipation of Ted Healy trying to get back one or more of the boys," Moe explained. "He attempted by telegram to take Larry Fine out of the act, in my mind to disrupt this combination. That was the reason that I wrote in there that anyone leaving this group for any reason other than illness or death would pay a penalty, because I would have to go looking for two other fellows, which would take time and effort."

In all likelihood, neither Fine nor Howard read the agreement very carefully, because Moe was not only taking care of the business but even did their tax returns. Why, though, would they freely give up ownership of the Stooges name, he was asked in court.

"Because I came up with the name based on the fact that I thought of it, because we were three and we were stooges, that I thought that was the appropriate name. And in view of the fact that I came up with the name, that I would own the rights to the name." Even though Larry recalled in his memoirs that the name predated Moe's recollection and was a team effort, Moe said he came up with the name during a brainstorming session that occurred right outside the MGM offices the day they were free of Healy.

In some ways, Moe had become Ted Healy. He assumed his role onstage, the perpetually angry older brother who dished out the discipline.

"He bullied them around just as Ted had, only Ted did it with more class," said Mousie Garner.

Maybe, but Moe was a fair guy when it came to sharing the proceeds. And after seeing Healy destroy the act, and himself, through his drinking, Moe never touched a drop, not until the 1960s.

Moe testified that even before they signed the first Columbia contract, his partners relied on him to take care of all the business arrangements.

"Well, I imagine they relied on my good judgment," said Moe. "In many cases, it came back to me that the boys would say, 'Well, Moe will do it.'"

That went double for Curly: "Curly was my brother, relied on me, trusted me and knew that I had good judgment and would do the best for all concerned."

CHAPTER TEN

THE GOLDEN AGE
OF STOOGE SHORTS

The boys display what became one of their funniest comic assets:

six of the homeliest gams in movie history.

BY 1936 MOST OF THE SHORTS WERE IN THE CAPABLE DIRECTING HANDS OF DEL LORD AND PRESTON BLACK, WHO WAS JULES WHITE'S BROTHER. THOUGH JULES WHITE WOULDN'T BEGIN DIRECTING SHORTS HIMSELF UNTIL 1938, HE WAS CERTAINLY EXERTING HIS INFLUENCE AS PRODUCER.

As the shorts caught on, several things became evident. One was that Larry's lines were limited. In personal notes he furnished for a biography at Fox, Fine defined up front that he had a short attention span and that his favorite hobby was sleeping. Curly, too, often forgot his lines.

But the second thing that had become clear about the Three Stooges was that Curly had physical comic abilities that put him in a class with the likes of Charlie Chaplin and Buster Keaton. Even Sam White, who feels his brother introduced the Stooges to a lot of their mannerisms, acknowledged that he just let Curly do his thing.

"There were all different types of comedians who Jules worked with," said White. "Curly was comparatively fresh and new. Charley Chase and Buster Keaton and Harry Langdon and many of the others were old hat. Those old-timers pretty well knew every slapstick move there was to do, but not one iota of Curly's comedy was derivative."

While the Stooges were a fresh act, much of what they did in their shorts was familiar. Lord for one was quick to borrow gags he'd directed in the early Sennett shorts.

"Del had been one of the mainstays at the Sennett studio, and like all of those guys, he had a long memory," said Leonard Maltin. "He'd reach into that bag of tricks and reuse them again. Clyde Bruckman, the writer, even got sued for doing it. He'd written a short for Harold Lloyd called *Movie Crazy* in 1932 and reused a key gag sequence in a Universal B feature that he wrote in the forties. Lloyd did sue and he won. Bruckman borrowed from himself over and over again, he was kind of notorious for it."

The Stooges adopted a lot of gags that were being used a decade earlier. "There was the Sennett short with Billy Beven, who was a stalwart Sennett comic, and there's a scene where he starts eating clam chowder and the clam starts spitting up back at him, shooting the stuff into his face," said Maltin. "That's a specific gag that Del Lord reused with Curly. Del directed the original as well. There are some you can trace precisely to earlier shorts, and others where it's a variation on a theme and they've used something similar. You wouldn't call it a direct lift, but it's out of the same lexicon. No one thought much of it then, they just did it."

Between takes, the Stooges talk shop with Jules White, who ran the Columbia short subjects department and produced and directed most Stooge shorts. According to many, White liked to be in control, so usually he spoke and the Stooges listened.

Even with the recycling—and the Stooges themselves would recycle that soup routine at least three times during their stay at Columbia—Maltin said that the Stooges managed to concoct distinctive shorts that at least equaled the others on the lot.

"There was nothing else quite like their humor, even at Columbia," said Maltin. "The Andy Clyde series was not quite like their series.

They had a lot of the same gags because they kept stealing from each other and they kept remaking the same scripts over and over again, but even within that realm, the Stooges stuff was different. Nobody created characters that were so absurdly unreal as they. The others were situational comedies, domestic comedies, but nothing else was the same as what they were doing, because of them. No one approached their personalities and the way they did what they did."

While it might seem that a large majority of the Stooge routines were improvisation, the trio stuck surprisingly close to the scripts as they were written, an assertion that is backed up by a reading of several of the original scripts.

Moe himself admitted that, partly because the shorts were cranked out so quickly, there were a minimum of takes, and the players stayed very close to the page. "There was no extemporaneous acting in these things," he said. "They were written by qualified writers and directed by qualified directors, although we added, each one, an individual touch of his own character."

The process was a streamlined one. A short was shot within the span of a few days, a thirty-five-page script being needed to create shorts that originally ran eighteen minutes but were shortened to sixteen minutes in later years. The operation was done on a shoestring; each short cost about $27,000 to make.

"Prior to shooting we would come in for a couple of days for the main reason that the writer sometimes wrote dialogue for one of the characters that didn't fit the character, as I saw it," said Moe. "In other words, you couldn't expect Larry to deliver a very tough line, addressing it to me, you see. A script had to be of a certain length in order to bring it in on the scheduled time period. This was left solely to the individual, within his lines—if it is said in the script that Moe smacks Curly, then it was up to Curly on his own to react the best way he knew how."

Bernds, who was the Stooge director least enamored of the onscreen violence that Jules White adored, said that when he wrote a script, he'd come to the part in which the Stooges would beat each other up and simply mark the notation "Moe punishes Curly" or "Larry punishes Curly." By that time, the timing of the Stooges was so dead-on, they were better left to their own devices.

Bernds said that while Larry and Curly seemed most concerned with scraping up a good card game, Moe was constantly interested in the process. He was always trying to get more involved—but knew his place and never tried to impose his will. The director was king on the set, and it was up to him how much input the actors could give.

"Del allowed the boys some input, and was the most easygoing guy you could meet," said Bernds, who was also highly collaborative. "But he didn't believe, nor did I, in allowing ad-libbing on the set. Jules insisted they do it his way and no other way. Del would let them use their ideas, as long as they didn't spring them on him during a take. They had to be discussed beforehand."

Almost as important as the visuals in the Stooge shorts were the sound effects that accompanied the slapstick, which became a Stooge trademark.

By all counts, credit for those went to a sound editor named Joe Henrie.

"Joe loved the Stooges and always tried to make the sound good," said Bernds. "When we'd run a rough cut of the picture, the next thing we'd do was run it for sound effects. Once in a while we'd ask Joe for something else, but generally, he was always on the ball. Joe had a cutting room with racks, a whole library full of sound effects. He could get you any kind of sound effect you wanted. If you needed something new, he'd often try to get in when a shooting company finished earlier, and keep his sound crew there to shoot some new sound effects. When he was working in his cutting room, I'd pass by and he'd be in there, all alone, putting sound effects into a Stooge picture and laughing. He'd laugh even while he was doing this routine work."

Henrie was like an orchestra conductor, plucking a violin string when a hair was being tugged out of Larry's forearm, a kettledrum for a blow to the stomach. He'd crack a whip to replicate a slap, use sandpaper when the blade of a saw was run over Curly's stubbled cranium.

It wasn't just timing and sound effects that made the Stooges the favored two-reeler stars of their day. Another was that they were the comic equivalent of the blue plate special. Like Charlie Chaplin before them, the Stooges generally began their shorts as guys who were down-and-out on their luck but inevitably found themselves in close proximity to the upper-crust social set. By the time the Stooges were done, the entire snooty lot had been taken down a few pegs, whether having their house destroyed by inept handymen or gaping wide-eyed like gaffed fish with bits of pie stuck to their kissers. Moe called the formula "deflating comedy," and they never wavered from it.

"The working-class people like to think of us as being a real part of them," Moe once said in an interview. "The middle class enjoys our work because they don't dig opera and art and they think they're better than we are. The few upper-class people who watch us like to see what happens on the other side of the tracks. That's why we're so popular. We specialize in upsetting dignity. We only throw pies at guys wearing top hats—obviously high-class people. We never throw pies at old ladies."

They also never shrank from what they considered their responsibility to pound each other believably during filming. While Moe was reputed to be gifted at delivering his signature eye poke so quickly it was hard to notice that his fingers landed almost two inches above the eye sockets, the boys worked rough and accidents did happen.

"Once we did a scene with Moe on a table, and Curly and I were sawing a piece of wood on a table and we were sawing right through the table with the wood and it was wired so it would break away," said Larry. "And Moe knows that, and as they pulled the wire, it failed to work and the jerk of the wires threw Moe off the table and broke his ribs. It was in one of the Columbia pictures in 1937, and he got up and finished the scene and then collapsed."

"In another scene for another picture, Moe accidentally broke my nose," Larry said. "He was supposed to hit me with a rubber hammer, but the handle was wooden, and accidentally the handle hit my nose in about 1939." Legend has it that Larry's face grew so accustomed to the slapping that his cheek was callus-tough, but by most accounts Moe was even gifted at pulling most of the sting out of the slaps.

"Moe was very skillful," said director Edward Bernds. "He said the secret of the slap is not to have the fingers stiff. Sometimes he belted them pretty good, but not nearly as vicious as it looked. On the eye poking, he never poked the eyes, he never missed. I objected to the violence. When I was assigned to direct the first one, I wanted to have a talk with him and I said that I didn't like it, that the idea that if one kid anywhere damaged another kid's eyes, I'd die. And he kind of agreed with me. It was forbidden in the ones I did, except once in a while in the heat of the action they would revert to it. Actually it was Larry who did that more, you know, in the stress of combat."

Larry recalled once getting a fountain pen embedded in his forehead which created a bloody

mess, during filming of the 1948 short *Heavenly Daze,* as he and Moe were trying to sell the unlikely invention of a fountain pen that would write under whipped cream. He once tried to run through a breakaway brick wall only to hit the real bricks next to the phony part and get knocked cold.

Three Little Pigskins featured a scene in which the Stooges were running downfield for a score, stopping for a sideline photo. The other team

catches up and levels the boys and the shutterbug. Larry recalled refusing the stunt. The doubles he insisted on and the photographer were hospitalized with broken arms, legs, and internal injuries, Fine said.

Stuntmen were fine for some gags, but not the slaps, and those blows had to look real. Moe once recalled a take in which he was to deliver a hard slap to his brother Curly.

"On one occasion, I slapped him and it was just a little bit off line, was a little low, and it didn't make quite the noise that he liked," said Moe. "So when we redid the scene, he said to me outside, outside of the door we were entering, 'Come on, do it a little harder so they can hear it.' " Moe obliged.

Moe's daughter, Joan, said Curly was a regular Rocky Balboa during live shows. "When my dad hit Curly, he'd always say, 'Hit me harder,' " she said. "He wanted them to be able to hear it in the back row. I'd actually be able to see the saliva flying out of Curly's mouth. I'm sure it hurt."

Audiences certainly were convinced. During the thirties, the *New York Times* reported on just how much trouble Curly's ability to take hits caused him with drunks and children. Drunks routinely walked up to him just to belt him in the kisser. While Curly could defend himself against those attacks, the kids were more difficult because he never knew whether he'd get an autograph request or an assault by a half-pinter. Once in Atlantic City while he was on the boardwalk admiring the ocean, Curly was recognized by a cane-carrying eight-year-old who promptly swung his stick and belted Howard in the back of the legs. Turning for a fight, he was met with the adoring look of a mother and her youngster, and could do little but smile.

For all their success, the Stooges were stuck in

FOUND—IN A STORM OF LAUGHS!
The 3 STOOGES
MOE LARRY CURLY
TUNIS 1500 MI.
TUNIS 1500 MI.
TUNIS 1500 MI.
TUNIS 1500 MI.
WE WANT OUR MUMMY
Directed by DEL LOR
Produced by JULES WHIT
A COLUMBIA
2-REEL COMEDY

The boys play detectives on the hunt for the cursed corpse of the mummy Rootentooten in this 1939 short.

the two-reeler genre, which didn't have the level of prestige accorded full-length features.

Abbott and Costello, who learned their craft by watching stooge vaudeville routines, eclipsed their fame when the duo stepped into the feature work the Stooges could have had if they'd followed Larry's original Universal deal instead of the Columbia pact Moe had signed.

Larry with a blond Lucille Ball in Three Little Pigskins, 1934.

and didn't mean as much. They felt there wasn't much of a reward to be reaped from it. I don't think shorts were that big a profit center for the studio."

The Stooges did the occasional feature, which was included in their contract and for which they didn't really receive extra money. But it never became their prime focus. Most performers used two-reelers as stepping-stones to the higher-profile features. Talents such as Lucille Ball and Lloyd Bridges show up in shorts on their way to features, and Del Lord and writer Charles Lamont also moved on to features. Not the Stooges.

"Moe talked to Harry Cohn about that and I guess Harry didn't believe in them," said Bernds. "I mean they had the example of Abbott and Costello and Laurel and Hardy and I think it kind of put them off and I think the Stooges continued for a number of years with the hope that Columbia would let them do a feature."

In truth, the Stooge style of manic slapstick would have been difficult to sustain for the length of a feature. Larry acknowledged as much once when he said, "We can make six short features out of material needed for one long comedy. Look what happened to Harry Langdon and Buster Keaton when they tried to be funny for seven reels. We're satisfied to keep 'em short."

"They weren't treated second-class, it was more like third-class," said Leonard Maltin. "It wasn't really a matter of treatment, but there wasn't as much attention or publicity. The publicity department, if they had a starlet under contract they were trying to build up in the feature unit, they would plant items, get photo layouts, send out pinups. There was a whole regimen of things they would do. With the short-subject stars, they hardly did anything. That's not to say they did nothing, they tried to give them some publicity. They weren't fools, they wanted to support the product. But it was just on a much smaller scale

THE STOOGES FIGHT WORLD WAR TWO— FROM HOLLYWOOD

The Stooges lacerated the Nazis and Mussolini's Italy in <u>You Nazty Spy!</u>

THE STOOGES MOVED UP TO CONTRACTS THAT BROKE THEIR PAYCHECKS UP INTO WEEKLY SALARIES. ACCORDING TO A CONTRACT THE GROUP SIGNED ON APRIL 11, 1936, THE GROUP REUPPED AT $750 PER WEEK. OTHER OPTIONS THAT COVERED THE NEXT FOUR YEARS CALLED FOR RAISES TO $1,000, THEN $1,500 THE FOLLOWING YEAR, $2,250 THE NEXT YEAR, AND $2,750 THE FIFTH YEAR. IT PROVES THAT THE MYTH ABOUT THE STOOGES NEVER GETTING A RAISE WAS JUST THAT; BUT IT ALSO SHOWS THAT THE WAY NOT TO GET RICH IN HOLLYWOOD WAS TO BE A LONGTIME STAPLE OF THE TWO-REELER GENRE.

Perhaps a better barometer of what the Stooges earned comes in a studio accounting dated May 21, 1937. It covered the period between July 1, 1936, and May 15, 1937, during which Columbia paid the trio a total of $21,000. That included $2,250 over three weeks for *Grips, Grunts, and Groans* and the same sum for the next six shorts.

Essentially, the Stooges were made to sweat out contract renewals each year. Moe, who lived to work and who constantly fretted over his finances, hardly seemed the type to make a fuss over pay.

"Columbia played a game with them every year," said Edward Bernds. "They kind of let it be known that two-reelers were on the way out and that they didn't know if they'd renew. Most contracts in the picture business, if you pick up an option, there's a raise with it. If you picked up the option on a team like the Stooges, that means you want them, they're good, and you give them a little more money. What I heard is that Columbia kind of mounted a campaign of saying that two-reelers weren't making money, that they might be phased out. So Moe, for several years, signed at the same money. According to the contract, they were

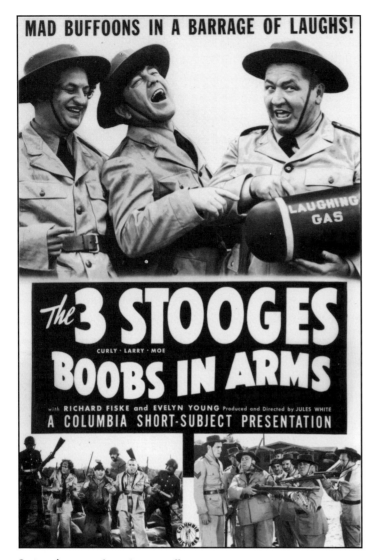

Boobs in Arms, one of several wartime efforts.

due for more money. But knowing Moe, he didn't want to take a chance of the series being terminated. He wanted to work. He didn't really need the money desperately, but he did want to continue making Stooge films."

In the late thirties and early forties, that threat seemed a hollow one. The Stooge shorts were the strongest sellers Columbia had. But that doesn't mean that Moe knew it.

"Every year somebody would come to my dad and say, 'I don't think the shorts are doing well, but we'll talk to the powers that be and see what we can do for you,'" said Joan Maurer. "Every year they had to wait to see if the option would be renewed. I don't think my father realized how popular they were from a monetary standpoint because he was working all the time. But I remember him coming home one time in the late forties, telling my mother that he found out Columbia was forcing theater owners, if they wanted the Stooge comedies, they'd have to take all these lousy B movies. Had he known that earlier or had he gotten an agent who was really on his side, I think my dad would have had much more confidence. He would have known that the studio really needed him."

The other reason Moe and the Stooges were reluctant to make a major case over their paychecks was the intimidating presence of their Columbia boss, Harry Cohn. Remember, the Howards and Fine worked nearly a decade being underpaid by the prickly Ted Healy. But Healy was a marshmallow compared to Cohn.

By most accounts, Cohn could be a brutally hard man who seemed to enjoy reducing a writer or staffer to a shell with his browbeating. According to Bob Thomas's biography *King Cohn,* Cohn was invited to meet the Italian dictator Benito Mussolini in 1933, after the studio released a successful documentary, *Mussolini Speaks,* at a time he was most famous for making the trains run on time.

Cohn was captivated by the setup of the iron-man's office and replicated it exactly because it made a clear statement that he was the man in charge and a man to be feared. There was no knob on the outside of his office door—only a buzzer activated by his secretary—and visitors, who often waited hours after being summoned by the boss, had better push the door before the buzzer stopped. Or else face the wrath of Cohn. It was all for intimidation purposes, of course. Cohn was a man who, an oft-repeated joke in Hollywood goes, had a funeral that was packed to the rafters. Explained director Phil Berle, "It was proof that if you give the people what they want, they show up in droves."

Cohn apparently adored the Stooges, and especially Curly. But this was a man who reputedly bugged offices and who would dress down employees if they exited work the day before and left a light burning, which he would discover during daily rounds he'd make of the premises for that very purpose. Cohn wasn't about to fancy the Stooges' feature aspirations when their shorts were driving his two-reeler department and making him money—their highly physical slapstick style made them salable even in foreign markets. And Cohn wasn't about to pay them any more than he had to.

Aside from the contractual games, Cohn left the Stooges, and the running of the entire shorts department, to Jules White, who oversaw all the two-reelers the studio supplied to theaters. That included the Stooges and the Screen Snapshots newsreels. By the early 1940s, White would become a regular director and producer of the Stooge shorts as other short-subject franchises fizzled out. And he was exerting more influence in their direction.

White favored the hard slaps and outlandish physical slapstick that taxed the team. But he also produced some of its funniest shorts, giving sound mixer Joe Henrie plenty of opportunity to employ his seemingly endless library of odd noises that perfectly accompanied any form of physical torture that White and the writers could dream up for the Stooges.

The Stooge shorts continued to evolve and improve. Though the airborne pie was considered a staple of the Stooge comedy diet, it wasn't until 1939 that the troupe engaged in the first heated pie battle. That occurred in *Three Sappy People,* about a fun-craving eccentric woman who gets more than she can handle when the Stooges, phone repairmen, show up at her birthday party masquerading as supershrinks Dr. Z. Ziller, X. Zeller, and Y. Zoller.

Adrian Booth Bryan played the eccentric woman, going under the stage name Lorna Gray. As was common in the shorts game, Bryan was a newcomer who made her debut with a few lines when she played a gorgeous Southern belle in *Oily to Bed, Oily to Rise.*

"They put me under contract because I'd made a picture, *The Man They Could Not Hang,* with Boris Karloff, and they liked me," said Bryan. "They put me in that first Stooge comedy, and it was only a couple of lines. But I had to speak with a Southern accent and I put on the most Southern accent I could come up with and Jules White got tickled by it. That got me the lead role in the next two shorts."

One of the countless Columbia actresses who endured pie facials to act in Stooge shorts. From Three Sappy People, 1939.

Both were Stooge milestones.

Three Sappy People demonstrated to White that pie as projectile was funny.

"When I did *Three Sappy People*, Jules was laughing right along with us, and he said that in his twenty years of directing, one of the funniest things he'd ever done was a scene in which they were throwing small pies," said Bryan. "The first was thrown at me when I was sitting at the end of a table. He told the propman to throw the pie at me while my mouth was open. I really laughed and I didn't know it was going to happen. So he threw it and it went right down my throat but I just went on talking. Jules said it was one of the funniest things he ever saw in his life and he printed it. I don't remember what they used in the pie, something heavier than whipped cream. I just remember that it made me choke."

Her next short was even more of a milestone in Stooge history. *You Nazty Spy!*, filmed in 1939 and released in 1940, was one of the very first showbiz assaults on Adolf Hitler's Nazi Germany. Though Charlie Chaplin rightfully drew acclaim for his Hitler parody, *The Great Dictator*, and clearly Chaplin had worked for several years on the film, the fact is, the Stooge short came out first.

Early Stooge shorts often made topical references to the Depression and FDR's New Deal, but the Stooges had been largely apolitical, except that they were a lower-class crew who made a living by giving a comeuppance to the upper-crust set. That would change with the advent of war with Nazi Germany and the Japanese, both of whom were lampooned viciously.

In *You Nazty Spy!,* Moe played Moe Hailstone, who became dictator in the kingdom of Moronica. With his stunted mustache (Hailstone called it "my personality"), Moe was closer to a dead ringer for the menacing facial features of Hitler than was Chaplin. Accompanied by Curly and Larry in parodies of Hitler's minister of propaganda, Joseph Goebbels, and Field Marshal Hermann Göring, the short depicted the thinly veiled Nazis as cruel buffoons. Hailstone becomes dictator when he's promised that the requirements of the job were to "make speeches to the people, promising them plenty. He gives them nothing and then he takes everything." Moe quickly warms to the clipped speech of Hitler. Moronica gets a new flag—snakes entwined into the shape of a swastika—and he orders books to be burned and an innocent man to be sent to a "concentrated camp." In the epitome of what could be called a happy ending, Hailstone and his aides are eaten by lions. They would show up again, however, in a sequel episode, in which they wind up getting killed, their heads mounted on a wall as trophies.

Bryan played Mata Hari in *You Nazty Spy!,* and though she said she moved so quickly from shorts to features that it all blended together, she recalled the short creating quite a stir when it showed in theaters. "None of the studios had done that kind of thing at that time," she said.

That assertion was backed up by Don Morlan, chairman of Dayton University's communications department and an expert on war propaganda films. Though it later became fashionable to knock Nazis and the Japanese, the Stooges were at the forefront. And their genre allowed them to tee off on both countries.

"There were some movies that predated *You Nazty Spy!,* such as *Confessions of a Nazi,*" said Morlan. "But there was great criticism leveled at the producers of those dramas by the isolationists in Congress, who were opposed to U.S. involvement in the war. It led to Congress actually holding hearings about the movie business. For some reason, they left the comedies alone. Some studios didn't want to rock the boat either, because the foreign market for their films was high."

Hollywood, initially reluctant to make political films because of its own theater and film interests abroad, only began to warm to the task after the United States declared war on Germany. There were exceptions before then, such as the message in a film like *The Man I Married,* which starred Lloyd Nolan as an American war correspondent in Germany who says, "Perhaps war was the only way to make an end to these lunatics who spread fear and hatred over the world." Films such as *Confessions of a Nazi Spy, To Be or Not to Be* with Jack Benny, the Veronica Lake-starrer *I Wanted Wings,* and even the Abbott and Costello comedy *Buck Privates* began a trend of anti-Nazi films.

But the Stooges were first. Sam White attributed the aggressive propagandizing to the patriotism of the Stooges and especially his brother

Jules, who directed all of the politically charged shorts. All of them were Jewish, and had become aware of the toll the Nazis were taking on Europe and the Jewish population there.

"We all felt strongly during World War Two," said White. "We lived through that war, and the feelings ran so high you can't believe it. Everyone here, with the Japanese colony nearby, we'd look at every one of them and suspect they were spies for Japan and that they were going to destroy us. When the little submarines came and lobbed two or three bombs on the Santa Barbara pier, it scared the hell out of us. Jules had a very strong feeling about it, and he and my brother Jack joined up to create those things together, even though Jack didn't take credit for them. They weren't the only ones. Warner Bros. made *Confessions of a Nazi Spy,* and there were quite a few others that followed, very powerful ones that were anti-Nazi and even anticommunist."

After the bombing of Pearl Harbor, the filmmakers took their ire out on the Japanese with several shorts that depicted the Japanese as mute, brain-dead villains with slanty eyes and sugar-cube-sized buckteeth. In one, the Stooges wipe out a bunch of "Japs" after they escape from a relocation camp. Given the stories of cruelty to Japanese Americans who were herded up, stripped of their possessions, and detained in relocation camps when anti-Japanese fever raged at its high-

I'll Never Heil Again, 1941.

est, those shorts appear to be racist and are difficult even to watch, much less laugh at, today.

Sam White argues that the shorts that used the Japanese as villains must be judged within the context of the times, right down to the stereotypical physical appearance of the villains.

"They were caricatures of what we visualized

the Japanese to be as they were painted through propaganda and especially after they bombed Pearl Harbor and killed all of our boys," said White. "It was enough to make your blood boil, and the newspapers had many, many cartoons depicting them in that same way that Jules did in those movies. I went to Japan to make a feature in 1986, and the crew and people I got to work with were the most wonderful people you'd ever met. But they, like the Germans, said, 'We did what we were told.' You can be sure those shorts were the result of our feelings running so high about the war that it was just frightening."

After Vietnam, most filmmakers today would rebel at being used by the government as tools for propaganda. Back then, with the existence of the United States at risk, the film community lined up for duty. In fact, there was an armed services office right outside of the Columbia lot, and filmmakers were regular visitors.

"Everybody in the film business, all the guys I worked with, all went into the service in various capacities and got commissions because of their knowledge of making propaganda films," said White, himself the director of many films, and episodes of the series *Perry Mason* and *My Friend Flicka,* which he also produced. "I tried to join, but was told to stay home because I had two children, but I made a lot of anti-Nazi kinds of features which they ran for the armed forces. They wanted films made by professionals, which is why Frank Capra went in as a general and John Ford went in as an admiral. George Stevens was a colonel and they made him a general."

Stars did their parts. Jimmy Stewart flew combat missions over Germany; megastars of the day like Bette Davis volunteered to stump for war bonds to support the war effort; Carole Lombard died in a plane crash when returning from a war bond tour. Her devastated husband, Clark Gable, enlisted in the service shortly after.

CHAPTER TWELVE

CURLY'S COLLAPSE

Curly offscreen. A dapper dresser and graceful dancer,
his love of nightlife eventually caught up to him,
and his health began failing.

THE STOOGES FLOURISHED DURING THE WAR. THE POPULARITY OF THE SHORTS MADE FINDING STAGE WORK EASY FOR MOE, AND THE TRIO REGULARLY TOURED DURING THEIR ANNUAL TWELVE-WEEK LAYOFF FROM THE STUDIO. CONTRACTS INDICATE THAT THEIR COLUMBIA SALARIES HALTED DURING THOSE PERIODS. BUT THE STOOGES GOT PAID MUCH BETTER ON THE STAGE AND DOUBLED AND TRIPLED THEIR SALARIES BECAUSE OF THEIR ROAD WORK.

Their burgeoning popularity in the foreign market convinced Moe to plan an overseas tour for 1946.

Unfortunately, their meal ticket, Curly Howard, was beginning to show the strains of his wild lifestyle.

Curly was an anomaly. Onscreen, he stole every scene he was in, this wildly talented man-child with the high-pitched voice and the distinctive physical mannerisms. Offscreen, he was largely withdrawn, particularly when he was in the company of his brother Moe. Though Moe once described his relationship with Curly "as close as it's possible to be without sleeping with him," even Moe acknowledged he didn't really know what Curly was doing when he wasn't working.

"Socially, he was as hard to contact or grab as a wild rabbit," said Moe. "He just went his own way, did what he wanted. Socially, he never consulted anyone."

It has often been reported that Curly, who once cut a dashing and relatively svelte figure, developed a poor self-image as a result of his Stooge persona as a heavyset cueball-crowned clown. He'd be no different than Fatty Arbuckle, or in later years John Belushi or Chris Farley. All were wildly gifted overweight comics who died from excess that was a combination of a lack of self-discipline and the urge to fill some emptiness inside.

Curly's offscreen passions included stray dogs, which he seemed to collect in every town he visited. Though he was quite shy when sober and described in several accounts as a mama's boy, he fancied the ladies and seemed to collect wives with the same enthusiasm he did dogs.

Curly got married four times, and though he died as the husband of Valerie Howard, most of his other marriages lasted about as long as a Stooge short. The June 8, 1938, *Beverly Hills Citizen* described a four-month romance with Elaine Ackerman that culminated in marriage, with Moe serving as the best man. This was his second marriage, the first having lasted just six months.

Moe, who knew Elaine well, arranged the divorce.

"I was the one that made the settlement, and gave more than she ever asked for, for Curly," Moe said. "He left it to me to handle."

A *Los Angeles Times* article dated June 20, 1946, broke news of Curly's divorce from his third wife, Marian Howard, whom he had married the previous October after a two-week courtship. Even though Curly had given her $250 for clothes, a $3,750 mink coat, and an $850 wristwatch,

The Howard Brothers laugh it up, before Curly suffers his stroke and Shemp returns.

his wife and her lawyer served up twenty charges in the divorce complaint which netted her a $5,200 settlement.

"She said he used filthy, vulgar and vile language, kept two vicious dogs which she was afraid would bite her; shouted at waiters in cafes; pushed, struck and pinched her; put cigars in the sink," the article reported. Though Curly claimed

she had refused to live with him and called him a "bad name" at least once, the judge ruled in her favor on the cash, though she vacated the home he owned in North Hollywood.

Moe got Curly out of that mess as well, recalling that "to all appearances, she made him miserable. Obviously taking him for whatever she could."

Though painfully shy in private moments,
Curly was the life of the party after hours.

Moe's children, Paul and Joan Howard Maurer, recall Curly as being very demure when he visited their home. "He was a quiet, charming guy," said Paul. "I remember once he went on a tour of a military camp and brought me back a Japanese rifle. As a kid, I didn't see much of the humor he displayed in his work, but I've seen him in the family films, Curly with a bunch of kids at a birthday party teaching them how to salute."

Curly would occasionally display a wild side. In his office, Sam White has a framed Christmas card from Curly which features Curly's head superimposed on the body of a naked little boy in a crib. It reads "Merry Christmas from an Itty Bitty Stoogie."

"I'd say the wild part of his lifestyle was when he was on the road," said Joan Maurer. "He stayed up later than my dad, and if he'd been drinking

he'd come back to the hotel and yell 'Swing it' at the top of his lungs. He might wake a few people up but my dad would breathe a sigh of relief, know he was okay, and my dad would go to sleep. I didn't think of him as an alcoholic. He never drank onstage because my dad wouldn't have worked with him. I don't think he was the happiest guy, though, and he tried to find some happiness in women. He loved women. Because they were in that milieu, he usually didn't find the most intelligent women."

The seemingly indestructible man-child began slowing down gradually. He took medication for high blood pressure. And he began suffering what would later be determined to be small strokes. Larry

Curly is Señorita Cucaracha in the Stooge classic Micro-Phonies.
While Curly went drag in many Stooge shorts, this 1945 short was his
last great performance.

Fine suspected that immunity shots the Stooges were required to get for their overseas tour could have contributed to his deteriorating condition.

Whatever the cause, the erosion is readily evident to anyone willing to take the time to watch his last ten shorts. In some he's Curly, in others, sickly.

Edward Bernds, the longtime Stooge sound-

man, got his big chance to direct with the Stooge short *Bird in the Head*. Unfortunately, that was one of the shorts in which Curly was clearly suffering.

"He was a hard liver, and he drank too much," said Bernds. "It was an awful tough deal for a rookie director to have a Curly who wasn't himself." Bernds made the movie, but Hugh McCollum, the former secretary of studio president Harry Cohn, was now responsible for half of the Stooge shorts. Bernds never got along well with Jules White, and both he and McCollum feared that if Bernds made his directing debut with *Bird in the Head* and a half-strength Curly, his Stooge directing career would be over as soon as it had started. So they shuffled the order and pushed back the release date of *Bird,* replacing it with *Micro-Phonies.* That short, which featured Curly at full strength with a hysterical stint in drag lip-synching to a record, is remembered as one of the best Curly efforts. It allowed Bernds to keep working.

Bernds directed five shorts with Curly and said that he never knew which Curly would show up. At times, it was the ebullient comic genius who bounced off the walls; others, it would be a tired old man who moved slowly and whose voice was clearly strained.

"My main recollection of that first one is Curly, what we later all decided had been a slight stroke," said Bernds. "He was not the same Curly, and I believe that Moe was as surprised as me. Of course, as a rookie director, this was dismaying. I was very well acquainted with Curly's work. Like most of the rest of the crew, we were crazy about Curly. He did the kind of things that delighted the crew. So, directing my first one, it was not the same Curly, this was a considerable blow."

Moe helped his brother with line readings, said Bernds, because Curly grew forgetful. While it seems unfathomable that Curly would not have been carted off to a doctor immediately, Jean DeRita, the widow of later Stooge Joe DeRita, recalled Moe saying years later that Columbia brass didn't want to interrupt the output of the shorts and wouldn't allow Curly time off to recover. The Stooges gamely continued on, hoping he'd come around. It was a disastrous course of action.

"He couldn't remember his lines, his motions were slow," said Bernds. "I made five shorts with Curly, and the last one, thank goodness, was *Three Little Pirates,* the one where he is the rajah, and he was almost his own self in that. But then a week or ten days later, he was making a picture with Jules White and that's where he passed out and they finally realized it was a stroke and he never really worked again."

Curly suffered his debilitating stroke on May 19, 1946, waiting to do the last scene of the day on *Half-Wits Holiday,* a remake of one of the very best Stooge shorts, *Hoi Polloi.*

"He was sitting in a chair and had a stroke," Moe later recalled. "I completed the scene for him. He was taken home."

It was clear to his brother that Jerome was in seriously bad shape.

"His mouth became distorted, and when he got up from the chair he fell to his knees," said Moe. "One side of him seemed to be slightly paralyzed."

While it seems difficult to believe Curly had to deteriorate so far before being hospitalized, it was in keeping with his childlike manner.

"He was the kind of man that if my dad didn't tell him to do something he didn't do it," said Moe's daughter, Joan. "The only way he would ever go to a doctor is if my dad chased him there. He wasn't that kind of man, he was like a big kid. Do kids take themselves to a doctor? My dad might have made it worse because Curly was so dependent on him. But I know my dad loved him and treated him the way a dad would a son. Curly was not an alcoholic but he liked to drink and he ate too much and his weight was too high.

Moe, Larry, and Curly mug on the Columbia lot during No Census, No Feeling, 1940.

And he liked the ladies. I think he just burned the candle at both ends and it caught up with him."

Curly's unexpected stroke left his longtime partners, Moe Howard and Larry Fine, reeling. And though Columbia boss Harry Cohn had told the Stooges they'd always have a place at the studio while he was there, they were genuinely worried that they wouldn't last very long without Curly.

Thinking that Curly might recover and rejoin the act, Howard and Fine brought Shemp Howard, who had preceded his younger brother, back into the fold as a temporary replacement. Shemp was a natural choice because he'd accumulated a solid performing record and knew the routines dating back to his vaudeville days.

Curly's health, unfortunately, did not improve. His comedy depended on his high-pitched delivery and his overwhelming physical abilities. The stroke left him with impaired speech and dragging one foot.

Trying to boost his morale, the Stooges gave Curly a cameo in *Hold That Lion,* the third Shemp short.

Curly, who'd grown back his full head of hair, is shown sleeping in a Pullman car. The Stooges are looking for a crook who stole their inheritance, and when they lift his hat, they seem to recognize him, but put the hat back over his face and move on.

"We tried to build his morale . . . but it didn't work out right," said Moe.

Columbia brass was clearly rooting for Curly's recovery, as evidenced in a contract dated September 31, 1946, that reupped the Stooges for another year of two-reeler duty. Curly was still on the contract, as was Shemp. A section of the contract dealt with Curly's illness.

It is acknowledged that presently Jerry Howard is incapacitated and that Shemp Howard shall render his services in place and stead of Jerry Howard . . . Jerry Howard agrees at such time as he is physically able to render his services under this agreement to give us written notice of such fact . . . to enter upon his employment under this agreement upon the termination of the term of Shemp Howard's employment as hereinabove provided.

But Curly was finished as a Stooge for good. He retired, later married Valerie Howard, had his second child, another daughter, and passed away at the Baldy View Sanitarium on January 18, 1952.

As was the case with Ted Healy, Curly left very little money behind, prompting his daughters to eventually sue Moe.

Revealed in the 1961 court case was the fact that Moe had gotten his infirmed younger brother to basically renounce all rights to the Stooges. Moe again might have just been trying to protect the group's interests, but the letter is heartbreaking. Dated September 30, 1946, and addressed to "Dear Bro. Babe," Moe wrote:

I trust that you are feeling better at this writing. It might encourage you, and in a way delight you to know that Brother Shemp was agreeable to step into your boots, in the act, and finish the comedies that were intended to be made by you, I and Larry. Until such time as you are well enough to return to the trio. It may further delight you to know that I have made arrangements with Shemp and Larry, so that during your illness, you will receive $150 per week to assist you for a time towards the extraordinary medical expenses that you have and are still incurring. And further in view of the fact that Shemp is now operating with us in your place, I will need from you, by your signature underneath attesting to the fact that you give me, as owner of The 3 Stooges, the perpetual rights to use pictures of your face and recordings of your voice for all future advertising, commercial tie-ins, merchandising and any other way needed, and the right to assign these rights to others if and when the need may arise. The first picture in which Shemp operates in your place was very good, but although Shemp is a great comic in his own right, Larry and I miss you very much and we are hoping and praying to have you back with us soon now.

Babe, please sign your name to the bottom signifying your acceptance of my using your face and voice for the purposes I have stated above. Hope you will soon be well enough so that we can be together again. Your loving brother, Moe.

The ailing Stooge signed the letter with a shaky "Jerry Howard," but the payments lessened after about two years, by Moe's own admission. "Vaudeville theaters were closing up," he said. "We weren't going on personal appearances as much. And I felt at that time that I couldn't afford to make such weekly payments. Shemp stopped sooner than I did and so did Larry." That happened in late 1948, though Moe later brought his younger brother in on a real estate deal that proved profitable.

It's clear that Moe was shattered by his brother's demise, and worried perhaps more than was necessary about the future of the act that dominated his life.

While a spirited comic onscreen, Moe was the exact opposite of what most people would imagine a famous Hollywood star to be. When he was not out touring, he was a genuine homebody. His hobbies were hooking rugs, gardening, and presiding over weekend family barbecues. The other thing he did was worry.

"To me, my father was this very nervous, anxiety-ridden person," said his son, Paul. "I believe, in retrospect, that he was worrying about his career. His partners, while being very creative and nice people, did not have the same sense of responsibility that he did, and perhaps he even overreacted. I remember the anxiety he was always going through, this guy sitting at what he called his captain's table, this wonderful Early American table he'd sit at with his checkbook. I could hear him brooding and grunting and worrying about finances. This was roughly the period when his younger brother, Curly, got sick."

Paul Howard recalled that his parents put the house up for sale at this time, when his father was worried about a downturn in business.

"I was about eleven or twelve and my folks were away on a trip, and Doris Day was looking for a home," said Howard. "We had the house up for sale when my father was having trouble in the business. A Realtor came and I decided I didn't want that house sold. I hid under the bed, and I could see legs as she looked through the house. I remember trying to light firecrackers to make them go away, which, fortunately, wouldn't light. Finally, when they did leave, I did throw firecrackers out the window. Part of me always wanted to meet her and ask if she remembered me."

But while Paul Howard recalled some childhood turmoil, for the most part Moe provided a very stable home. "The perfect analogy of my father is that he was the practical pig of the trio," said Paul. "He literally built his world as a brick home, not a straw home or a home of sticks. By the standards of that time, we certainly lived comfortably. In our neighborhood, our house was clearly not like that of Bob Hope, who lived nearby and whom we trick-or-treated and found a security man and a fence. We went to Frank Sinatra's house nearby as well, and that was a very modest house. I remember his wife coming to the door, giving us candy and telling us that Frank was recording and couldn't see us. A lot of those people lived in the neighborhood. We had a nice house, a pool man, and a maid, and we lived very comfortably."

Moe slaved in his beloved vegetable garden. Family barbecues were the week highlight. "If you walked in the yard on Sunday afternoon, my father would be barbecuing, people would be swimming in the pool," said Paul. "Women played gin rummy by themselves, the men would play the same game by themselves. I have no idea why they didn't play together. They'd come together later for coffee and Danish and they'd tell jokes. My father was a wonderful joke teller."

Mostly, the attendees were family. Joan Howard could recall seeing Phil Silvers, a family friend. Paul recalled seeing Bowery Boys stalwart Huntz Hall, a close pal of Shemp's. For the most part, Moe kept business out of the house. The only clear reminder of who he was, was the black wrought-iron silhouette of the Stooges taken from an MGM still photo that Moe's wife had made for him while Moe was on tour during the 1940s. It hung on the garage. Other than that, the homelife suggested that Moe was more likely an accountant than a stooge.

"The only time I was aware of the business at all was when my father was worrying and messing with his finances," said Paul. "I think they had preproduction meetings where they discussed routines, but they were formally planned meetings outside, and I can't remember anytime the business infiltrated the house. I know that was very important to my father."

Moe had plenty of reason to worry when his baby brother took sick.

"The big question, what would happen to the Stooges, was the subject of considerable debate," said Edward Bernds, who was right in the middle,

since he was directing many of the shorts during that period. "Shemp had made a whole series of singles at Columbia. I had directed a couple of them and liked his work very much. I was not consulted on the process, that was for the front office. But some of the people in the front office said that Shemp looked too much like Moe, that his series would probably do very well by itself. They would have to sacrifice it.

"But in the end, I think it was at Moe's insistence that Shemp take Curly's place." Bernds then directed the first short Shemp appeared in, a boxing short called *Fright Night*.

"It was kind of Curly material but Shemp did it very well," said Bernds. *"Fright Night* turned out to be a pretty good picture and it was apparent that Shemp would get by very nicely. And I considered the Stooge comedies I did with Shemp as the best of the bunch I did."

Though they sorely missed Curly, replacing him with Shemp allowed them to continue with no break in continuity. Shemp, after all, was an original Stooge who knew their timing and routines, which he had helped develop. And he caught on lightning quick, even though he'd been gone almost fifteen years. While his shorts are considered second-tier to those that starred Curly, Shemp had his own distinctive comic voice and more than held his own. And it seems unanimous that he was a lot funnier offscreen than his brooding and troubled brother Curly.

In fact, he was nearly as much a character as Ted Healy.

"As far as I'm concerned, because Moe was dead serious about everything and Curly never really made any comedic moves, I think as a personally funny person, Shemp was funniest," said

Sam White, who often saw the group socially. "He didn't come across on the screen that funny, not like Curly, because Curly was visually funny."

Shemp was peculiar in ways all his own. He was quite a hypochondriac, recalled Sam White, who used to play poker at Moe's house, partly to catch up on stories about the eldest Howard.

"He was scared of his shadow, really, and wouldn't go to a hotel room because of bedbugs and things unless his wife, Babe, checked it out," said White. "He used to live over near Toluca Lake, where they all settled down. All the Stooges bought houses and Shemp and Babe lived in one and I don't know how or why but they had some chickens in their yard. He liked chickens. One day one of the chickens got out and flew over into the neighbor's yard and started pecking away at everything. The neighbor was just very upset about it. So Shemp was scared to go in the neighbor's yard. He climbed up on a wooden fence that separated their yards and first he went in the house and got a fishing rod with a hook on it. He tried to hook the chicken," said White, "and he kept casting that thing out and he never got it onto the chicken. His wife came home and she went next door and brought it back. She asked why he didn't, and Shemp muttered that they would have been mad at him."

Shemp was an enormous fan of the prize-fights. Watching with him was an adventure, Jeffrey Howard recalled. "Shemp was funny in ways he couldn't even help. Around when the first TV sets came out, he had the first television set in the family. He lived two blocks from my house, and when he couldn't go to the fights in person, he'd watch on TV. One night we all went to his house for dinner, and I asked to bring a friend along because the fights were on and I knew we'd be totally entertained by Shemp."

To Howard, it seemed his uncle worked harder than the pugilists. "Rather than the fighters being the focus, he was the center of attention. He'd go through all the bobs and weaves and ducks and grunts. It was amazing and hysterical to watch him. He was like a punch-drunk fighter, and there was as much perspiration on my uncle as there was on the fighters. And he didn't even realize what he was doing."

Howard said life around Shemp was never dull. "To a ten-year-old, he was really quite something to see. I remember he'd ask if we wanted to see his war wound. He'd pull down his sock, and on the shin of one leg, he had this growth. I'd say it was about the size of the tip of a thumb to the first joint. A lump. He said there was a bullet lodged there from World War One. Of course, it was some kind of growth that he was afraid to have removed because he was quite a hypochondriac."

Shemp loathed flying, and he wasn't much for driving, either. "The only person he'd get into a car with was his son, Mort, my father, and myself," said Howard. "My father once was teaching him to drive. He was in the car, going down the street on a quiet morning. The brake was on the outside and Shemp was behind the wheel and in a panic. He pulled the wrong thing and the car crashed right through a barbershop plate-glass window and ended up right alongside one of the chairs. Thank God nobody was there. That ended his driving career. How he traveled professionally is to this day a mystery to me."

His peculiarities aside, Shemp's temporary stint would become a permanent one, and his presence clearly saved the act.

A Western Union telegram arrived on August 28, 1946, when Shemp was just beginning the difficult task of replacing his more talented younger brother.

"Shemp Howard. Our heartfelt wishes for your success. Stop. Kill the people. Love, Harry and Phil Silvers."

Shemp, who had left the act back in the Healy days at the urging of his wife only to become a show business journeyman, finally found a home at Columbia for the next decade. It would only become evident how difficult it is to replace a Stooge when Shemp was no longer there.

CHAPTER THIRTEEN

TV EYE-POKES THE TWO-REELERS

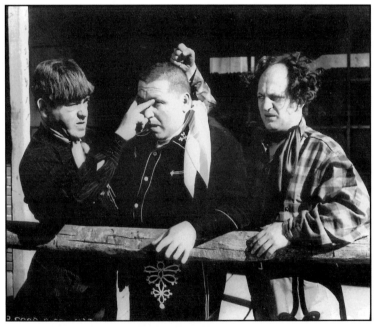

Yes, We Have No Bonanza.

THE STOOGE SHORTS BEGAN TO CHANGE FOR THE WORSE IN THE LATE FORTIES AND EARLY FIFTIES, AND THERE WERE SEVERAL TANGIBLE REASONS FOR THE GRADUAL EROSION.

The output of Stooge stalwarts like Del Lord and Charles Lamont and Charley Chase faded when they moved up to features. And television, initially as derided as the talkie movie twenty years earlier, was gaining a foothold. More people were buying televisions or visiting neighbors who had one. It shrank the demand for two-reelers as exhibitors were now demanding double bills with features topped by recognizable stars. The days when an admission to the theater meant an all-day program were ending.

Predictably, margins tightened, and stock footage from earlier Stooge shorts began showing up more and more frequently during the latter part of the Shemp era. This was made possible by the fact that Larry and Moe never seemed to age physically, making the transition to early footage less clumsy.

That hardly means that the Shemp era didn't have its quota of memorable shorts, particularly in his early years. A solid cast of supporting players that included Vernon Dent, Christine McIntyre, and the irrepressible Emil Sitka kept the shorts vibrant and the gags sharp, even if they left one with the feeling of déjà vu.

To Edward Bernds, who came to prominence as a director during this period, the cost-cutting merely forced a filmmaker to be more clever. If there was a big-budget feature shooting on the lot and using an interesting set that would lend itself to a period short, they would quickly adapt the script to any period necessary.

"I remember we made *Square Heads of the Round Table* and *Hot Scots,* and then Jules made another one, all in a beautiful castle that was built for the feature picture *Lorna Doone,*" said Bernds. "We had to get permission from the front office, and very often I wondered why they'd let us do it. Imagine if *Lorna Doone,* with its big beautiful castle set, was followed on the same program with a two-reeler using the same beautiful castle set?"

The Stooges also filmed shorts on sets for *The Caine Mutiny* and *Pal Joey.* To survive in the second-class two-reeler genre meant being resourceful. Though the phrase "If you build it, they will come" is most readily applied to the 1989 Kevin Costner film *Field of Dreams,* it might well have been the mantra for feature producers on the lot. If they built the sets, inevitably the two-reeler makers would come, hoping to sponge period looks that would enhance the production values of their shorts. They'd shoot until they were chased away.

The catch-as-catch-can nature of the shorts gave opportunities to talent. Diana Darrin, who'd later star with Jack Nicholson in the feature *The*

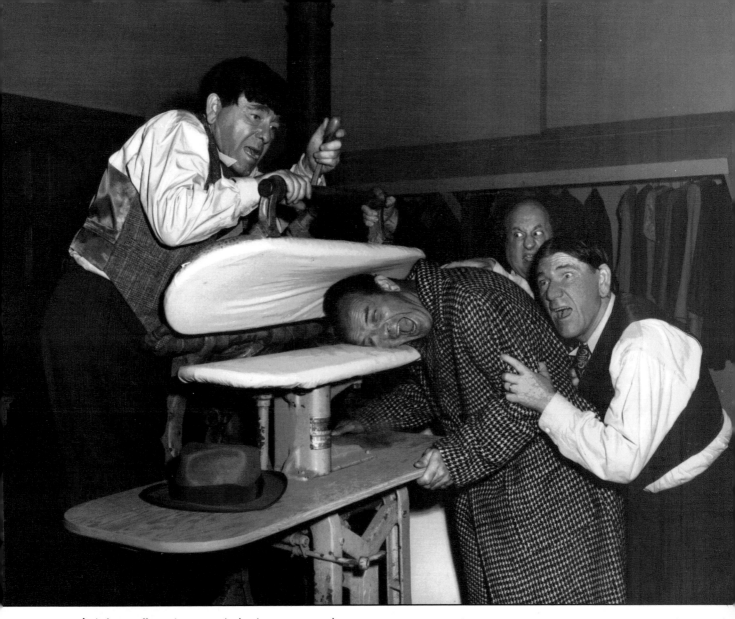

Aside from an effective shirt presser, the dry-cleaning press proved a durable form of punishment in Stooge shorts.
From Rip, Sew & Stitch, 1953.

Broken Land, broke into film with the Stooges. She screen-tested in an actual scene from the short *He Cooked His Goose*, in which she plays the perky secretary of pet shop owner Larry Fine and sits in his lap taking dictation. Jules White, not standing on ceremony, christened her with the stage name Theila Darrin and said action. Fitting the model of gorgeous girls who populated Stooge shorts, she would go on to appear in many Stooge efforts with Shemp and later Joe Besser. She recalls getting numerous pie facials.

"They would make the shorts in three or four days, and it was a lot of pressure but great training, because if you could handle that you could handle anything," said Darrin. "I'd had some stage experience and that helped. I had a few pies in my face. You kind of keep your eyes shut. They tried to do it on one take because it's a lot of pies, and you'd get it all over you and your hair had to be done again, you'd have to change your clothes and start all over again."

Injuries on the set weren't uncommon, but Bernds said that it would have to be cataclysmic to halt work on a short, such was the work ethic of the Stooges.

"Hurt gags were naturally a staple of the two-reelers," said Bernds. "In the very first one I directed, *Bird in the Head,* Moe hurt his knee, really banged it. All through the picture, he had to run and he didn't beg off, he knew the show had to go on. But if you see that picture, you'll notice Moe ran with a limp. And Shemp was not quite as good as the other boys at, say, going through a door, opening it and hitting the door instead. Moe and Larry and Curly knew how to fake that bump, but Shemp didn't have that knack. He too was a willing trouper. I remember one time when he was supposed to bump into a door and he cut his head. The scene was all right because the blood didn't show until the scene was over. But always the comic, he put his hand to his head, saw blood and said, 'Waddaya know, tomato ketchup.' He was kinda shaky, though."

The Stooges watched the fading fortunes of two-reeler business and saw their other major revenue outlet dry up as vaudeville houses closed across the country. That cut down their opportunities to tour in between films. Rather than fight TV, they tried to join it.

Perhaps tiring of sweating out the renewal of their two-reeler contracts each year, the Stooges tried their luck with a TV pilot in 1949.

The show was called *Jerks of All Trades,* and it was produced, written, and directed by Phil Berle, whose brother, Milton, was just becoming known in households across the country as "Uncle Miltie."

Berle, a sharp-minded ninety-seven when interviewed for this book, was a friend of the Stooges and talked them and their regular player Emil Sitka into doing the show, which Berle described as the very first of its kind to be staged before a live studio audience.

The pilot featured the boys as the proprietors of a jack-of-all-trades business. It was highly reminiscent of the Columbia shorts, with the boys pressed into duty as interior decorators who need to paint and wallpaper before a man's boss comes to the house for dinner. Naturally, they do an awful job.

"There was a lot of slapstick, which was their forte," said Berle. "This was the first time a show like that was ever put before a live audience, done with a comedy idea. And it was shot in Kinescope, which meant that once you started, you went right through to the end. There was no stopping if something went wrong."

Though they had become used to working take by take in films, the vaudeville stage training, and plenty of rehearsal, made the Stooges perfectly suited for live TV, even though they were performing precision gags.

"We rehearsed for weeks and weeks to get it down to the second," said Berle. "Kinescope was tough. I had a situation where NBC sent a guy from New York to be an emcee in a show I was doing called *Comedy Matinee* and the guy was out of line from the camera and I told the floor manager to move him over. He waved him over and the guy stops working and says, 'Nobody waves to me.' As soon as he got off, he was fired and I don't know if he ever worked again. Another time, on my brother's show, there was this Italian singer, a barber, who put this can over Milton's head and he ripped Milton's nose, opened it wide open, and Milton kept right on going. That was Kinescope, and what I attempted with the Stooges had never been done before. Even though there was a lot of rough stuff in it—they were slapping each other all over the place—it went beautifully. These three were so professional, it was like they did it in their dreams. They knew exactly what the other guy was going to do before he did it."

Unfortunately, ABC didn't pick up the pilot to series, and Berle moved along to NBC, shelving the entire effort.

"The day we did it, everybody was cheering this thing, but it just died," Berle said. "I shouldn't say it died, because it was good. But the audience just was not ready."

Snubbed by the small screen that was squeezing their shorts, the Stooges returned for another season at Columbia in 1950. Around this time, a power struggle was beginning to break out between Jules White and Hugh McCollum, who by this time was responsible for roughly half of the Stooge shorts. All of the Stooges had problems with White's tough-guy style, which left them little room for collaboration. While Larry and Shemp were happy-go-lucky, Moe wanted a greater say in the comedy. Shemp didn't quite mesh with White mainly for the

same reason he shrank from Ted Healy. Shemp loathed confrontation.

"One of Jules White's faults was that Shemp was a very sensitive guy, and he disliked intensely working with Jules White because Jules insisted on showing him how to be funny," said Bernds. "The really ridiculous thing was when Buster Keaton came to Columbia I walked on the set, and Jules was directing a two-reeler with Buster Keaton. And he was showing Buster Keaton how to be Buster Keaton. So Shemp approached doing a two-reeler with Jules White with distaste, to say the least. But because I gave him full reign for doing his thing, he liked working with me."

Bernds credits Jules White with much of the Stooge success, but he was hardly a fan of White. There was increasing tension between White and McCollum, and it led to a turf battle that ended in an ugly split, with McCollum exiting, Bernds and his stable of filmmakers along with him.

Since Jules White passed away, it falls on his brother Sam to give his version of that internal split.

"It wasn't really what you'd call a power struggle because Jules was glad that he didn't have to make all of the shorts himself," said Sam. "Before the Stooges he made a great number of comedies and big programs, producing them all. He hired directors for some, but directed a lot of them himself. The friction came because each had entities to fulfill. I used to see McCollum at Jules's house and they had a friendly rivalry relationship. Each wanting to do more. Hugh had a different kind of a relationship with the Stooges. He kissed their ass and Jules wouldn't. Hugh let them have their way on almost everything."

Ultimately, White prevailed, and he would take an even greater role in the steering of the Stooges. It was a tough call for Harry Cohn: he was close to both men. While White might have sought administrative opportunities in features, he had built a profitable shorts department and stayed there. McCollum, in turn, had been Cohn's loyal secretary before being made first a production manager and then a producer.

Though Jules White continued the output of Stooge shorts, even he began to tire of the creative falloff caused by continuing budget cuts. Whole scenes were being recycled, with White tapping his brother Jack to script transition scenes that would turn a recycled scenario into something resembling an original short.

"Reusing that footage became the only way he could make them," said Sam White. "Columbia would say, 'Look, this is all we're going to spend on these shows this coming season, because we're not getting the bookings we used to on account of television.' The theaters just weren't booking them like they used to, and that's why they would gradually fade out. Jules was a film editor before he became a director. When you're an editor, you learn how to finagle film. He knew he could take certain sequences, and instead of having to shoot four or five days, he could shoot a whole short in one day."

At that time, nobody seemed to notice that old footage was being reused. Sometimes, though, it proved to be quite awkward. Featuring a post-stroke Curly in *Hold That Lion,* a move done to bolster his spirits and quicken his recovery, was touching. It's hard to feel that sentiment seeing that exact same footage of a sleeping Curly in the patchwork 1953 short *Booty and the Beast,* which came out the year after Curly died.

Belt tightening and infighting were not the worst of the problems faced by the Stooges in 1955. That was the year that the rubber-faced Shemp, star of seventy-eight Stooge shorts over a nine-year period, dropped dead while riding home in a car after a prizefight. And this time, Moe was out of brothers.

STOOGES SANS SHEMP

Shemp Howard. To many, he was not the equal of his younger brother.
But he kept the Stooges going until his own untimely demise in 1955.

WHILE CURLY LINGERED FOR SEVERAL YEARS AFTER HE SUFFERED A STROKE, SHEMP'S FINAL CURTAIN FELL ABRUPTLY.

A lifelong fight fan, Shemp was returning home after watching a fight card at the Hollywood Legion Stadium, smoking a cigar with two pals, when he fell over on one of them. He died instantly of a heart attack on November 22, 1955, at the age of fifty-nine. The official cause was acute coronary occlusion, according to his obituaries.

"I never knew this, but he was taking nitroglycerin pills for a condition which I knew nothing about," Moe said years later.

While losing another brother was a shattering experience for Moe personally, Shemp's sudden passing could not have happened at a worse time professionally. Once again the Stooges were on the verge of extinction. And while Columbia always pleaded poverty when the Stooges renewed their contracts, this time the demand for two-reelers was really waning.

Days after he buried a second brother, Moe Howard returned to Columbia, where he and Jules White had to decide the fate of the Stooges. Moe and Larry could have continued as the Two Stooges, but they all agreed the act worked better with a third man. While this was going on, Moe did something to further solidify his position as top Stooge.

In a letter he sent to Larry dated December 12, 1955, Moe wrote:

It is hereby understood and agreed between us, that I am to have the sole and final say in the selection of any new partner that might be asked to join with us as a "Third Stooge" in the combination known as "The 3 Stooges." This is in no way any reflection on your professional knowledge of talent values, but merely reiteration of clauses of an agreement drawn between us in 1934, and which is still in force, which expresses the fact that I am the sole owner of the name "The 3 Stooges" and the manager of the act, and do all business and sign all contracts for "The 3 Stooges," which as you know has worked out so amicably and so successfully over these many years.

It is further acknowledged that you rely, as in the past, on my good business judgment to finalize all deals pertaining to "The 3 Stooges." This does not in any way mean that I will not consult with you on all major problems that arise. Your signature under mine will signify your agreement and acceptance of the above.

There were no signatures on this particular copy of that letter.

But this didn't mean that Moe had final say in choosing the new Stooge. That ultimately fell to the studio, as reflected in a December 21, 1955, interoffice memo from Jules White to the front office regarding the new contract for the Stooges:

> I feel it would be advisable to insert a clause stating that Moe and Larry will work with whomever we mutually agree upon as the replacement for the third Stooge. Furthermore, that if for any reason the Company chooses to do so, they have the right to stop making Three Stooge films and can make any remaining two reel films unfinished in any option period with Moe and Larry as a team, or with either Moe or Larry as individuals.

Neither Moe nor Larry had any solo aspirations, and so the search for the third Stooge was on. Among the comics they canvassed was Mousie Garner, the wild-haired onetime rival to the Stooges who replaced them as one of Ted Healy's foils. Garner said they offered the job to him, though Moe's own later testimony doesn't bear that out.

"When I was with Spike Jones, they wanted me to take Shemp's place," Garner recalled. "They wanted me more than any of them because I knew the material and I had my own style. The way Curly would make all those funny noises? I had my own style of making noises. Faces too. I could make more faces than Curly, I had a rubber face." While his face might have been made of rubber, his contract was ironclad, and it shackled him to his employer, who wouldn't let him leave.

They also contacted an old pal, the roly-poly longtime vaudevillian Joe DeRita, who bore more than a passing resemblance to Curly Howard. Jean DeRita, Joe's widow, recalls Joe getting the call right after Shemp died.

"They still had a year on their contracts with Columbia to make two-reelers, and they went to Vegas to talk to my Joe to join them," she said. "Harold Minsky had Joe under contract, and he wouldn't let him out. So Joe couldn't do it. It was after that they went after Joe Besser."

After a series of meetings and with little other choice, Jules White and Moe Howard decided to draft Joe Besser, partly because he was already under contract to Columbia. Besser was a curious choice to complete the trio. Moe and Larry knew him from the vaudeville circuit, where Besser was a veteran who had begun performing on the stage at the age of ten. He was an errand boy for a song plugger in St. Louis, where Besser grew up. He adopted the vagabond lifestyle of the stage shortly thereafter when he was stolen away by a magician named Howard Thurston. Unlike most veterans of the hardscrabble vaudeville slapstick comedy, Joe Besser did not like to get hit.

While that seems a fairly common trait for the average human being, it was highly aberrational for the Three Stooges, who were still boxing the ears off each other in 1956, even though its members were at least fifty years old.

Moe acknowledged that Besser was much different from his predecessors.

"His was an entirely different characterization as far as movements were concerned," said Moe. "In contour, I would say Joe was a fat boy, cute, who had his own mannerisms."

Despite his wimpy persona, Besser was certainly a gifted comic in his own right; he would never have lasted so long if he hadn't been. Moe and the studio decided Besser was their guy. Despite the assertions by both Garner and DeRita, Moe's recollection was that Besser was the first guy they approached.

Joe Besser, already under Columbia contract, is installed as a Stooge and finishes out their twenty-four-year run in the short subjects department. Fifi Blows Her Top, 1958.

HOWARD, FINE AND BESSER
STAGE SCREEN AND RADAR

"We had conversations to the extent that they thought he would be a good substitute because he, too, was making a series of his own at Columbia studios at the time . . . He was talented enough to carry a series of his own; therefore, they felt that he was competent to carry his part through from his comedies into ours."

Howard and Fine readily accepted Besser into the fold, though it meant reorienting the act. Besser made it clear up front that he had no interest in taking the punishment willingly accepted by his predecessor, Shemp.

Joe's shtick was to deliver nothing harder than love taps, usually delivered to the shoulder and accompanied by a whiny "Craaaaazy." He did develop a mildly amusing belly bump, which could be coordinated to a bass drum sound effect.

"Joe Besser had it in his contract that they couldn't hit him, and Larry had to play the Curly role," said Moe's daughter, Joan. "At the time, my dad was so desperate to keep working. Not for the money, but because he just loved what he was doing."

Larry assured Besser that he would happily take the blows, which meant that Fine would be taking punishment for two men. The changes were reflected in an interoffice memo sent to the front office by Jules White. It established that Besser would become a Stooge, maintaining his own contract separate from Moe and Larry. The new deal called for the Stooges to be paid exactly the same as they had been the previous year. That amounted to about $20,667 each.

While that seems to be an appallingly low sum of money for a veteran team going into its twenty-third year of business, there is no evidence that either Larry or Moe complained. Fact is, the writing was on the wall; the short subjects department and the Stooges were only in business because Columbia president Harry Cohn wanted them there. Just about all of the other acts had been let go by then.

Besser's shorts are considered the weakest of the Stooge lot, partly because compared to him, Shemp and Curly were full-fledged gladiators. While they absorbed punishment like a sponge soaks up water, Besser abhorred violence. Indeed, his most famous line was, upon getting even a pinch, "Not so haaaaaaaard!"

He appeared in fifteen shorts over two years, five of them remakes of earlier, and better-executed, Stooge shorts. During that time, Jules White, with the help of his screenwriting brother, Jack, hatched stories that allowed them to steal scenes wholesale from early shorts and reuse them. In the Besser shorts these are easy to detect, because the new footage looks clean while the older scenes were much grainier. And the mother of all continuity errors would come after Joe Besser replaced Shemp as the third Stooge. He starred in the 1957 short *Rusty Romeos,* which was a rip-off/remake of the 1952 Shemp short *Corny Casanovas.* Both shorts revolved around the story line that had all three boys unknowingly in love with the same girl and planning to pin an engagement ring on her. The woman, who takes the rings from Larry and Moe before stashing the suitors in adjoining rooms, takes a ring and a photo of Besser, whose smiling mug she places on a coffee table. When the boys figure out her duplicity and begin fighting each other, they move into her living room. The photo is in plain view, and it's very clearly Shemp's grinning puss in the frame.

If Shemp's passing wasn't traumatic enough, another death would ultimately doom the Stooges at the studio.

Columbia studio chief Harry Cohn passed away in 1958. Though known by many as a tyrant, Cohn had staunchly supported the Stooges. He didn't exactly pay them a king's ransom, but he renewed them for twenty-four consecutive years. When he died, the Stooges, along with the entire short subjects department, lost their advocate. Columbia shuttered the department in 1958, leaving the Stooges without a place to punch in for the first time in over two decades.

Columbia unceremoniously shut the door on the Stooges and ended its business with them. Unbeknownst to even the Stooges, the studio was ending a chapter of its history that would come to be regarded as one of the most memorable Columbia ever produced.

CHAPTER FIFTEEN

OUT OF BUSINESS, OUT OF OPTIONS

Rhythm and Weep, 1946.

THE STOOGES STAYED TOO LONG AT THE DANCE, AND THE MUSIC ENDED ABRUPTLY. THEIR INABILITY TO CROSS OVER TO EITHER FEATURES OR TV SERIES LEFT THEM ENTIRELY DEPENDENT UPON COLUMBIA. AND UNEMPLOYED WHEN THE STUDIO STOPPED MAKING SHORTS. AND THAT HAPPENED ALMOST IMMEDIATELY AFTER HARRY COHN PASSED AWAY.

Once it became clear that their contract would not be picked up, all that was left was to reflect upon the unparalleled productivity and the memories of filming 194 shorts over twenty-four years, mostly on Studios 3 and 7 and on the Columbia ranch when the story was a western that was filmed outdoors. Surely, the Stooges figured, closing out the longest uninterrupted run of a comedy team would merit some attention, maybe a party lined with grateful executives. Even a lousy watch.

But though he had died, this was Harry Cohn's Columbia, where there was little room for nostalgic sentiment. The Stooges were put off the lot with as much regard as the sets scrapped from yesterday's production.

According to a report in *Parade* magazine at the time, Moe's anticipation of a farewell ceremony left him hopeful as he and the boys completed their last short on their familiar haunt on Stage 5.

"By 6 P.M., which is closing time in Hollywood, no executive had appeared," wrote *Parade's* West Coast correspondent, Lloyd Shearer. "The Three Stooges checked off the lot without so much as a front-office goodbye. There simply was no longer a market for their type of two-reel comedies, and the studio wanted nothing more to do with them. In Hollywood this maxim has long held true: when there is no profit potential, courtesy flies out the window."

It would get worse the following day. Moe returned to the lot, per *Parade,* to pay his respects.

"He planned to tell the executives how genuinely pleasurable it had been for him and his partners to work for a production genius like Harry Cohn," wrote Shearer. "When Howard attempted to enter the studio, he was stopped. 'Sorry, Moe,' the gateman said. 'As of yesterday you and your buddies are finished here.' "

Bill Dyer, who would become the Stooges' soundman on live shows during the sixties and a regular traveling companion with Moe, would hear the head Stooge tell the exit story numerous times over the next six years. The version was always the same.

"It was there's your hat and there's the door," said Dyer.

Though hardly unexpected, the shuttering of the short subjects department left Moe and Larry devastated. Moe had smartly saved and invested his money and was financially secure. But after working almost nonstop practically since boyhood, he could not even contemplate the notion of not showing up to work each day.

"Moe was heartbroken," Edward Bernds recalled. "He liked to work. It was his whole life, being an actor. I cast him in a little low-budget science fiction film I directed called *Space Master X7,* cast him as a taxi driver. A straight part, he was supposed to be a New York taxi driver. He did very well, he was a good actor, and he appreciated it. He needed to work."

"The Stooges . . . found themselves unemployed for the first time in a quarter century and were shocked to realize that they were considered by all as useless as yesterday's newspaper," Norman Maurer, Moe's son-in-law, wrote. "Three stars that had succeeded worldwide were suddenly considered over-the-hill has-beens. All attempts to book them met with instant rejection."

Moe and Larry could not tour with Besser, who, according to Moe, "claimed that his wife was ailing and he didn't care to leave town."

Some, like Bill Dyer, said that the Stooges didn't really want Besser anyway. Though undeniably a gifted comic whose whiny routine would make him a standout as the effeminate bully character Stinky when he worked with Abbott and Costello, Besser in the Stooges was like a priest in a brothel—he wanted no part of the rough-and-tumble stuff going on inside.

"Moe would say they never considered him to go on the road with them because he was just not part of the act. He had been forced in by studio executives who said, 'Here's the new guy, he's well known, he's under contract, and that's the end of it,' " said Dyer. "He didn't help the act, even though he was a good performer. So they made the excuse for him not joining."

Truth is, there was nothing to join. The Stooges had stopped touring during the latter days of Shemp. Moe, so driven to work, found his way back onto the Columbia lot. But the circumstances were absolutely humiliating.

For seven weeks, Moe was hired to work for Harry Romm, the Stooges' agent whose cozy relationship with Harry Cohn might explain why he never pushed that hard to get the boys raises or feature work as they toiled in two-reelers.

"One of Harry Cohn's best friends was my dad's agent," said Joan Maurer. "They used to play cards together, they traveled together on vacations. My dad never accused him of anything, but my feeling is they were just too close. I don't know how the Stooges could have had the right representation when their agent was Harry Cohn's buddy."

Romm was a former vaudevillian himself, who once served as the personal East Coast rep for Columbia boss Cohn. But in fairness to the man who once agented Ted Healy and represented the Stooges since 1943, Romm was merely trying to help Moe out by giving him a job, which the Stooge leader didn't have to take if he felt it beneath him. But down on his luck and unwilling to stay home in his garden, Moe worked as Romm's lackey, on the lot where he had once been considered a star.

"Moe complained bitterly about this associa-

Moe, Emil Sitka, Joe DeRita, and Larry
with their favorite audience—the kids.

tion as he was not only working for his former agent and manager in a menial capacity, but was doing so at the studio where for twenty-five years he had been a star and consequently was in daily contact with all of the familiar personnel, the guards at the gate, the crews, the executives, etc., with whom he had been associated as an important star for so many years," Moe's son-in-law, Norman Maurer, once wrote. "Moe was hurt by the fact that in this association with Harry Romm, he was nothing more than a messenger boy." It should be noted that Maurer replaced Romm as the Stooges' manager, and for a time the two competed for the loyalties of Moe. Maurer mounted a lawsuit against Romm and Columbia when the studio later did the film *Stop, Look and Laugh,* a patchwork of Stooge shorts for which the boys got no money. Maurer wouldn't be the most objective judge of Romm.

Moe's anxiety and desire to work had little to do with financial need. He had made a number of wise investments, and he was also thrifty. He lived comfortably most of his life in a gorgeous four-bedroom home at 10500 Kling Street in Toluca Lake that had a built-in swimming pool, a pool man, and a maid. But he was legendarily tight with the buck.

"Larry would tell a story that Moe would send home most of his money when he was on the road and live on twenty-five dollars a week," said Bill Dyer. "So someone figured out that after all his expenses, Moe ended up with three dollars left over, and asked what he'd do with it. Larry said, 'Ah, he just pisses it away.'"

Actually, Moe was not thrifty when it came to people less fortunate than he. Both he and his wife were heavily involved in charitable causes, and Moe was president of the Spastic Children's Guild for kids with cerebral palsy. It was a charity he got into with Jules White, and Moe took his duties seriously. He'd push the Stooges to make appearances in hospitals. He was also helpful to friends such as Emil Sitka. While Sitka would go on to become one of the more memorable members of Stooge costars, the work was not steady and he had five children to support. According to Sitka's son, Saxon, a shopping trip with Moe was an annual holiday occurrence during those lean years for his family.

"I remember being about four or five and going with my dad and brother to meet Moe at the supermarket," said Sitka. "We'd fill the cart with groceries, and it was Moe's holiday gesture when my father was going through rough times."

That doesn't mean Moe had grown profligate.

"I remember one year my brother and I got hip to the fact Dad wasn't paying for this stuff, and we threw in all these boxes of Twinkies and cookies," said Sitka. "Here's Moe, in a hat and sun-glasses and looking grumpy, taking us into the supermarket. And he'd be putting the cookies and stuff back on the shelf, like he wasn't ready to be totally taken advantage of by us."

While Moe's motivation to work was mainly to keep busy, Larry was driven by a more pressing need. After twenty-four years of absorbing punishment, Fine was broke.

"Larry blew all his money," said Bernds. "He gambled, his wife gambled. He had some in-laws who sponged on him. When the Stooges were terminated at Columbia, Larry was broke.

"He managed to throw it away on horse races and baseball games and football games," said Bernds. "When we were working, Larry, who had a short attention span anyway, would tend to wander off to listen to a radio and see if a horse that he had a bet on won. Of course, during World Series time you had to drag him away from the radio."

Larry and his Mabel were as happy-go-lucky offscreen as Larry appeared on.

"They had a home on each side of the country," Joan Maurer said. "Their home was the Knickerbocker Hotel in Hollywood and the President Hotel in Atlantic City. Mabel loved that type of crowd and life. She didn't have to cook, she could just send up for whatever she needed, and there were maids. They were very extravagant. My dad would be putting away money to invest in property, while Larry was happy spending his money as he made it."

As for Jules White, the man who galvanized the short subjects department for more than two decades, he was ready to retire.

"Theater distribution was becoming limited for some time, and after two or three years of weaving together all that old footage in the shorts, he'd had enough," said Sam White. "He was tired and wanted to stop working. He had enough money. He spent most of his time fishing at the lake we belonged to in Palmdale."

Though Joan Maurer said she had no recollection of this, Sam White said that his brother did one last thing for the Stooges. He used his close relationship with the Cohn clan to convince the Columbia subsidiary Screen Gems to test-run the shorts on television.

"Jack Cohn and Jules were such good buddies, and their sons Ralph and Bobby came out to the studio," said Sam White. "Ralph ran the syndication end of the business, Screen Gems, and Jules said to him, even before they closed the department, that the Stooges should be on TV. Ralph said, 'Christ, nobody will watch them.' Jules pressed them to take a TV station and give them some of the segments and see what happened, just try it out. It was somewhere in Boston, and the people went wild. Suddenly, all these stations around the country were saying, 'Where can we get these shorts?' "

As quickly as the Stooges were washed up and considering retirement, they would suddenly be back and bigger than they had been during their entire career at Columbia. Resurrected, ironically enough, by the very medium that drove them out of business in the first place.

CHAPTER SIXTEEN

TV RESURRECTS THE STOOGES

The Stooges packed stadiums for their live
appearances in later years.

WHEN THE THREE STOOGES WERE IN THEIR PRIME AS STARS OF THE TWO-REELER GENRE, THEIR BEST AUDIENCES WERE THE SATURDAY MORNING MATINEE CROWD. THAT MEANT CHILDREN.

But there was no way to predict that a new generation of children was ready to embrace thirty-year-old black-and-white shorts that were grainy and crude-looking compared to the modern cartoons kids were watching. But the impact was nearly instantaneous.

"Screen Gems initially released a batch of approximately forty of these shorts and having no idea of their value, sold them to stations at a very low price," wrote Norman Maurer. "The ratings were astronomical, and of course, they quickly released an additional block of shorts at a much higher price. Thereafter they gradually released additional films at increased rentals as the Three Stooges skyrocketed into the top of the ratings. The trade papers reported that Columbia made $12 million profit from the first release of these shorts. The Stooges did not get a penny."

Nor did Jules White, as neither the Screen Actors Guild nor the Directors Guild contracts called for residuals to be paid for product made that far back.

It was a double-edged sword. Sure, Moe Howard and Larry Fine lost out on a lot of money. After spending twenty-four years slapping each other around with the most physical comedy Columbia ever witnessed, the Stooges were on the outside looking in as the studio reaped millions of dollars in found money.

But the surge in interest allowed an overnight rebirth of the Three Stooges. The shorts were airing weekdays in 165 markets, and the kids wanted to know: who were these grown men who were slapping each other silly, eye gouging, and braining one another with just about anything found in the hardware section of a department store?

"Suddenly, the Stooges were on the top of the heap, with offers pouring in every day for fairs, shopping centers, theaters, circuses, at salaries ten and twenty times in excess of what they ever dreamed possible," wrote Maurer. "From $2,500 per week in the Bakersfield nightclub to $25,000 for one day to dedicate a new shopping center in New York."

To Maurer, the reason was obvious. The Stooges were the live-action equivalent of the wildly violent cartoons kids craved.

"I recall several fan letters to Moe which clearly indicated why this phenomenon had occurred. Basically it was due to the fact that the children had been exposed on television for many years to the insane, wild, exaggerated antics of Popeye, Tom and Jerry, Krazy Kat. All animated cartoons wherein the action was of extreme, unreal, unlifelike exaggeration. Finally, and for the first time in their lives, these children were exposed to real, live human beings doing what hitherto only cartoons had done, and the results are now history."

The Stooges, who had seemed like they were history, quickly set about to reform the act and capitalize on the luck.

The first order of business was finding a third Stooge to replace Besser, which they had been in the process of doing just before the shorts began to catch on again. They had not worked live in about four years, not since the last days of Shemp.

According to Moe, they first approached Mousie Garner, but Garner, who now calls himself "the Lost Stooge," once again missed out on the chance to be a real Stooge. As Moe recalled, it was Larry's idea, and this time Garner was available.

"We did rehearse with him for three days," said Moe, who called the results "completely nonacceptable."

It was at this time that they called another old friend who had also been under contract when they searched for a replacement for Shemp. His name was Joe DeRita.

Born in Philadelphia on July 12, 1909, as Joseph Wardell, DeRita was born to the stage. His father was a stagehand, his mother a dancer called "the Girl in the Moon" because, suspended by a wire, she'd swing across the stage, over the audience. DeRita traveled across the United States

Moe Howard signing autographs for a new generation of Stooge fans.

with them, and once he caught the whiff of greasepaint, he, too, became hooked on the stage.

DeRita made his stage debut at the tender age of seven, at a Red Cross benefit during World War I, and soon was teamed with his mother and sister in a stage act called DeRita Sisters and Junior. That led to seven seasons spent playing the title role in *Peck's Bad Boy,* once again alongside his mother and his sister, Phyllis.

DeRita went solo by the age of eighteen. Able to sing, dance, and tell jokes, he became a staple of the burlesque circuit and moved up to films, making his debut in *Dough Girls* for Mark Hellinger at Warner Bros. But DeRita's first love was performing before live audiences, and he was a regular participant in road shows staged for U.S. servicemen, teaming up with everyone from Randolph Scott to Bing Crosby. Once back, he settled into a contract with Minsky Burlesque in 1950, working at the Rialto Theatre in Chicago and the Dunes Hotel in Las Vegas for eight years.

DeRita didn't exactly jump at the chance to join the Stooges. His widow, Jean DeRita, recalls that Joe was in Mexico, playing the villainous hangman alongside Gregory Peck in the Fox film *The Bravados*.

"When he finally got back to L.A., he had a lot of messages on his machine from them," said DeRita. "They decided to put something together to see how it would work. They got some routines out, and well, they were old routines that Moe had, and Joe didn't like them. They put some together and they went somewhere and tried them out but they didn't go very well. They were all disappointed. Joe and Moe got out the old trunks of Joe's with the burlesque things, and they picked some old things out from there, put a new act together."

Though history dictates that DeRita was lucky to land with the Stooges, that was hardly evident at the time, said Bill Dyer, who became the Stooges' soundman around this time.

"I'd gained some weight and was seeing a fat doctor in the Valley, and on my way out I saw Joe in the waiting room," said Dyer. "We had coffee and he told me they'd come to Vegas while he was working for Minsky and asked if he'd join the act. He told me Moe had offered him a third of the act, but that he'd taken a major cut in pay. He joined in September, and they didn't have any bookings until December. It was a tough time for

Joe DeRita was a top burlesque star before joining the Stooges.

him—he was living hand to mouth—and he said if he knew it was going to be like this, he'd have turned them down. Minsky was not a great payer, but the work was steady."

But DeRita was a comic journeyman who wanted the chance to set down roots and develop an asset that could be worth money someday.

DeRita had worked onstage with the likes of Abbott and Costello, and his trunks of memorabilia contain a slew of moldering but carefully clipped news write-ups from papers across the country. All touted DeRita for stardom on the big screen.

Though he did numerous features and shorts for MGM during the 1940s, he did not become the franchise star MGM hoped. He signed a deal at Columbia in 1946 calling for him to make shorts at Columbia Pictures, some directed by Jules White, at a weekly salary of $600. But stardom never happened, and he returned to the burlesque stage, where he remained until the fateful visit from Moe Howard and Larry Fine.

While it might seem that DeRita would have the same inattention to detail that Curly Howard, Shemp Howard, and even Larry Fine displayed, a search through his burlesque memorabilia strips that away.

The trunk contains volumes of carefully typed routines that DeRita either wrote himself or picked up during his long stage career. There are jokes, cataloged by subject, for nearly every occasion. All of them are impeccably typed on onionskin paper and filed alphabetically. His widow said Joe typed them all himself, using one finger, and nary a typo can be found. There's even a verbatim copy of the "Who's on First" routine made famous by Abbott and Costello.

A letter written to DeRita from his agent, Al Kingston, indicates that joining the Stooges wasn't an easy call. Kingston was against DeRita joining and turning his back on his own opportunities as a single. He wrote:

There is a great deal to be said about your departing from a career on your own. You were getting established very nicely, and just prior to committing yourself to the boys, there set in a tremendous demand for your services. There was no question in my mind that the career you were seeking as a top performer was on its way. There were about six good opportunities including a star role at Desilu Playhouse that would have developed into a television series. This choice assignment alone would have done a great deal to further your opportunities.

But DeRita had made up his mind. He shaved his head to closely resemble the original Curly, whose shorts were the favorites on TV. According to Jean DeRita, it was a decision he never regretted.

Actually, there was little time to reflect, once the shorts became the top-rated series across the country for children. The Stooges were in demand all over. The tour began in Pittsburgh, with children and their parents packing shows all day. From there, they guest-starred on *The Steve Allen Show*, with "Curly Joe" performing the nearsighted rajah routine first done by Curly Howard in *Three Little Pirates*. The skit ended with DeRita throwing a knife that wound up in the stomach of Allen, who closed the gag with a deftly executed triple slap of Stooge faces.

Touring was amped up and the Stooges played everywhere, though Larry Fine preferred it when they avoided the casinos, since, by his own admission, he'd end up losing more at the tables than he was making in salary.

Multiple appearances followed on *Ed Sullivan,* highlighted by one stint in which Sullivan introduced them as the Ritz Brothers, only to realize he'd made a mistake and say, "Oh, it looks like the Three Stooges."

At that point, he might have been about the only person in America unclear who they were.

CHAPTER SEVENTEEN

LAST LAUGH FOR THE STOOGES

A crowd awaits a live appearance by the Stooges, 1962.

THE STOOGES WEREN'T THE ONLY ONES BENT ON CAPITALIZING ON THEIR SUDDEN FAME. COLUMBIA, MAKING MILLIONS OF UNEXPECTED REVENUE, PUT THEM TO WORK IN THE FEATURE HAVE ROCKET, WILL TRAVEL, WHICH HARRY ROMM PRODUCED.

When the Stooges held out for better terms from Columbia for the first time in their careers, Romm and Columbia went around them, recycling vintage Stooge footage with vignettes featuring the ventriloquist Paul Winchell. The Stooges, who by that time had parted company for good with Romm, were now being steered by Moe's son-in-law, Norman Maurer, an artist. Maurer led a lawsuit against Columbia that gave the Stooges a small cash payment and a three-picture contract. Not only did the deal call for them to get paid more for each film than they received in their best year filming shorts at the studio—they even received a back-end percentage for the first time in their careers.

The feature films that followed, and an animated series that mixed cartoon with live-action introductions by the Stooges, showed a marked change from the frenetic slapstick of the early shorts which had so captivated the kiddies. The second film was *Snow White and the Three Stooges,* a takeoff on the fairy tale, which starred figure skater Carol Heiss and was directed by Walter Lang (who, aside from his Oscar-winning job in *The King and I,* also helmed the 1933 MGM Stooge feature with Ted Healy *Meet the Baron).*

The film was barren of physical punishment and leaves little to recommend it. But there were two very good reasons why the Stooges had to tone it down.

"They were by then in their sixties and it would have looked just terrible for these old men to be beating each other up," said Joan Maurer. The other reason was a concern by parents that a steady TV diet of Stooge mayhem was not good for the half-pint set.

Moe in particular brooded over the possibilities that kids would emulate the violence and hurt each other. Personal appearances always began with Moe's admonition that they were professionals and the kids shouldn't try to copy them.

Not that Moe was totally apologetic for their earlier efforts. Remember, the Stooge shorts were totally irreverent. Babies were given the barrel of a loaded handgun to suck on in place of a pacifier, and the butt of a loaded handgun would be used as a hammer to hang a picture, with Moe having his part creased by an errant bullet. A villain was dispatched by having his head stuck in a dry-cleaning press and his tail scorched with a hot iron. The sharp blade of a tree saw would routinely be ruined from a run across Curly's cranium. Power tools were employed for the cruelest forms of punishment.

But nobody ever got hurt, unlike a lot of other programming during the sixties.

"Kids watch the Popeye films constantly," Moe said in an interview during the Stooge comeback. "They can watch one Popeye film ten and twelve times without ever getting tired. They don't mind if he gets hit over the head with a mallet because they know he'll always get himself back in shape. But underneath their adoration, they know that Popeye isn't real. He's make-believe. When they see us, they know we're real and they also know that nothing is going to happen to us.

"We're not as sadistic as westerns, which to my mind are as violent as gangster movies," said Moe. "Kids don't mind seeing somebody get it over the head so long as they know that person will get right up. In westerns, kids are likely not to understand or not to like it when somebody doesn't get up . . . You take a look at your westerns, you can count the dead at the end, or the broken necks and crushed jaws. And social groups and organizations don't say a word, at least as far as I know."

There was little objectionable in the Stooges' stage show during that period, in which kids would pack theaters and, for the price of $1.50 during the day and $3.75 at night, would get either lunch or dinner and a soda pop along with their beloved threesome. Rich Safire, who would later become the manager of Spanky McFarland, the Our Gang member who like the Stooges watched the owner of that serial make millions of dollars, played on a bill with the Stooges during an East Coast swing. He was a fifteen-year-old magician.

"They did a bunch of stuff that might well have been written for the original Curly because Joe DeRita did not have the timing, and I was able to tell that the jokes weren't playing the way they were written because he had a slow kind of delivery," said Safire. "Curly Joe would come out and have two pieces of wood hinged together and he would say he invented a new railroad track, and when two trains are coming into each other [he] would lift up one part of this hinged piece of wood and say the train goes underneath and the other one flies right over it. All the kids would start to laugh even though it wasn't very funny. And of course Moe would smack him in the head and that was what made it funny. Actually, none of the jokes they did were that funny, but they didn't have to be because the kids ate it up. They cut down on the hitting because of a backlash by parents, and they really didn't need it because the kids loved them so much. They just had to stand there and that was enough."

Safire also noticed Moe's efforts to keep his Stooge character separate from his offstage persona. It was all in the hair.

"Moe had a hang-up about his hair, and in all the pictures I took with him, his hair is combed back," said Safire. "He would always have the hair combed back until about ten seconds before he went onstage. He would comb it down, go onstage, and do the act. Almost every single performance, before he got offstage, you could actually see him—he put his head down, put his hands to his forehead, and he would whip his hair back."

Safire said that Moe was clearly the leader of the clan, and he seemed to genuinely care about the small-fry set who fueled his resurgence.

"Moe was the businessman, he kept the timing together, and if the show was running a little late, you would see him smack his hands together and run them and pace back and forth and say, 'When are we going to get on with this thing?' " said Safire. "Not that he had anyplace else to go, but he didn't like hearing the kids banging their feet—you know how kids behave if you're even two minutes late. He was interested in the show. Curly Joe, I think, would have sat there for an extra hour playing cards. He was always looking to scrape up a card game."

To the hard-core Stooge fans who loved the sheer irreverence and unbelievable violence of the gags, the reborn Stooges became the equivalent of watching an old-timers' baseball game, with fleshy former Major Leaguers trotting around the base paths at half speed, cheered by a crowd who remembered their former greatness.

And traveling with a trio who had about 150 years' worth of vaudeville and burlesque experience made for great fun, said their soundman and driver Bill Dyer.

Each Stooge was a character in his own right.

"Larry was a great storyteller, but he seemed to be unattentive onstage," said Dyer. "He would just walk away from the others, walk downstage, and start making faces. Moe would chew his ass out backstage. Larry was a charming guy, and he'd long stopped drinking when the shorts stopped. Before then, he'd be drinking and carousing, and Mabel would catch him with notes in his pockets from women. By the time we were working together, it was Mabel who was the drinker, and we had a running joke that if the phone rang late at night, it would be Larry. Earlier in the evening, she'd get drunk and have only a few bites of food, then go off and fall asleep. She'd wake up at mid-night and always send Larry out to find an all-night Chinese food place, which is why he'd call us. More often than not, he'd come back with the food and she'd be asleep. But Larry loved her and took all of it. I think it was all the guilt for those years that he was on the road and cheating on her. It was something to watch them. He drove a four-door Lincoln and she'd get in the backseat and make him wear this chauffeur's hat."

Larry was also notorious for borrowing money and forgetting to pay it back, per Norman Maurer.

"The boys and I were on our way down the hall toward the elevator at Columbia to go to lunch when Larry asked Moe to lend him five dollars so he could pick up his laundry," Maurer recalled. "Despite the fact that Moe had already experienced a quarter of a century of Larry's borrowing money and forgetting to return it, he agreed instantly to lend Larry the money and handed him the five. At this point, I almost fell apart from embarrassment. Moe grabbed Larry and stopped him, then Moe unzipped his own fly, took out his you-know-what, waved it at Larry, put it back, and zipped the fly back up."

While Maurer and Fine both thought their companion had lost his marbles, Moe was being a shrewd businessman.

"Flabbergasted, Larry asked him what he was doing," Maurer continued. "Moe replied simply, 'Every time I lend you money you forget, and when I ask for it you say, "What? When? Where?" Now you won't forget.' "

Curly Joe was good for a surprise or two himself, said Maurer.

"The Stooges and I were staying at the Hampshire House on Central Park South when I had to call an important meeting that required the presence of all Three Stooges," said Maurer, who led them on a promotional tour of *The Three Stooges Meet Hercules.* "I was in Moe's room when we called Curly Joe on the phone and said that we had something very important to talk about. Joe asked us to come on down to his room, pick him up, and go on to Larry's room for the final conference. Moe and I went down in the elevator and knocked on Joe's door."

DeRita drew from his burlesque background to surprise his cohorts.

"The door opened immediately and there was Joe stark naked, from the top of his shaven head to the tip of his clipped toenails. With his hairless body and roly-poly weight, it was difficult to tell whether he was a woman or a man. To our amazement he stepped out into the center of the hall and insisted on having the conference then and there. Moe and I almost died until Joe finally felt that he had carried the joke far enough and went back into the room to dress."

And Moe was also a character. An unparalleled joke teller, he would regale the group with gags and stories from the Healy heyday. He'd also inevitably attempt to set the single Bill Dyer up with whichever waitress was taking their food order.

Dyer also recalled Moe's unwillingness to part with a buck. "Larry and Joe took me aside one time and asked me to handle the tipping instead of Moe. We'd take a cab from La Guardia to New York City and Moe would give the guy ten cents and thought it was a good tip. It embarrassed the hell out of them. So I'd say, 'I got it, Moe,' and if I gave fifteen cents, that was a 50 percent increase over what Moe would give."

During that period, the reconstituted Three Stooges followed their 1959 first feature, *Have Rocket, Will Travel,* with *Snow White and the Three Stooges* in 1961 for Fox. After settling the *Stop, Look and Laugh* suit, the Stooges came back home to Columbia, where they made the 1962 feature *The Three Stooges Meet Hercules,* a well-received effort in which they reteamed with their longtime friend and former Stooge director Edward Bernds, with a script from Elwood Ullman, a former journalist who scripted many of the Stooge shorts and was a regular collaborator of Bernds. The same creative team followed with *The Three Stooges in Orbit.* Moe's son-in-law, Norman Maurer, now the act's manager, directed the 1963 comedy *The Three Stooges Go Around the World in a Daze* from an Ullman script, and Maurer also directed the 1965 feature *The Outlaws Is Coming!,* again from an Ullman script.

While the features stacked up poorly compared to the shorts filmed while Moe Howard and Larry Fine were in their prime, the rebirth of the Stooges was a lucrative one. The boys were paid $50,000 for *Have Rocket, Will Travel* and $75,000 for *Snow White and the Three Stooges.* Stage revenues were steady. The boys even reaped merchandising revenues and got money for making phonograph records.

According to internal documents, the Stooges brought in $80,357 from personal appearances in 1959, when the shorts came to television. The following year, the personal appearances made them over $97,000, which grew to more than $114,000 the following year and didn't dip again until 1964, when the appearance schedule began to dwindle. Merchandising money was worth over $16,000 in 1959 and jumped to more than $33,000 in 1960.

Comedy III Productions, Inc., the company the trio formed to handle their licensing, reported $137,619 in revenues in 1960, a figure that remained steady through the 1960s.

In short, Mabel Fine could once again order room service in her beloved hotels, and Larry could lay all the bets he wanted. In a business that had long exploited the Stooges, from paltry Ted Healy paychecks to missing the millions Columbia reaped by recycling their shorts, it was nice to see the Three Stooges, and especially Moe Howard and Larry Fine, still able to get laughs. And have the last laugh.

CHAPTER EIGHTEEN

THE FiNAL CURTAiN

Husbands Beware, 1956.

AFTER STAVING OFF A FORCED RETIREMENT IN 1958, THERE WAS NO WAY THE STOOGES WERE GOING TO QUIT NOW. MORE MONEY THAN EVER WAS COMING IN, AND AUDIENCES LINED UP FOR MOVIES THAT COULDN'T HOLD A CANDLE TO THE VINTAGE SHORTS.

Though TV brought them back from the dead and the Stooges had a series on the small screen that was largely animated, the boys decided to try once more to land a series. Moe's son-in-law, Norman Maurer, hatched an idea he called "Kook's Tour."

The pilot, narrated by Moe, featured the Stooges taking a much-needed vacation, touring national parks around the country. The Stooges put up their own money—Joe DeRita's widow, Jean, recalled the figure being $250,000. Maurer saved some money by making a deal with Chrysler for the use of a pleasure boat. While the idea for a TV series might have seemed a good one, the results were vastly underwhelming. The pilot is like watching someone's unedited home movies, an exercise for only the most hardened Stooge fan.

Norman Maurer's widow, Joan, said a decision was made to shoot the pilot without a script, relying on situations the boys might get into while fishing and hiking through the woods to create humorous opportunities. In fact, there was very little humor, and the shoot proved to be a nightmare. Moe and Joe DeRita took falls, not advisable for men in their late fifties and sixties. Several times the boys got lost in the boat. Once, they got caught in a torrential downpour far from shore.

Another time, while they were shooting footage of Snake River, where rapids had earlier taken the lives of eleven explorers, the engine died. The boys had to sit for five hours, praying that the tide wouldn't turn and send them into rapids they'd have no hope of surviving.

Aside from costing the boys a lot of money and more aggravation, "Kook's Tour" was never really completed, because during the tail end of shooting, Larry Fine suffered a debilitating stroke. The tour was over. For all intents and purposes, so were the Three Stooges.

Larry's beloved Mabel had died in 1967, and Fine, after living for a time above the garage in the home of his daughter, Phyllis, retired to the Motion Picture Country Hospital. There he entertained the showbiz veterans and had a visitor list that included James Cagney. Larry, who was a free spender to the last, got to continue living in the lavish way he had grown accustomed to. One of the best-known entertainers America has ever produced, he had $776.45 in the bank when he turned over his estate to his daughter, and was worth $20,541.82, most of that being assets of his share in Comedy III Productions. Fine died of cerebral thrombosis on Friday January 24, 1975, at the age of seventy-three.

Even with his partner of nearly fifty years permanently out of the picture, Moe Howard still tried to keep working. It was impossible to replace Larry Fine, but Moe tried with Emil Sitka. Of all the stalwart character actors who spent years working in the Stooge shorts, Sitka was perhaps the most humorous.

Sitka, who passed away in 1998 after lapsing into a coma, had remained friendly with Moe Howard and was thrilled to finally get his long-awaited chance to be a regular part of the act. He had gotten close when he costarred with the Stooges in the TV pilot "Jerks of All Trades." Here he would finally become a member of the storied threesome.

"My father felt funny about filling in for Larry, but once he spoke to Larry about it, my dad was all pumped up," said Sitka's son, Saxon. "It was to be a triumph, a milestone, but it never materialized. He had two opportunities. The first involved a Philippines production company and everything was coming together. But Dad said Moe had misgivings, that the Philippine connection didn't sit well with him. Moe felt he was being boxed in by Norman Maurer. Then there was another deal involving another production company, and this time it seemed like they would go forward. They signed contracts, and my dad was packed and ready to go. Again, this was his major triumph. And every week, he'd get notification that Moe had fallen ill and they were waiting for him to recover."

Sitka kept his luggage ready, because it looked like Moe was rallying and that the ironman would come through as he always had in the past, when he completed a short even after his brother Curly suffered the stroke.

"Emil waited for that call that would put him on a plane," said Sitka. "Then, one weekend, he got the call, only it was to tell him that Moe had passed away. He was in total shock. It could be argued that Emil was a Stooge; he was certainly very proud of that association and enjoyed the warmth he got from Moe and Larry. The only thing he got acclaim for was participating in those Stooges shorts. It's ironic, because he had great respect for other comics he'd worked with like Andy Clyde, and maybe he regarded that work with more esteem than the Stooge. But only the Stooges gained immortality."

Sitka would have to settle for that.

Moe Howard, the hard-faced soup-bowl-haired scowler who was the backbone of the Three Stooges and the reason the act lasted forty-five years, died May 4, 1975, of lung cancer at the Hollywood Presbyterian Hospital, less than four months after Larry Fine succumbed. It figures that for a blue-collar troupe, the only thing that could break up its members was illness and death. Howard had kept his illness to himself, and died just after completing his memoirs, *Moe Howard & The 3 Stooges,* which was published by Carol Publishing after his death and is still on bookshelves.

Surviving Stooge Joe DeRita attempted one last time to carry on the act, giving Mousie Garner one last chance to become a Stooge. DeRita tried to join with Garner and a veteran comic named Frank Mitchell in an act called the New Three Stooges. But the act was scrapped before it got off the ground. Moe Howard's death effectively marked the end of one of the most durable acts in comic history.

DeRita lived until July 3, 1993, when the comic succumbed to pneumonia at the age of eighty-three. His widow, Jean, recalled that before her husband was placed in the Motion Picture & Television Hospital, he enjoyed sitting on his porch with his beloved cigar, regaling the neighborhood children and passersby with tales of what it had been like to be a member of the legendary Three Stooges.

Joe Besser, the gentle Stooge who stayed with the act the least amount of time, lived until March 1988, when he died in North Hollywood after a long illness. Though Besser seemed ill suited for the Stooges, he did the boys proud when the Stooges finally received their long-overdue plaque on the Hollywood Walk of Fame after radio personality Gary Owens got twenty thousand signatures and prompted the Hollywood Chamber of Commerce to plant a plaque in their honor.

Before a crowd of two thousand fans and such longtime Stooge pals as Milton Berle, Besser was the lone Stooge on hand to accept the accolade. He considered it the greatest achievement of his career, after marrying his wife, Ernie.

Moe Howard was long gone by the time the Three Stooges got that star, and it says something about his workmanlike attitude that he wasn't there to take the bows. For years, the boys would be asked why they hadn't gotten a star when just about everyone else in Hollywood of any repute had. Shemp would shrug off questions by saying he didn't want people walking on him anyway.

Bill Dyer also got the brush-off from Moe and decided to try to help correct the injustice. "I said, 'How come you guys aren't on the boulevard,' and he said, 'Those assholes,' and just brushed it off in the conversation. I went down and checked, and there were all these people who had two or three stars, because you could get separate ones for records, radio, and theater. I was trying to build a case for him. Then I found out you had to pay for

your own star, and knowing how much Moe liked to spend money, I understood completely."

Moe could certainly have afforded a boulevard full of stars, but it would go against every fiber of his being to buy an accolade for egotistical reasons. For the man who wanted to be a serious actor and traded Shakespeare on a Mississippi riverboat for slapstick on a soundstage, Moe Howard's reward came from knowing that he did good work and was remembered and respected for it by his peers.

"Once, we went to dinner in those later years in Beverly Hills and this fellow came over to the table with sunglasses on," said Moe's son, Paul. "He excused himself from barging in on our meal and said, 'Mr. Howard, I just want to let you know you have been an inspiration to me all my life, and I just want to shake your hand and thank you.' It was Bill Cosby, and I could tell it meant everything to my father. That was the kind of thing that pleased him."

At the writing of this book, the last man standing who orbited around the Three Stooges was Mousie Garner. Garner said he still entertains in stints near his Las Vegas home, calling himself "the Lost Stooge." Asked if he was bitter that he'd missed being part of such a storied troupe, Garner's answer was surprising.

"I'm kind of glad it never happened," he said. "They took terrible beatings which could have caused those strokes. I had to have an operation on my brain because my memory was leaving me, and it was from the smacks and all the stuff I took from Healy. Larry died from a stroke, and so did Curly, at a very young age. Shemp also died young. I got onstage last night and I died. But," said the almost Stooge, "I'm still here talking to you."

PART TWO

THE LEGACY

Dizzy Pilots.

SOME SIXTY-FIVE YEARS AFTER THE THREE STOOGES BACKED INTO A DRAWING ROOM IN THE 1934 COLUMBIA SHORT <u>WOMAN HATERS</u> AND SLAPPED, EYE-GOUGED, AND BRAINED EACH OTHER WITH A CRESCENDO OF BONKS AND BANGS, THE STOOGES' FOLLOWING IS AS STRONG AS EVER. THANKS TO THE TV-FUELED STOOGE RESURGENCE OF THE SIXTIES AND SEVENTIES, A SURPRISINGLY LARGE NUMBER OF PROMINENT FILMMAKERS AND STARS COUNT THE SLAPHAPPY TRIO AMONG THEIR GREATEST COMIC INFLUENCES.

That hardly means that the Stooges are being widely imitated today. In fact, the Stooge formula of simplistic plots, outrageous sight gags, and high content of bloodless but seemingly lethal violence is rarely seen today, outside of some *Jerry Springer* episodes. In comedy, highly physical slapstick has found itself in the same low rung as the two-reeler genre the Stooges toiled in. Sure it made people laugh and was profitable, but it never measured up to the prestige of full-length features.

Some of the biggest names in Hollywood count themselves as touched in some way by the Stooges, from Mel Gibson to Quentin Tarantino to Robert Zemeckis. But it is also clear that while everyone admires that work, nobody really wants to do it, or at least not for long.

Much of that has to do with how much has changed in how comic stars are now treated, which is a far sight better than when the Stooges spent their twenty-four years at Columbia. It seems laudable that they had the longest tenure of any act at any studio, but in reality, this implies that they were taken for granted. And they surely were. In some ways, the Stooges were treated much like Hall of Fame baseball players whose performances have been immortalized and who, people say, would be paid fortunes today. They weren't back then, shackled to the same team their entire careers by a reserve clause. The Stooges had no such restrictions; they were shackled, instead, by working-class paranoia that left them fearing for their jobs, and by representation that never encouraged them to test the waters elsewhere.

For more than two decades, they worked hurt, enduring weekly bruises and mishaps. Curly Howard kept working even when it was obvious he was ill and in need of serious medical attention. But that would have required a work stoppage, and by all indications, studio brass didn't want it. With his brother Moe helping him through line readings when his little brother couldn't remember even full sentences, the Stooges hoped he'd just start feeling his old self again. It turned out Curly had suffered a small stroke, which was followed shortly after by a second that was serious enough to partially paralyze him and end the career of one of the greatest physical comics this country has ever produced.

The Stooges never troubled the Columbia brass for a raise, constantly worried each year whether they'd have a job the next. Studio brass would engage in an annual round of head games about the viability of short-subject films that left the boys relieved to be back for another season.

In this day and age of high salaries and high-powered agents, that kind of treatment doesn't exist for stars of even minor note.

The kind of contemporary comics who most qualify as throwbacks to the physical gifts the Stooges displayed are limited to performers like Jim Carrey, Steve Martin, and Michael Richards of *Seinfeld*. The latter's manic pratfalling and herky-jerky movements were most effective when limited to short doses. And Martin long ago swapped his physical comedy prowess in favor of a more cerebral form of comedy. The man who got his film start playing the title character in *The Jerk* is now a columnist in the *New Yorker* and collects art. The films he creates are gentle, clever comedies like *Roxanne* and *L.A. Story*.

Carrey, the elastic comic with perhaps the greatest physical gifts seen onscreen since Jerry Lewis, catapulted in a three-year span from being the white guy on *In Living Color* to the first actor to be paid a $20-million film salary by a studio. That meteoric rise came because of his outlandish comic work in blockbuster comedies like *The Mask, Dumb and Dumber,* and *Ace Ventura*. But much like Martin, Carrey has pined to be taken seriously as an actor and has begun moving away from the frantic work that defined his ascent.

The fact is these performers use physical comedy as a stepping-stone for weightier fare. That was a move the Stooges didn't make. Comics today don't hang around the slapstick game long enough to develop signature moves. Indeed, compared to Carrey or Martin, Curly Howard had more signatures than the Declaration of Independence, if one considers all the gestures and noises still considered his trademark.

Even the Stooge formula that allowed working-class guys to get revenge against the socially superior upper-crusters seems out of date. Though a common plot structure for Depression-era shorts, the Stooges patented it. The last major contemporary proponent was Eddie Murphy, who became a star playing the underdog who used razor-sharp wit and street smarts to make fools out of much better educated adversaries.

Until he outgrew it, the formula worked in films ranging from *48 Hrs.* to *Beverly Hills Cop* to

Trading Places. In that film, Murphy played a street hustler made into a successful stockbroker by two arrogant brothers who wager whether success is made by heredity or environment. That is practically a carbon copy of the plot for the famous Stooge short *Hoi Polloi,* which was remade several times by the Stooges during their shorts years.

The reason these comics move on from Stooge territory is that they can. Highly physical comedy is hard work, and people get hurt. Small wonder an actor like Chevy Chase, who became the first break-out star on *Saturday Night Live* by pratfalling all over the stage as the bumbling President Gerald Ford, gladly traded those aches and pains for much better paying roles in films like *Caddyshack, Fletch,* and the National Lampoon's *Vacation* series. In those films, the spills are taken by stuntmen.

There's no evidence that Moe, Larry, and the various third Stooges ever had a representative who presented that kind of game plan. The shorts perfectly suited the Stooges' manic style of slapstick, but two-reelers were the bastard stepchild of the studio system. But for Moe Howard, Larry Fine, and Curly Howard, the trio of pint-sized dropouts with bad haircuts, it was steady work. And the fact that their longtime agent was one of Columbia chief Harry Cohn's best friends probably didn't help matters.

The prolific output of the Stooges and the fact that their shorts were sold piecemeal to any station that would broadcast it led their transformation from card-carrying members of the Amalgamated Association of Morons (Local 6⅞) to American icons.

"The very thing that agents and managers fight to protect is often the thing that stops pop-ularity," said Mel Brooks, director of such comedies as *Blazing Saddles* and *Young Frankenstein* and a lifelong Stooge fan. "The Three Stooges had bad agents and bad managers and they became famous because of it. No one protected them and that enabled them to be seen everywhere and by everyone at all times. A good manager or agent wouldn't let his clients be used like that. Back then, their agents either didn't understand or otherwise sold the Stooges out every chance they got. And we're the lucky recipients of those bad agents. They got nothing for the Stooges, they allowed them to be put everywhere, and we all got to see them. A lot of guys were handled more skillfully, like the Plover Brothers. Thanks to their managers and agents, you couldn't get near them and no one remembers them now. I just invented the Plover Brothers, of course, but there were teams just like this who were handled too skillfully. The other two-reelers, I don't know who those guys are."

As a youth, Brooks watched the Stooges when their original shorts were sandwiched between features and admits that he "probably consciously or unconsciously stole a lot of their moves. They were incredible," said Brooks. "They just stood out from all the rest. The guy doing the sound effects must have been a genius. Those bings, bangs, and bongs are the best hits ever recorded in sound.

"And Curly just made the best sounds, natural noises that were the best ever. And here they were, just program fillers between a movie like *A Night at the Opera.* But they were so good. You believed that Moe was sticking his fingers into Curly's eye sockets, and the sound effects made it utterly convincing."

Despite their poor handling, Brooks, who hailed from a family of brothers, considers the Howard clan film history's top sibling team. He qualifies them because Moe, Curly, and Shemp Howard were brothers and Larry Fine might well have been.

"They were always considered the B movie brothers, compared to the Marx Brothers and some others," said Brooks. "But the prodigious output made the Three Stooges history's most important brother act. Nobody did more shorts than they did and every living being has seen them. They are so ingrained in our memories."

Unlike Brooks, most of the Stooge-influenced writers and directors plying their trade in Hollywood were introduced to their slapstick on television. "Screen Gems put together a package of syndication that included the Three Stooges, Little Rascals, and Japanese cartoons like *Speed Racer*," said Quentin Tarantino, writer/director of *Pulp Fiction* and *Reservoir Dogs* and writer of such films as *True Romance* and *From Dusk Till Dawn*.

"They offered it so cheap, so dirt cheap, that any one-kilowatt TV station could afford it," said Tarantino, who won an Oscar for his *Pulp Fiction* script. "So from 1971 to 1976, at least one ratty-assed station around the country had the Stooges. In L.A., where I grew up, it was the UHF station Channel 52. It wasn't on the regular dial—you had to flip over to UHF—and it was the only thing besides PBS that had programming. And everybody I knew watched it."

Since there are so few proponents of Stooge comedy nowadays, why are the antics of a troupe that critics once dismissed as little more than professional wrestling with a laugh track now recalled so fondly?

It is the very thing that comic actors seem hell-bent on getting away from: simple story line, uncomplicated character motivation. That has allowed it to translate lucratively to foreign markets. Whether one lives in South Dakota or South America, there is a global understanding of what it feels like to get hit in the head.

George Carlin, who has spent a career dissecting what is funny and why, feels the Stooges perfected the distinction of which forms of violence worked for laughs.

"First of all, slapping people is very funny, even funnier than hitting a guy with a pipe," said Carlin. "Although hitting a guy with a pipe is also really funny—there's humor in that too. Granted, it's low, but so are a lot of other things about human beings."

Another interesting trait about the Stooges is that they've managed to remain popular despite appealing almost exclusively to males. With few exceptions, fans of the fairer sex are as rare as female members of the Woman Haters Club.

Figuring out why males would find the Stooges appealing does not require heavy sleuthing. There was plenty of violence, which guys like. And the Stooges were a beacon of hope to the average underachieving male who could watch a trio of homely midgets with comical haircuts romance stunningly beautiful platinum blondes a foot taller than they, even though they were either unemployed or absolutely incompetent in menial jobs.

That might also explain why there isn't much there for women, most of whom find the appeal of the Stooges as confusing as the triangle offensive scheme that propelled the Chicago Bulls to six NBA titles.

This is hardly a new phenomenon. Moe's daughter, Joan, recalls keeping her famous lineage quiet during her teenage years when she was with her girlfriends or meeting new people. "I didn't know how my friends would react, because slapstick was the type of comedy that was looked down upon by a lot of women. Even those who loved them probably wouldn't have admitted it. Sometimes I got bad reactions. I'd mention who he was and get 'Oh, isn't that wonderful,' or other times I'd hear, 'Eeew, I can't stand them.' So consequently, it would be better not to say anything."

Stooge fan Danny Jacobson, who with Paul Reiser created the long-running sitcom *Mad About You,* is so resolute in the single-gender appeal of the trio that he made it a running joke between Reiser and Helen Hunt. The story line grew from personal experience.

"I would sit there with my wife, and she would turn on the news every night, and you'd hear all this depressing stuff. One guy leaves his kids in a Dumpster, another guy beat his wife. Finally, she heard the weather and turned it off, and I turned on a tape, the one where the two guys have made a bet of whether they can make gentlemen of the Stooges. Vernon Dent says, 'I want to introduce you to my daughter, Lulu, who's in from college.' She's this thirty-year-old knockout who was probably sleeping with the studio executive back then. The Stooges come in and say, 'What a lulu,' and Curly just goes, 'Awooooo,' and when his mouth is wide open, Moe flicks this big wad of ash that's on the end of his cigar into Curly's mouth."

Jacobson roared with laughter, while his wife just stared at him as she might a petulant child.

"I said, 'Honey, just watch this one bit.' I run it back and laugh again, and she just looks at me like I'm the biggest schmuck in the world. So periodically, Helen finds Paul watching the Stooges and laughing his head off, and she just stares at him. He says, 'Honey, you got to watch this, they're in the cow, they're inside this cow,' and she just looks at him and says, 'I don't get it.' "

Comedy that was just blatantly crude would never have withstood the test of time. One reason the Stooges have lasted while other two-reelers have been long forgotten had to do with the trio itself.

To George Carlin, one key was that each Stooge created his own reality in an unreal situation and never wavered in it, which is why they lasted those twenty-four years. Moe, the stern disciplinarian. Larry, the dim-witted punching bag. Curly, the precocious child.

"What I discovered on my own and I'm sure has been talked about by the scholars is the durability and believability of those characters," said Carlin. "The interesting thing to me is how you just could not please Moe. The only smile he would give is the sarcastic smile. If Larry gave him $1 million, Moe would slap him anyway. Occasionally, for the sake of the plot, he'll go along with an idea, but he'd only smile to bait Larry or Curly into a slap. That state of constant agitation, irascibility, or dissatisfaction. See, I'm dissatisfied with my species, my particular nation. In a general sense, I'm Moe."

Mad About You cocreator Danny Jacobson also hailed the character consistency. "They just had their own reality and they were really true to it. It's a lot like John Lithgow in *3rd Rock from the Sun.* Here was an actor who was not a standup comic but totally committed to the material and wasn't afraid to stand up there and be a clown. And Moe, Larry, and Curly were the ultimate clowns. It didn't matter if they were the leaders of some country, or what period they were supposed to be in, they always delivered what they promised. Larry's timing was among my favorite stuff. When Joe Besser joined and he didn't want to take hits, Larry said, 'I'll do it,' and he ended up with a faceful of callus. That's the kind of commitment to his character that I'm talking about."

Jacobson counted Fine as one of the three great characters he saw on TV, after Jackie Gleason and Danny DeVito, the latter in his portrayal of the loathsome Louie in *Taxi.*

Equally passionate about Fine is Peter Farrelly. He and brother Bob have come closest to making films in the slapstick style patented by the Stooges. Those films include *Dumb and Dumber, Kingpin,* and the 1998 hit *There's Something About Mary,* which actually had a Stooge homage involving a dog blocking an eye poke, a move right out of Curly's repertoire. The Farrellys grew up watching the Stooges in Boston, and for Peter, the highlight was Larry Fine's understated stoogery.

"I started out loving Moe and then moved to Curly, but as I got older Larry became the guy I loved the most," said Farrelly. "You could watch an episode and see Curly or Moe do their thing and then watch again, just to see Larry and the way he reacted to them. He's such a ham. He reminds me of Chris Farley during the years he was on *Saturday Night Live* and wasn't getting parts, but I always noticed him. He'd be in the background, off to the side, but his reactions were memorable. That's why for me, as much as I love Jim Carrey in *Dumb and Dumber,* Jeff Daniels is

the guy to watch. Just the way he reacts off of Jim is brilliant. That's why Larry became my favorite."

Steve Oedekerk, a former standup comedian who directed Jim Carrey in *Ace Ventura: When Nature Calls,* also cited the reality of the group and its trio size as the reason the Stooges have endured.

"You don't run into the three-guy team a lot, but they really felt like a family," said Oedekerk. "Most teams, whether it was Martin and Lewis or Abbott and Costello, were guys who hooked up and went in opposite directions in real life. But with the Stooges, you felt like they were a family, hung out together all the time. They ate together, slept together, dressed together. You got the sense they never did anything alone, ever, like they were one guy. And the comedy is so grounded that you can show it on another continent where they speak an entirely different language and still get laughs. It's truly the most basic slapstick, which is pounding the crap out of someone else and making it funny. There's a fine line. It's the adage where a guy slips on a banana peel. It's funny, but if he breaks his neck it's not funny."

The bloodless violence and fact that nobody ever got hurt helped the Stooges keep on the right side of that line. In only one scene in the shorts did a character actually bleed—1951's *Merry Mavericks*—and that was used to show that the strappingly handsome, heroic guy who takes credit for corralling a bunch of bad guys (the Stooges actually did the hard work) was a coward. The man, as soon as he sees a trickle of blood coming from the ringleader's mouth, faints dead away.

"It's the kind of comedy that can be a total

crash and burn, and fail miserably if the guys aren't good at it," said Oedekerk.

There is subtle evidence of Stooge influence. Bruce Willis used Curly as inspiration for some of his comic antics as the fast-talking David Addison on *Moonlighting.* Howard Stern's top-rated morning radio show is populated with joke-enhancing sound effects which could have come right out of the library of noises Joe Henrie used for the Stooge shorts at Columbia. Michael Jackson's moonwalk was inspired by Curly's distinctive shuffle, and Jacko is such a Curly fan that he once wrote a song about the Stooge.

Mel Gibson, the Australian star of the Lethal Weapon series and the Oscar-winning director of the eleventh-century Scottish war epic *Braveheart,* is such a big fan that he used two different Stooges as inspiration for two recent movie roles.

"I'm playing this character as Moe Howard on acid," Gibson joked between scenes of *Payback,* a drama he was shooting one fall day on Stage 20 of the Warner Bros. lot. He was playing a deadly guy with a deadpan expression who hunts down an accomplice who made off with his conniving wife and his share of stolen loot. Forget the wife and the fact his partner tried to kill him; Gibson's character wants his money back and is willing to commit mayhem to get it. His character is more abusive than Moe Howard on his crankiest day, but his straightfaced dispensing of punishment does remind one a bit of the sourpuss Stooge.

"I play this low-voiced totem pole of a guy who just brains people trying to get his money," said Gibson as he waited for director Brian Helgeland to set up the next shot. "I actually poke a guy's eye out. A little like Moe, in his deadpan way."

Gibson's kidding, but if that's Moe Howard on acid, then his *Lethal Weapon* persona was Curly Howard on Viagra.

Martin Riggs, introduced in the 1987 film and three successful sequels, is a virile but suicidal former government-operative-turned-police-detective whose dark, violent side is offset by outrageous bursts of humor and physical comedy which he drew from years of watching the most watchable Stooge. In a key scene early in the original film designed to show just how crazy and fearless he is and how far he'd go to stop a group of gunrunners, Gibson pulled a Curly routine right out of the hat, eye poke and all, reminiscent of the 1934 short *Punch Drunks.* That was the second Stooge short at Columbia, and Curly's first break-out effort, the one in which he became a maniacally effective fighter—only upon hearing the tune "Pop Goes the Weasel."

"It was a scene where I'm slapping a bunch of guys around, and there are three of them in front of me and I had to get the drop on them," Gibson said. "I thought, 'Let's go the whole hog with the Stooges.' The guy was supposed to be crazy, this couch potato drunk who couldn't sleep and spent his nights watching late-show reruns. It seemed right that the Stooges-style movie slapstick violence would be on the top of Riggs's watch list. He'd laugh at that stuff."

Gibson's Stooge passion led him to try using the Stooge mayhem as the model for the Mad Max movies, the post-apocalyptic trilogy that launched him as an international star. His director was George Miller, who, while unarguably a most intelligent filmmaker, since he happens to be a medical doctor, seemed to develop a medical affliction right on the spot when Gibson suggested the Stooges.

"When I was working on *Mad Max,* the Stooges popped to mind, because anything that involved violence with blunt instruments—which those Road Warrior films did—would make you think of the Stooges," said Gibson, who got hooked on reruns he watched as a boy in New York before his family moved Down Under. "They were the original commit-violence-on-each-other-with-blunt-instruments-and-make-it-funny-with-funny-sound-effects team. They always had loud jobs as plumbers or carpenters, and they always had chain saws and claw hammers, stuff like that, so they would naturally come to mind. I remember telling George about this on the set, and he kind of looked at me funny. He said, 'You know, I didn't like that guy.' I said, 'What guy?' He said, 'Moe. I didn't like him. He scared me when I was a little kid. I used to have bad dreams about that guy.' He told me that Moe Howard haunted him. He had confessed to me that Moe, this five-foot-tall guy, was his own personal id as a child. He liked Curly, though."

Another Oscar-winning director who counts the Stooge shorts as a major film influence is Robert Zemeckis, who won his Oscar for *Forrest Gump* and also directed such films as *Back to the Future, Contact,* and *Who Framed Roger Rabbit.*

"I'm probably typical of many people, in that I've seen every single episode, watched them as I grew up in Chicago where they played every afternoon, and have most of them memorized," said Zemeckis. "They were always great, great gags."

Zemeckis attributed much of that quality to producer and director Jules White. "I was sort of joking when I once mentioned Jules White was the director who had the biggest impact on me,

but in a way it's true. He had a spectacular sense of timing, and he knew how to use sound to make the jokes work. And his style was elegant and imaginative."

Since his films are often complicated, Zemeckis said the evidence of influence on his own work is subtle. "They certainly influenced the development of my sense of humor. I wouldn't say I've used a lot of Stooges technique in my films but I watched them with great affection. What I loved most was the social irresponsibility, like watching a baby sucking on a revolver, using it as a pacifier. I think how wonderful it would be to be able to do this stuff without having people complain about being offended. Or the one where they're trying to fish, and they hang out a white distress flag that has a red paint spot in the center, and the aircrafts overhead say, 'They're Japs all right, let 'em have it.' "

When Zemeckis wrote broader comedies like *Death Becomes Her* and the Back to the Future films with partner Bob Gale, they used the classic Stooge short *Punch Drunks* as the model for seamless comedy. "They were masters at using neurosis and dysfunction as a plot point," said Zemeckis. "The best is where Curly goes crazy when he hears 'Pop Goes the Weasel,' and Larry drives a sound truck trying to get the song to Curly so he can win the fight. That was the tightest plot from a story standpoint. That kind of setup, where character triggers all this stuff, definitely influenced Bob and my scripts. We'd always say it's got to be tight, seamless, just like the Stooges."

Quentin Tarantino's Stooge passion led him to work the trio into a pivotal scene in *Pulp Fiction,* just before John Travolta plunges a needle full of Adrenalin through the breastbone of Uma

Thurman to restart a heart that had flat-lined because of a fatal snort of heroin. That heart-starting feat was easier, he says, than what he had to go through to display the scene in which Emil Sitka warbles, "Hold hands, you lovebirds," his signature line from the 1947 short *Brideless Groom.*

"That's probably my favorite Stooge line of all time," said Tarantino, "and I just knew I had to put it on TV during that scene. But you cannot show the Three Stooges without paying beaucoup bucks to Columbia, which not only makes a small fortune but actually makes it prohibitive to include them. I knew this was one of a few shorts available in public domain, but even then you cannot show the Stooges, whose images are copyrighted. Four days before that scene, I called my friend Scott Spiegel, who wrote the Evil Dead films with Sam Raimi. Those guys are such huge Stooges fans that they include 'Fake Shemp' in the credits of all their movies after they saw that credit when Joe Palma played Shemp after Shemp Howard died. I asked Scott to take the three public domain shorts and cut together all the stuff that doesn't show the Stooges in it. It's funny, everybody remembers that the Three Stooges are in *Pulp Fiction,* only you never see the Three Stooges."

Tarantino, a film buff who has resurrected the washed-up careers of actors like Travolta by plucking them from obscurity and putting them into his features, said he could easily have found a place for Moe, the one Stooge who always harbored aspirations to be a serious actor.

"I can see the actor in Moe, if just for the simple fact that more than the other guys, Moe is playing a character," said Tarantino. "Curly is too,

but he's more like a completely comic persona. I think Larry is very underappreciated as a straight man, but Moe is the one with the full-on character. And while everybody loved Curly, Shemp was just as good taking his place. I'd seen Shemp in the W. C. Fields Bank Dick movies, and so he was a big movie star to me. I think that, to me and my friends, and people of my generation, the Stooges sound effects have become the sound track of our lives. The woop-woops, nyuks, nyuks, they're in our psyche, we've been marinated in it. That's one of the reasons the Stooges are getting newfound respect, because my generation grew up with them and loved them, and now we're old enough to do something with it."

Phil Hartman, the former star of *Saturday Night Live* who moved to the hit sitcom *NewsRadio* and such films as *Sgt. Bilko* and *Small Soldiers,* also counted the Stooges as a major comic influence. Well before his life was tragically ended by a gunshot from his wife in May 1998, Hartman said that his major career goal was to play Moe in a screen version of the Stooges.

"I thought, God, me as Moe, Jon Lovitz as Larry, and maybe Chris Farley as Curly would be so good in the nineties," said Hartman, interviewed before the tragic death of his pal Farley, whom many saw as a throwback to Curly Howard, a man-child who exuded innocence and unusual physical abilities for a man his size. "I've analyzed the Stooges, and besides the fact it's great mindless entertainment, the thing that stood out to me was that whatever happened to the Stooges, whatever incident provoked violence, whether it was Moe slapping Larry, or Moe slapping Curly, they always got over it quickly and went on with their business. They never held a grudge. To me, it was like a subliminal message that it's not so bad to express your emotions, dispense the beating, and get on with your life.

"They skewered snobbishness, gave it to those snobbishly matronly society women, which made them lowbrow and performers for the meat-and-potatoes blue-collar crowd," said Hartman. "There was something so accessible about the Stooges, down to Curly cataloging all of his hand moves, and Moe with his slaps and eye pokes.

"But the heart of their appeal is what I try to achieve in my craft and what the best people in my game accomplish in character comedy. That's to try to achieve funny, fully realized characterizations, and that's what they did. Moe Howard was such a strong character. Curly was the one who stood out with his noises and physicality, but I identified with Moe. I'd like to play all three, but when I jut my jaw forward, put on the bowl-shaped wig, wrinkle my brow, and say, 'C'mere, what's the matter with you?,' I just know I could hit it out of the park."

Tarantino feels that the combination of Moe's madness and the childlike trust of his partners linked the Stooges to the kids who fueled their renaissance in the sixties.

"The Stooges and Abbott and Costello are similarly linked in their appeal to kids," said Tarantino. "Kids responded to Lou Costello because he's a child, and Bud Abbott wasn't a straight man as much as he was a nasty guy, the worst big brother a kid could ever have. That is a direct parallel to Moe and his relationship with the other Stooges, especially Curly. The only negative aspect of the Stooges for me was that I wished Moe wasn't so mad all of the time. I wanted him to have one moment of bliss. These guys spent every moment together, and he could have shown one moment of enjoying that camaraderie."

While *Dumb and Dumber* might be the film that is most reminiscent of the Stooge shorts, Tarantino's filming style of setting a scene, introducing an unimaginable burst of violence, and then returning to the plot as though nothing happened is also reminiscent of the Stooge style. *Pulp Fiction, Reservoir Dogs,* and *From Dusk Till Dawn* are peppered with such scenes. Tarantino embraces the similarities, to a degree. "Their violence never failed to crack me up," he said. "The poking, the slapping, using a pair of pliers to twist Curly's nose off, banging Curly over the head with a pickax. In my films, I try to wait more than a few lines for the next violent thing to happen."

The difficulty in sustaining that high level of violent comedy for the length of a feature not only hampered the Stooges from crossing over beyond the two-reeler format during their early years, it has also taken sixteen years to mount a film about the Three Stooges—their antics leave an audience exhausted after sixteen minutes, let alone one and one-half hours.

With so many comedians hooked on the Stooges, it makes one wonder why it has taken so long to mount the movie version of the Three Stooges. There is no easy answer and many valiant, albeit unsuccessful attempts.

The first documentable attempt to turn the Stooges into a feature came courtesy of Mel Brooks, who wanted to make the film with himself, Marty Feldman, and Dom De Luise. Early on, he felt as he wrote it that it just wouldn't work. Instead, he turned the teaming into the 1976 hit *Silent Movie,* in which an alcoholic producer decides a silent movie is just what Hollywood needs, and sets about to make one. Brooks made the film silent—mime Marcel Marceau uttered the only line of dialogue in the film. While this seems the most extremely unlikely scenario for a comic film, Brooks felt that the Stooges would have been even more difficult.

"I wanted me to be Shemp, Dom to be Curly, and Marty to be Larry, but it was just too hard to do a Three Stooges movie that was two hours or even ninety minutes," said Brooks. "It's such physical humor and so hard to sustain a plot that could withstand their antics for that long. I felt it was better to go with a simple story within a story, about a silent movie made to save the silent movie."

Brooks wasn't the only filmmaker whose attempt to turn the Stooge characters into screen stars has been silenced.

Next up was Stooge manager Norman Maurer and Howard West, who later became an executive producer of *Seinfeld* and managed such comic talent as Jerry Seinfeld and Andy Kaufman. In 1983, when a lot of marquee names expressed interest in starring in a Stooge feature film, West took his shot with "Oh, Oh, 3 Stooges."

"There was so much Stoogemania at the time that I thought that a Stooge movie with the proper casting could be another *Rocky Horror Picture Show,* where kids would go to see it again and again at midnight shows," said West. "There could be sequels. So Norman, who was an artist, drew the Stooges in a takeoff on James Bond."

The elegantly drawn one-sheet bills Richard Pryor in the role of Moe—though it was unclear whether Pryor was even aware he'd been tapped to sport Moe's soup-bowl haircut. Still, it made the desired impression.

"We walk into Columbia, where Guy McElwaine was running the studio at the time," said West. "We present him with this beautiful rendering of the Stooges emulating a James Bond one-sheet, and Guy calls down his head of marketing, Ashley Boone. All Guy does is point to the rendering we did and say, 'Can you sell that?' Ashley gets this shit-eating grin on his face, smiles, and nods his head yes. Guy says, 'Hey, we're in business.'"

That proved to be the easy part.

"Next came the pulling and tugging over who owned what rights and who was screwing who, and I was in that hell a long time," said West. George Gallo was signed to write the screenplay. Gallo, whose credits include *Wise Guys,* the Brian De Palma–directed gangster comedy starring Danny DeVito and Joe Piscopo, and *Midnight Run,* describes himself as a lifelong Stooge fan who grew up watching the shorts on WPIX in New York, introduced by a weatherman who threw on a beat cop's uniform and became Officer Joe Bolton.

"I thought the script was a riot, but as I recall, it got tied up in lawsuits that involved family fighting," said Gallo. "I'm a big fan and we worked in a couple of Stooge references into my script for *Wise Guys.* The plot of this movie took an old Stooge idea. They were exterminators supposed to take care of a cockroach problem. At the same time, a top-secret jet is stolen by a country in South America called Guano. The Stooges show up as three guys who are brought in by the NATO brass as exterminators, hit men who are supposed to kill General Roberto Alou, or Bob Alou. He's modeled the country after fifties TV shows, and what he wants in return for the jet is a billion dollars, plus every episode of *Sky King* on VHS. It was madness, was way out there, this take-off on James Bond. 007 had Octopussy, we had Connie Lingus and the Russian operative Bitya-cockov."

"It looked like something would happen, and there was this nationwide casting call," said Gallo. "People would call up all day doing Curly, doing Moe. But it stalled, and I went on to *Midnight Run*. It's too bad. I think the idea could make a fortune, only nobody seems to be able to get their heads out of their asses long enough to make it happen."

West acknowledged the difficulties that had little to do with the movie itself: "Finally, we developed a script and then a second one, but we could never get it off the ground. We'd gone from the extreme, from casting Dustin Hoffman to Bruce Willis or whoever had expressed interest, to getting unknowns who looked like them. I remember some agent submitting a young actor to play Curly who starred in a show called *Fridays* and who was Larry David, who would cocreate *Seinfeld* with Jerry. But it just never worked out. All I've got is about eight pounds of deal memos."

Ace Ventura director Steve Oedekerk also smells a can't-miss prospect, if the spirit of the original shorts is kept intact. "There's this scene in *Dumb and Dumber* where Jim Carrey cracks the back of Jeff Daniels's legs with a cane, and there are just huge laughs. Then you think, that's what the Stooges used to do all the time, and by today's standards, if these shorts were in theaters, people would react the same way. You'd need the right type of guys, and it could work again. One could argue that Jim Carrey succeeded Jerry Lewis and it took years for him to come along. It might take that long for another guy to be accepted acting as goofy as Curly. But I think if you make a Stooge movie and get out within seventy-five minutes like we did with *Ace Ventura,* you can do it. Just don't stay a moment too long."

Some directors, such as Tarantino and David Zucker, who with brother Jerry hatched films like *Airplane* and *Kentucky Fried Movie,* feel that even attempting a Stooge film would be tantamount to sacrilege.

Zucker's an avowed Stooge fan, though he puts them a cut below Abbott and Costello and the Marx Brothers, whose routines, he feels, were cerebral enough to sustain a feature. "The Stooges could make you laugh hard, but you could never do it for one and one-half hours," he said. "In a movie you need a plot, characters, and story development, things you didn't need when you made a Stooges short. I know I was never interested in that kind of film. If I wanted to do it again, we'd make up our own characters. Even the Stooges couldn't duplicate Curly when he had a stroke."

Tarantino also felt the standards of the original trio in the shorts would be too much to compare to in a feature. "It's almost like saying let's do a Laurel and Hardy movie. How do you do it without Laurel and Hardy? Also, I don't think you can sustain it for the length of a movie. Even if you go to a revival house and watch Stooge shorts, you're burnt out by the last one. The first short you're on the ground, but by the fifth, you're ready to go."

The Stooge mantle currently resides with

Columbia and Interscope, the producer of *Jumanji,* and the revamped Comedy III Productions, Inc., a company originally formed by the Stooges themselves. At the writing of this book, the active script was one penned by *Mad About You*'s Danny Jacobson. He said his idea was to move the bloodless violence into the millennium. The idea is to make the Stooges losers with a grandmother who keeps pushing them into trying to find gainful employment.

In the opening scene, they start out as tow truck operators.

"It starts out with you thinking you're watching the elaborate opening robbery scene in *Heat,* with these guys setting up for a heist with a fire truck," said Jacobson. "Cut to the three guys in a tow truck. Curly hands Moe a hot cup of tea and says, 'What's this for?' and Moe says, 'For this,' and he pours it right down Curly's shirt, just as these gangbangers pull up right behind in a red BMW. Larry accidentally hits the knob and they drop the hook right into the hood. The Stooges drive off and the gang members are swinging behind them, the Stooges not even aware of them. They swing off, right into the hands of some cops who've been looking for them.

"Meantime, these bank robbers set off this smoke bomb so people think there's a fire, and the bad guys show up in a fire truck and zoom up to the bank, jumping out in oxygen masks and busting open the vault. They come out with a ton of money just as Moe sees the fire truck and says, 'What's the idea of parking in front of a fire hydrant?' Just as the robbers toss the money into the fire truck, the Stooges tow it away, and you're off and going into the movie."

One key to Jacobson's vision of contemporary Stoogery is to use the cutting-edge technological advancements of the millennium as instruments for Moe to brain his partners.

"The grandmother who thinks they're all screwups sends them out on a job interview and Curly does something wrong right away," said Jacobson. "Moe asks very politely to the person interviewing behind the desk if he can borrow the fax machine. She says, 'Please do,' and Moe breaks it over Curly's head. Cut to Grandma, who gets a beep, and then out comes a fax with Curly's cringing face."

Jacobson said he watched short after short and wrote draft after draft of scripts to come up with a movie Stooge fans wouldn't think the equivalent of flop film transformations *McHale's Navy* or *Sgt. Bilko.* As often happens in Hollywood, his efforts might prove as fruitless as the typical attempt by the Stooges to wallpaper a room.

Jacobson got skittish when he learned that Amy Pascal had become president of Columbia and overseer of the Stooge project, since women, for the most part, loathe the Stooges.

"One day I'm told there's a new executive in charge of the project, and she did *Sense and Sensibility,* and right away I know I'm in trouble," said Jacobson. "She says, 'I have some problems with the script. It's very funny but there are no characters in there that kids can relate to, and it's really violent.' I said, 'Amy, the Stooges are ten-year-olds in the bodies of forty-year-old men. It's *The Simpsons* with real people. Popeye eats a can of spinach, punches an alligator, and twelve suitcases appear. That's what this is! The fun is that they're irreverent.'"

Pascal hired director George Weisman, who turned the Jay Ward cartoon *George of the Jungle* into a hit Disney film and grossed over $100 million. But the fear of filmmaking Stoogephiles is that his view of the Stooges will be as toothless as his jungle foray.

"Amy wanted the director of *George of the Jungle* because it was a successful kiddie movie," Jacobson said. "This has been heartbreaking for me. I get offered movie stuff all the time. My feeling is there's as much shit in movies as there is in television and there's as much good stuff in TV as there is in movies. I've put more time into this than anything, and I couldn't wait to get to my office and work on it. I told Amy that I have kids, and if you took the watered-down version and had Moe hit Curly with a tomato when he's angry, the kids are going to fall asleep. These guys, they hit each other with saws, things like that."

But Pascal is in fact eager to move forward aggressively. She renewed overtures to bring in Peter and Bob Farrelly to work up a new draft of the script that Weisman will direct.

The Farrellys have something of a tortured past with Columbia over the Stooge movie. They so badly wanted to direct a Stooge film at one time that they offered to forgo up-front salary for a sizable participation in the film's revenues. Columbia, which continues to make money from TV and video residuals from the 194 original shorts and which controlled the screen rights at the time, would only permit that gross deal until the Farrellys recouped what would have been their original deal. Sensing a sucker deal on the scale of those annual Stooge contract renewals at Columbia, this smarter brother team balked.

"To me, this is the biggest slam dunk ever," said Farrelly. "But when we went in to meet with the people at Interscope, they freaked us out because they had such low expectations and weren't willing to do it right. I've got to tell you, if anybody directed this movie right, it's going to make $100 million guaranteed. Imagine if you did this right and had Jim Carrey, Bill Murray, and someone like Chris Farley, it could be a classic, classic movie."

The fact that *There's Something About Mary* became one of the most profitable films of 1998 has cast the Farrellys, and simple low road humor, in a new light. And Pascal responded by trying to bring them back, at this point as writers and producers. The average Stooge fan would be hard-pressed to complain, because if any filmmaker has upheld the Stooge spirit in their work, it has been the Farrelly tandem.

Dumb and Dumber, their smash hit which starred Jim Carrey and Jeff Daniels as nice guys with box-of-rocks brainpower, was a close cousin to the Stooges. The ten or twelve shockingly hilarious visual gags that distinguished *There's Something About Mary* were the kind of politically incorrect visuals that often made Stooge shorts so laugh-out-loud funny. Peter Farrelly, for one, vowed that their script will be true to the tone of the original shorts they love so much.

"If it's done right, no guy in the country would miss this movie, and they'll drag their girlfriends," said Farrelly, solving once and for all the female problem that has become part of Stooge lore.

As this book was being completed, the Farrellys fell out again and the studio hired as its writer Chris Matheson, whose credits include *Bill and Ted's Excellent Adventure.* Clearly, the Stooge movie will take several years to get off the ground if ever. But it seems clear that the audience is there. Is it a coincidence that, after *There's Something About Mary* became a summer sleeper hit, the Adam Sandler film *The Waterboy* became the fall sleeper, grossing a shockingly high opening weekend of $31.9 million, far more than its $19-million budget? Sandler is a student of comedy and a big Three Stooges fan, and his persona is much like the man–child Curly Howard, his vehicles formula physical slapstick, which proves itself with audiences time and again. As long as movies like these continue to ring up the cash registers, the Stooge movie has a fighting chance.

For now, though, fans are lucky to have the original shorts, which feature some of the best physical comedy that movies have ever seen, and which continue to influence and inform modern comedy.

PART THREE

The Shorts

 THE FOLLOWING IS A CHRONOLOGICAL SUMMARY AND CRITIQUE OF THE COLUMBIA STOOGE SHORTS FOR WHICH THE STOOGES ARE BEST REMEMBERED. THE POINT HERE IS NOT TO INCLUDE EVERY TRIVIAL FACT, BUT TO PROVIDE A BREEZY BLOW-BY-BLOW OF THE PLOTS AND A CONCISE BLOW-BY-BLOW OF THE BLOWS. THE REVIEW IS A WAY TO FOLLOW THE DEVELOPMENT OF THE STOOGE STYLE IN THE EARLY SHORTS AND THE SUBSEQUENT EROSION OF THE COLUMBIA SHORT SUBJECTS DEPARTMENT WHICH LED TO THE BLATANT REUSE OF OLD FOOTAGE AND STORY LINES TO SAVE MONEY.

There's also a count of the beatings dealt and the pies thrown. In a highly scientific formula, slaps were awarded for blows above the neck that were accompanied by a sound effect. Brainings with pipes, saws, or a variety of hand tools, while probably painful, went uncredited.

The Stooges would go on to top-line six feature films: 1959's *Have Rocket, Will Travel*, 1961's *Snow White and the Three Stooges*, 1962's *The Three Stooges Meet Hercules*, and 1963's *The Three Stooges in Orbit*, *The Three Stooges Go Around the World in a Daze*, and *The Outlaws Is Coming*. They also did bit parts in other films, most notably the Stanley Kramer–directed comedy classic *It's a Mad, Mad, Mad, Mad World*, in which the Stooges played firemen, same as their very first onscreen role, alongside Ted Healy in the 1930 Fox feature *Soup to Nuts*.

But the shorts are what etched the Stooges' place in comic history and why their fans still hold them in such high esteem. That's why this section is limited to the 190 done during the twenty-four years at Columbia.

So, as Curly Howard would say when he entered a room ready to party, **"SWING IT!"**

7.

Woman Haters,

1934. Columbia Pictures. With Marjorie White. Directed by Archie Gottler from a story by Jerome S. Gottler.

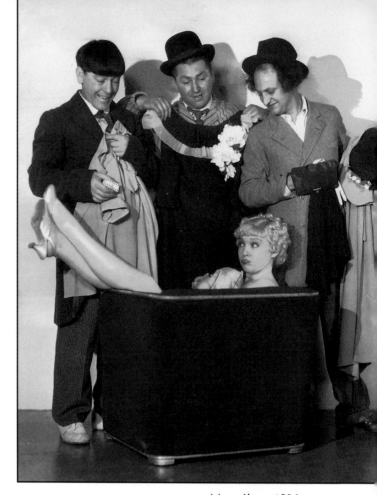

Woman Haters, 1934.

White, a budding star who died tragically shortly after filming, was given above the line credit. Below her, the Stooges were referred to as Moe, Larry, and Curley.

Set to the strains of orchestral music, the first Columbia short begins in the Woman Haters Club Room, where a meeting is going on. The dialogue is delivered in rhyming couplets, a most restrictive format. That's clear from the first line, when the club leader says, "Gentlemen, please / the meeting is called to order and we need quiet, not a riot / Otherwise, we can't proceed / Listen, you women haters / we meet for the seventh time / to convince each member that romance is a crime." Inauspicious start, but the short gets rolling the moment our trio enters the room, backs to the camera.

As though they were out to convince Columbia in one scene that the studio had made the right decision in hiring them, the boys start with a slaphappy flourish. Moe pulls on Curly's nose. The club initiation is an eye poke, and when Moe gets his, he slaps Curly, throws him into a full nelson, and delivers a flurry of punches. Curly hits the floor and delivers his signature rapid-fire hat rattle while Moe belts Larry, delivering a whirlwind twelve-slap barrage with his right hand that brings to mind Muhammad Ali working the speed bag. And that's just the opening scene.

Larry's name is Jim, Curly's name is Jackie, and Moe is Tommy. The physical comedy is sharp, as the boys clearly show they're more effective without Ted Healy. But the dialogue? Get me rewrite! Larry agrees to drop his spouse-to-be and tells his mates: "Either shine or rain, I'll meet youse at the train / and now I'll tell the lady I'll never see her again." Imagine Larry's whine, and you realize he's not the guy to hire for poetry readings.

The short is memorable for the precision honed from the vaudeville training. Curly is a scream when he boards the train. He's wearing the garb that would become his trademark: a suit so tight the coat could barely be buttoned. In one scene, he's got a split in the seam of his trousers in

the back (there must have been a tailor on the set because it is not evident in the next shot during the same scene). White plays the tossed-off lover, who gets hip to their vow and flirtatiously tortures them. When Curly tries to resist her advances, one can quickly tell he's poised to become the franchise. And a magnet for slaps, with White getting in a devastating shot of her own.

The moves are fluid, and one has to slow the picture down to see that Moe delivers his eye poke above the eyebrows. In fact, though Larry was the Stooge with boxing training, Moe has the hand speed of a welterweight as he expertly delivers multislap barrages. Again, slowed down, it's clear he knows how to pull his punches, sparing both Curly and Larry at least some of the punishment each seems to be absorbing.

As Larry is subject to a Moe combination of nose grab followed by a face slap, Curly issues his first "nyuk, nyuk, nyuk." And when Curly climbs from his bed trying to sneak out to woo the girl, Moe bites his toes, leading Curly to deliver the first "woop, woop, woop, woop, woop, woop, woop," just before the trio falls from the window of the moving train. Small wonder Columbia quickly picked up their option.

SLAP COUNT: 60 (mostly Moe)
EYE POKES: 11
CONKING HEADS: 1
MEMORABLE LINE: "Nyuk, nyuk, nyuk."

Punch Drunks,

1934. With Dorothy Granger. Story by Jerry Howard, Larry Fine, Moe Howard. Directed by Lou Breslow with Jack Cluett.

Though once again their credit was eclipsed by an actress, here the boys at least get to use their own names. And lines that would become staples of future shorts. Moe, ordering food from Curly: "Four slices of burnt toast and a rotten egg. I got a tapeworm and it's good enough for 'em." Moe's a fight manager in dire need of a fighter. He finds one in Curly, the waiter who becomes a fighter named KO Stradivarius. That occurs the moment

In Punch Drunks, 1934, Larry scratches out "Pop Goes the Weasel," and the ear puller is about to take a pounding.

Punch Drunks.

Larry, using his training as a violinist, plays "Pop Goes the Weasel," which turns KO into a punching machine. Curly slaps his face, stamps his heel, woop-woop-wooping as he gets in the ring with Killer Kilduff for the title bout. All's well until Larry's violin breaks and he tries frantically to get the song played as Curly gets knocked silly around the ring. The solution is hilarious, and by the time he's done, Curly has Kilduff, the ref, and Moe and Larry stacked up like firewood. A short that truly establishes Curly as a Stooge to be reckoned with.

SLAP COUNT: 30
EYE POKES: 1

3.

Men in Black,

1934. Story and screenplay by Felix Adler.
Directed by Raymond McCarey.

The Stooges' third Columbia short was nominated for an Oscar, the only such nomination the boys received during their long stay at the studio. They lost to the animated short *La Cucaracha*. At the Los Arms Hospital, they play three doctors described as not overly bright but who had been in the senior class too many years to stay any longer. Proud that they graduated "with the highest temperatures in our class," the dopey docs are dispatched to the hospital. Best known for originating one of the true classic Stooge routines, "Calling Dr. Howard, Dr. Fine, Dr. Howard," the boys rumble through the corridors of the hospital, crashing continuously through the glass window of the office door of hospital superintendent Graves. Each time they're paged over the intercom, the boys shuffle through the hospital with a different means of transportation. First, it's on bicycle, then horseback, next on go-carts.

Short is ripe with witty rapid-fire medical one-liners, such as Curly's diagnosis that one patient is "a victim of circumstance." When another is diagnosed as being in a coma, she replies, "No, I'm in a bed." Moe continues honing his methods of punishment. A combination punch to the stomach, followed by a punch to the head as Curly bows forward, becomes a Stooge staple.

SLAP COUNT: 14
MEMORABLE LINE: "Calling Dr. Howard, Dr. Fine, Dr. Howard."

In *Men in Black*, Dr. Howard, Dr. Fine, and Dr. Howard set the medical profession back a century.

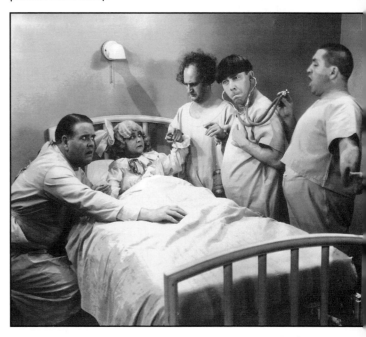

Men in Black diagnosis: the only Oscar nomination the trio would receive.

4.

Three Little Pigskins,

1934. With Lucille Ball, Gertie Green, Phyllis Crane. Story and screenplay by Felix Adler, Griffin Jay. Directed by Raymond McCarey.

Opens with a headline: "Joe Slack's Tigers to Meet Cubs in Professional Football Classic." Joe, a tough-guy gangster, has $50,000 on the game, but his "three backs got plastered and wound up in a ditch." A young Lucille Ball, who appears to be blond, suggests he head to Boulder Dam College to sign up the horsemen. Cut to the boys.

In what is to become a common entry to many shorts, they are begging, to no avail. Curly finally holds up a guy by using a finger in his jacket pocket, only to hear, "I haven't got a dime, it's the Depression." Curly replies, "You're talking depression, and me here with a gun without bullets." Curly winds up with a fist to the face, sprawled on the sidewalk. Larry tries his luck getting a job playing violin in a bar.

Asked for his credentials, Larry says to the barkeep, "Did you ever hear 'Snow, Snow, Beautiful Snow'?" "Did you write it?" he is asked. "No, I shoveled it," Fine replies. Soon enough, the trio, lured to the hotel room of Slack's three molls, is dressed in drag trying to woo the women. Slack and his two gun-toting pals chase them, leading to a hilarious fall down a dumbwaiter shaft. They're mistaken for the horsemen and are soon in football uniforms. Curly's number is ?, Larry ½, and Moe H_2O_2. Their incompetence on the gridiron quickly becomes evident, and the short ends with Slack shooting at the fleeing Stooges. Interestingly, the original script concluded with a scene in which the

Three Little Pigskins. The Stooges quickly prove their incompetence in the huddle.

In Three Little Pigskins, the boys are mistaken for football stars and bribed to play for Joe Slack's team.

Stooges recounted the story for their children, three pint-sized Stooge look-alikes who engage in their own battle at the short's close. If filmed, that footage remained on the cutting room floor.

SLAP COUNT: 30
EYE POKES: 1

5.

Horses' Collars,

1935. With Dorothy Kent, Fred Kohler. Story and screenplay by Felix Adler. Directed by Clyde Bruckman.

In Horses' Collars, the boys gumshoe for the Hyden Zeke Detective Agency.

Short opens with a glimpse at a door that reads "Hyden Zeke Detective Agency." That hatches a tradition of companies named with clever word-play which becomes as much a staple of Stooge shorts as the pie facial. Opening with signage is also a throwback to the silent era on which many of the writers cut their teeth. Not only did the signage establish location and context with a minimum of effort and film, it also birthed the likes of the memorable law firm of Cess, Poole & Drayne, which supported suspicions that upper-crusters like lawyers were out to swindle them. It bonded the Stooges with the commoners at whom the shorts were aimed. The undertakers Diggs, Graves & Berry, run by M. Balmer, is another example.

As the boss describes a case he wants the boys to work, Curly sits attentively, staring forward and not blinking, until the boss mentions that his client is a pretty girl about to lose her ranch to desperadoes. Then Curly's eyes flutter open, revealing that he'd painted eyes on his eyelids to mask his slumber, a classic Stooge gag. The short is full of strong one-liners. In a variation of the running gag in *Punch Drunks,* Curly goes crazy after seeing a mouse. When Hyden Zeke asks why, he's told Curly's "marked that way because his father was a rat." At the ranch, they try to get the ranch deed away from a desperado named Double Deal Decker. Asked by the client if they're good detectives, Larry points to his boot

The Stooges get hung up in Horses' Collars, 1935.

and says, "See that heel? I ran that down." The standout gag in the short comes when Curly sees mice in two pivotal scenes. In the first, it occurs as the trio is being strung up for thieving. Curly's fit ends up hanging the other Stooges from nooses. In the final scene, Curly again cleans house, knocking the bad guys silly, along with Larry and Moe.

SLAP COUNT: 29
EYE POKES: 1
MEMORABLE LINE: "Moe, Larry, the cheese!"

Restless Knights,

1935. With Geneva Mitchell. Story and screenplay by Felix Adler. Directed by Charles Lamont.

The story begins with a cameo from Walter Brennan, a bedridden, dying man who, with his familiar vocal stylings, says, "I would shpeak with my shons, and this wild tempest-laden night shuits the purpose besht." He confesses he had an affair with a chambermaid of the King of Anaesthesia and urges his sons to head to the kingdom to protect the queen and claim their royal lineage. Soon they're in a castle and wind up in a long and rather laborious wrestling match with one another. Finally, they're captured by the bad guys and sen-

Restless Knights, the 1935 short that featured Walter Brennan.

7.

Pop Goes the Easel,

1935. Story and screenplay by Felix Adler.
Directed by Del Lord.

The Stooges play royal grapplers in Restless Knights.

tenced to death. "You may either have your head cut off or be burnt at the stake," they are told. In what became a line used several times in Stooge shorts, Curly chooses burning, reasoning that "a hot stake is better than a cold chop." The best thing about the short is the continuing development of Curly, from his "soitenly" to his snapping fingers. The short has a rather clumsy ending; after an extended chase around the castle, the boys knock out all of the bad guys with a club, then inadvertently crown the queen as well. After she goes down, they knock themselves out too.

SLAP COUNT: 20
EYE POKES: 4 (another 1 blocked)
MEMORABLE LINE: Curly, questioning his royal lineage, asks his dying father, "Am I the Count of Ten?" "No," he's told. "You are Baron of Graymatter."

As in *Three Little Pigskins,* the Stooges once again begin the short as incompetent beggars. Larry holds a sign: "Must Have a Job. Will Do Anything, Position as Bridge Instructor Preferred." Asked by a prospective employer, "What would you do if you held the queen alone?" Larry answers, "That depends on when the king is coming home." They wind up stealing brooms and being chased by a cop into an art studio, where they quickly become mistaken for artists. There the one-liners are catchy. Moe: "My old man used to draw." Curly: "Sure, he drew twenty years with one stroke of the pen." Aside from a fetching Curly drag scene, the short is most valuable for two innovations. Curly executes for the first time the signature move in which he snaps his fingers together, then drums the fingers along the side of his outstretched neck, with four distinctive pops. The other innovation: a great fight with clay salvos that could be considered a precursor to the pie fights.

SLAP COUNT: 17
EYE POKES: 4 (another 1 blocked)

8.

Uncivil Warriors,

1935. Story and screenplay by Felix Adler.
Directed by Del Lord.

Stooges in Civil War mode in Uncivil Warriors, 1935.

The Stooges are unconvincing Confederate spies in Uncivil Warriors.

Short opens on Civil War battlefield. "Unless our Secret Service can get through the enemy, we will have to retreat," says the Northern army general, adding that the three spies are "the very brains of the Secret Service." Out comes Larry (Operator 12), Moe (Operator 14), and Curly (Operator 15), who become Lieutenant Duck, Captain Dodge, and Major Hide, respectively. They infiltrate the home of a Southern soldier and, as usual, woo the women. There are a few good verbal gags in the kitchen. Curly asks to help cook, boasting, "I used to work in a bakery as a pilot. I used to take the bread from one corner and pile it on the other," adding that he quit the job. "Oh, I got sick of the dough and thought I'd go on the loaf." Southern army intelligence knows the boys are spies and Curly winds up in drag as the matronly Mrs. Dodge, the wife of Moe. This leads to an awkward moment when she carries what turns out to be a black child, with Moe explaining he's sunburned. They crawl into a cannon and are shot back over enemy lines.

SLAP COUNT: 13

Moe and Curly break bread in *Pardon My Scotch*, 1935.

Pardon My Scotch,

1935. With Nat Carr, James C. Norton. Story and screenplay by Andrew Bennison. Directed by Del Lord.

Prohibition is over, and a draught drought is on. The boys begin as handymen in a pharmacy. They brain each other, and Moe takes a wicked spill after Curly saws apart the table he stands on. The boys are asked to watch the store and mix a potent concoction for a man who's desperate to get his hands on Scotch. Naturally, it knocks his socks off. Suddenly, the trio is sporting kilts and parading as Scottish Scotch makers at a formal dinner. Curly, with his ridiculously short kilt, is Mr. McSniff, Larry is McSnuff, and Moe is McSnort, all hailing from Lockjaw. In a routine that would be repeated memorably in *Micro-Phonies*, the boys torment the bug-eyed opera singer by shooting grapes into his mouth, open while he hits high notes—"What you try to make for me, a fruit salad," he screams. Dinner is destroyed, especially after the boys bring in a sample of their "Breath of Heather." When they tap the keg, the barrel explodes, leaving the guests splashing in a foam-filled room and scotching their careers as spirits makers.

SLAP COUNT: 17

In a Stooge classic, the boys are transformed into gentlemen in _Hoi Polloi_, 1935.

The Stooges mingle with the upper-crusters in _Hoi Polloi_.

10.

Hoi Polloi,

1935. Story and screenplay by Felix Adler.
Directed by Del Lord.

In what would become a frequent short theme (and later the basis for the Eddie Murphy/Dan Aykroyd film _Trading Places),_ two rich guys argue over what molds gentlemen, heredity or environment. The theme was written by Moe and his wife, Helen, originally conceived when Howard was a Healy stooge. When Helen suggested turning it into a short, she was offered story credit or fifty dollars. She took the cash.

The rich guys wager $10,000 and seek the most unlikely candidates for an experiment. One boasts he can turn three miscreants into gentlemen in three months. They choose a trio of garbagemen who've just showered them with a bunch of discarded food cans. Asked if they'll agree to be turned into gentlemen if the rich guys don't press charges, the Stooges first protest, but finally agree. "It'll break the old man's heart, but you've got the drop on us," Moe says.

When Curly grabs his coat from the garbage truck, he hits a lever that dumps all the cans on the convertible car and its occupants. "What happened? You're all canned up," says Curly. Moe flings a can, which shatters on Curly's cranium. Soon the trio is spoofing high society and given lessons in table manners, formal dancing. The slapstick is hilarious, such as when Curly (in a ridiculously tight-fitting tux) is matched with a heavyset female partner and winds up with a couch spring stuck to his tail. When he bounces off her, Curly falls to the floor and bounces up to his original position. The spring gets caught on another man and they both fall to the floor. Proving there's no chivalry in Stooge shorts, Curly engages his hefty dance partner in a slap fight. Soon Moe is pounding Curly with slaps and punches. The wager is over, with the real gentlemen braining the boys with champagne bottles.

SLAP COUNT: 48
EYE POKES: 4
MEMORABLE LINE: When Moe slaps both Curly and Larry, they complain: "What's that for? We didn't do nothin'." Replies Moe: "That's in case you do and I'm not around."

Three Little Beers, 1935.

Three Little Beers,

1935. With Bud Jamison. Story and screenplay by Clyde Bruckman. Produced by Jules White. Directed by Del Lord.

A door reads "Panther Brewing Co, A. Panther, President." He's hired the Stooges, but their jobs are in immediate jeopardy. Outside waxing over their plans to enter a golf tournament, Moe demonstrates his swing and causes a keg to crash down on Panther. All this is an excuse to get them creating mayhem on the links. When they get back to the beer truck, they go uphill, then lose all the barrels as they go crashing down the hill. Larry winds up stuck in wet cement, followed by his mates. "If I could get my hand out of this, I'd crack your head open," Moe tells Curly. "Can't get it out?" "No."

The Stooges deliver in Three Little Beers.

"Sure?" "Positive." "In that case, nyaaah," Curly says as he sticks his tongue out. Moe frees his hand, ending the short with a loud slap.

SLAP COUNT: 18
EYE POKES: 4

12. Ants in the Pantry,

1936. With Clara Kimball Young, Douglas Gerrard. Story and screenplay by Al Giebler. Associate producer, Jules White. Directed by Preston Black.

The influence of Jules White, a proponent of the hard physical gags, continues to grow. Director Preston Black is actually White's brother Jack. Open on a sign: "Lightning Pest Control Co. Exterminator of Mice, Ants, and All Household Pests, A. Mouser, Mgr." Mouser's nearly out of business. "Bills, bills, nothing but bills," he cries. "This rat-catching business is going to the dogs. Where are those three loafers?" An assistant says they're out talking politics. "Politics?" barks Mouser. "Yeah, I just heard one of them say, 'Let's have a new deal.'" Soon the card-playing loafers are dispatched to drum up business by supplying the ants and mice they'll exterminate once hired. They find work at a high-society party. Dressed in equestrian outfits, they're brought in by a matron who doesn't want her party guests to know her house is infested. Gags include cats stuck in a piano, a foxhunt, and Curly pulling out a skunk.

SLAP COUNT: 17
EYE POKES: 2
MEMORABLE LINE: Brought into the parlor of the house, Larry's asked, "What does this remind you of?" "Reform school," he replies, leading to a kick in the shins from Moe.

13. Movie Maniacs,

1936. With Mildred Harris, Kenneth Harlan, Bud Jamison, Harry Semels. Story and screenplay by Felix Adler. Produced by Jules White. Directed by Del Lord.

The Stooges open the short sleeping noisily on a train, with Larry and Moe sticking their feet in Curly's face. When he pounds their dogs, the trio awakens. It turns out they're stowing away on a train bound for Hollywood and have helped themselves to the furniture of someone moving west. "I wonder who loaned us their furniture without knowing it," Larry says. "If the cops come you'll find out," Moe says. After some solid sight gags involving the cooking of breakfast and ironing of clothes, the boys find themselves at the offices of Carnation Pictures and its general manager, Fuller Rath. They're mistaken for studio executives and given the authority to disrupt a love scene being filmed by a director named Swinehardt. When the actors and directors quit, Curly's once again cast in drag, this time as a blonde, his eyebrows plucked with a wrench. Soon the ruse is up, and the boys flee, escaping into a lion's cage. The lions follow them into a car, which takes off down the street, Curly "woop-woop-wooping" all the way.

SLAP COUNT: 7
EYE POKES: 1
MEMORABLE LINE: Asked by Larry how they're going to make it in pictures when they know nothing, Moe replies, "There's a couple thousand people in pictures now know nothin' about it. Three more won't make a difference."

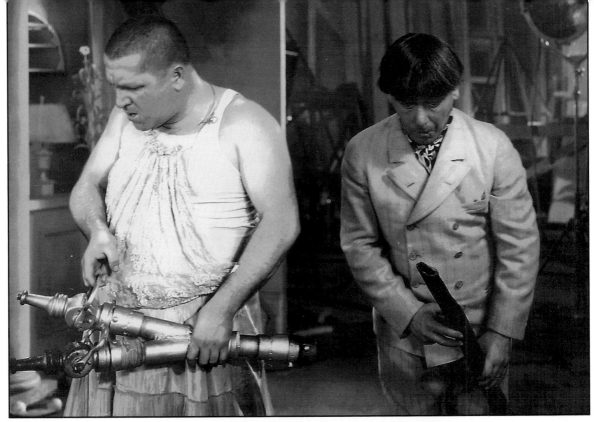

above: Stowaways on a Hollywood-bound train in Movie Maniacs, 1936. below: Larry woos Curly in Movie Maniacs.

The boys pull out the heavy artillery in *Half-Shot Shooters,* 1936.

14.

Half-Shot Shooters,

1936. With Stanley Blystone and Vernon Dent. Story and screenplay by Clyde Bruckman. Associate producer, Jules White. Directed by Preston Black.

It's World War I in 1918, and the boys sleep soundly despite the sounds of gunfire and exploding bombs. They're awakened by their sergeant, who growlingly tells them the war is over. After being abused by the sarge, the boys bring him down a few stripes by tugging his shirt over his head so that Larry can pluck out armpit hair as Curly whacks him with a plank with nails sticking out of it. Cut to 1935, and the boys are on the street in their familiar roles as beggars. They're recruited to enlist, and wind up with the same sergeant, who tortures them with glee. In one exercise with a cannon, the boys blast the major's battleship. The boys think they'll be decorated. The sarge lines them up, points the cannon at them. When he fires, all that's left is their smoking shoes, marking the first (but not last) short in which the Stooges actually get killed.

SLAP COUNT: 20
EYE POKES: 4
MEMORABLE LINE: Sarge, finding the trio asleep on duty: "So, you're still yellow." "No," says Curly, "I'm in the pink." Sarge socks him in the eye, saying, "Now you're in the black."

15.

Disorder in the Court,

1936. Story and screenplay by Felix Adler. Associate producer, Jules White. Directed by Preston Black.

Columbia switched the title cards used in the first fourteen shorts. For the first time, they've spelled "Curly" correctly. His billing goes from third to first, with Moe now bringing up the rear. Larry's head remains in the middle, looking as though he'd just sucked on a lemon. *Disorder in the Court* shows up often in news footage because someone at Columbia forgot to renew the copyright and established it as public domain. It was a watermark effort in Stooge shorts.

Set in a courtroom, the boys are witnesses in a murder case. Curly comes up to testify, leading to the Stooge equivalent of the "Who's on First" routine. Judge: "Take off your hat." After Curly takes it off with his right hand, he's told by the bailiff, "Raise your right hand. Now place your left hand [on the Bible]." Curly puts the hat back on. "Take off your hat," says the judge. The routine goes on several times. That finally squared away, the bailiff rattles off, "Do you promise to tell the truth, the whole truth . . ." Curly answers, "Huh, are you tryin' to give me the double talk?" After the judge asks if Curly will swear, he answers, "No, but I know all the words." "Take the stand," the judge orders. "Where'll I put it?"

Soon Larry is playing violin to reenact a dance scene; they murder the bailiff's hairpiece and hose down the courtroom trying to drench a parrot with the clues to the murder. Tying the hose in a knot before posing for a newspaper photo after solving the murder, the hose swells and bursts,

In Disorder in the Court, the Stooges taunt Bud Jamison, a fixture of Stooge shorts until his death in 1944.

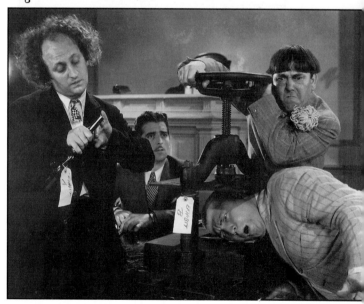

Disorder in the Court, 1936.

soaking the boys in the close to a most spirited episode. There is also a cameo made by Sol Horwitz, father of Moe and Curly. He showed up on the set to watch, and before he knew it, Preston Black stuck him in the jury box.

SLAP COUNT: 4
EYE POKES: 4 (another 1 blocked)

Nostril pulling in A Pain in the Pullman, 1936.

A Pain in the Pullman.

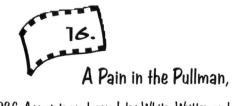

16.

A Pain in the Pullman,

1936. Associate producer, Jules White. Written and directed by Preston Black.

The boys are in a rooming house, Mrs. Hammond Eggerly's Theatrical Apts. They do a dancing act with a monkey and are so down on their luck Curly wants to eat the monkey. They're also behind on the rent. As they rehearse, it's obvious why they're unemployed, and the noise disturbs a neighbor, the Hollywood actor Paul Payne, self-proclaimed "Heartthrob of Millions." The Stooges brawl with the heartthrob, who's not quite as dashing when stripped of his tupe. The ethnic humor shows through here as the landlady takes a call. "This is Goldstein, Goldberg, Goldblatt and O'Brien, booking agents," says a heavily accented Yiddish voice. "This is O'Brien speaking." He's gotten the Stooges a job. In order to leave, they have to elude a back-rent-seeking landlady. She catches them and threatens to call the cops. "There's no need for that lady, I'm a G-man, what's the fuss," Curly says. He arrests his mates, orders Larry to take the trunk as evidence, and promises her they'll get "time and a half or overtime." They wind up on a Pullman car, en route to a vaudeville gig. They meet up with Payne again and steal his lunch of crab and champagne, which Larry thinks is a spider, Curly a turtle. They pull out the "stuffing" and munch on the shells. After some more gags in which the boys and their monkey destroy the train's sleeping quarters, they're thrown from the train and land on a trio of bucking broncos.

SLAP COUNT: 9
EYE POKES: 2
CONKING HEADS: 1
MEMORABLE LINE: When Moe sees Curly cooking his shoe and asks him what he's making, Curly says, "Well, that's filet of sole and heel."

17.

False Alarms,

1936. Story and screenplay by John Grey. Associate producer, Jules White. Directed by Del Lord.

This time they're firemen. They emerge from the shower fully dressed, only to be promptly fired by the fire chief for missing another fire. Told "If this was the army, I'd have you shot at sunrise," the Stooges reply, "But you couldn't, Captain, we don't get up that early."

They're assigned to clean the hoses, which promptly get cut when the boys roll them out over trolley tracks. Calling the severed segments "baby hoses," Curly picks them up and begins naming them, "Annette, Yvonne," before Moe comes across with the obligatory slap. The chief has gotten a new car, and through a variety of circumstances, Moe and Larry take off with it when

Curly, at his girlfriend's house, sets off the fire alarm to lure his pals to the party. "Where's the fire?" they ask. "She's right here, and she's got me all burnt up," Curly replies, pointing to his heavy-set babe, named Minnie, whom Curly calls Hercules. "Let's go places and eat things," she suggests as they pile into the car. She ushers in a Stooge tradition of fat women who get ridiculed. It would be offensive if it wasn't so damned hilarious. Of course, the Stooges wind up demolishing the cherished car. Once Curly engages in a slap fight with his Godzilla-sized mate, she huffs away, as does the car—with no driver. The Stooges trap it in a Bekins moving van and race off before the captain can kill them.

SLAP COUNT: 12

EYE POKES: 3.5 (One is delivered through a telephone; another got half credit because a single eye poke was delivered with a door key.)

Fighting fires in False Alarms, 1936.

Whoops, I'm an Indian,

1936. Story by Searle Kramer, Herman Boxer. Screenplay by Clyde Bruckman. Associate producer, Jules White. Directed by Del Lord.

One of the weaker episodes. Dressed in coonskins, the boys are caught cheating at a roulette-type game. Their mugs show up in a Wanted poster, offering $333.33 reward, "dead or in bad shape," for violation of game laws. They hide in the woods, trying to hunt game to survive. "You get a moose and a few meeces," Moe tells Larry, "and I'll run down an elk." "I'll try and find a Knights of Columbus," Curly says helpfully. Highlight is another drag turn by Curly, who gets married to a burly hunter named Pierre. About to embark on the honeymoon, Pierre says, "For you I have the grand surprise." Says Curly: "So have I, if you only knew it." The trio, now fleeing the hunter, hides in what turns out to be the Lobo County jail.

SLAP COUNT: 9
EYE POKES: 1

Slippery Silks,

1936. Story and screenplay by Ewart Adamson. Associate producer, Jules White. Directed by Preston Black.

The trio begins as antique restorers, and after destroying a rare Chinese cabinet valued at $50,000, they inherit the Madame de France gown shop. Soon they're making dresses. Sizing up one large customer who asks if the dress has a trifle too much train, Curly replies, "I think there's two boxcars and a caboose too many." When another suggests she'd look stunning in a riding habit, Curly says, "I think there'd be trouble picking out which one was the horse." Replies Moe, holding out his fingers: "Pick two." The boys wind up designing clothes in the style of furniture, complete with storage drawers.

SLAP COUNT: 6
EYE POKES: 5 (another 1 blocked)
CONKING HEADS: 1

Grips, Grunts and Groans,

1937. Story by Searle Kramer, Herman Boxer. Screenplay by Clyde Bruckman. Associate producer, Jules White. Directed by Preston Black.

The boys are assigned to keep the wrestler Bustoff from drinking before a big match. It becomes a variation of the "Moe, Larry, the cheese" short *Horses' Collars* or the "Pop Goes the Weasel" gag in *Punch Drunks*. This time Curly is set into a frenzy by the fragrance Wild Hyacinth. He knocks out Bustoff with dumbbells lying atop a locker, then stands in for the match. The ring mishaps are plentiful, with Curly nearly pinning his unconscious opponent until he revives him by using a real pin. Set off by the hyacinth, Curly brains everyone in the ring, including the referee and the other Stooges, topping the body count with his own after he is brained by a ring bell swung high into the air.

SLAP COUNT: 8
EYE POKES: 1
CONKING HEADS: 1
MEMORABLE LINE: "I'm a victim of coicumstance."

21.

Dizzy Doctors,

1937. Story by Charlie Nelson. Screenplay by Al Ray. Associate producer, Jules White. Directed by Del Lord.

After the layabouts go through the typically humorous exercise of preparing breakfast, the boys become salesmen of Dr. Brighto, which brightens old bodies. Proclaiming themselves "three of the best salesmen that ever saled," the boys ruin the uniform of a police officer and are chased by him. They end up in the Los Arms Hospital, site of their Oscar-nominated earlier

Brighto salesmen in Dizzy Doctors, 1937.

Skull session in *Dizzy Doctors.*

short, *Men in Black*. There they try to sell their medicine but get into medical mishaps instead. Turns out (as it always does) that one of the guys they abused with their Brighto runs the hospital, and he and his orderlies chase the Stooges around the place. They flee on a gurney, escaping by hanging a sail and using the wind to make it down the street until they crash into a car. They leap back through a window into the bed they never should have left that morning.

SLAP COUNT: 7
EYE POKES: 3

Curly plays dual roles as father and son in *Three Dumb Clucks*, 1937.

22.

Three Dumb Clucks,

1937. Screenplay by Clyde Bruckman. Associate producer, Jules White. Directed by Del Lord.

The boys break out of jail and are enlisted to bring their rich father home to their mother, before he marries a chippie out to steal his fortune. Curly, in dual roles, plays the father, differentiated by pork-chop sideburns. The con woman, who calls him Popsy, convinces him to shave them, marveling that he looks twenty years younger. And perfect for a case of mistaken identity with his son. The chippie has thugs who plan to bump off the father as soon as he ties the knot. They wind up dispatching one hubby down an elevator shaft, only to see the other surface immediately after. This mistaken-identity gag ends when the bad guys drop the boys off a building fourteen floors up. It might have been a fatal fall if they hadn't landed right on Dad, whom they promptly drag home.

SLAP COUNT: 8
CONKING HEADS: 3

23.

Back to the Woods,

1937. Story by Searle Kramer. Screenplay by Andrew Bennison. Associate producer, Jules White. Directed by Preston Black.

In Merrie Old England, the trio sports ball and chain. A judge says, "Order, order," to which Larry replies, "I'll take a sandwich." The Stooges are sentenced to the colonies "to fight the redskin and savage." That is great with Curly, who notes, "Mmm, I just love corned beef and savage." The short becomes a game of cat and mouse with hostile Indians. As Larry gets caught and has a date to be burned at the stake, Curly says, "I'll be back before thou can say Ticonderoga, if thou can say Ticonderoga." The boys wind up in a canoe that seems motor-powered and allows them to escape. It is actually stock footage from the earlier short *Whoops, I'm an Indian*.

SLAP COUNT: 6
EYE POKES: 2
CONKING HEADS: 2

24.

Goofs & Saddles,

1937. Story and screenplay by Felix Adler. Associate producer, Jules White. Directed by Del Lord.

With the Injun problem seemingly under control, General Muster dispatches his crack crew to catch cattle rustlers. Curly is Buffalo Billius, Moe is Wild Bill Hiccup, and Larry is Just Plain Bill. After a fairly entertaining card game with the desperado Longhorn Pete in the Longhorn Saloon, the boys are pursued by the rustlers to a cabin, where Curly shoots bullets through a grinder and thwarts the bad guys, who are captured by Muster. Once Curly's finished, a monkey takes over the task, which sends the Stooges fleeing a hail of bullets.

SLAP COUNT: 8
EYE POKES: 1
CONKING HEADS: 3

25.

Cash & Carry,

1937. Screenplay by Clyde Bruckman, Elwood Ullman. Associate producer, Jules White. Directed by Del Lord.

Ullman, a frequent scripter of Stooge shorts and later collaborator with Edward Bernds, makes his Stooge debut. Here the Stooges are gold prospectors housed in the city dump. Though they're sav-ing for "Jimmy's leg operation, so he can grow up like other boys," they're scammed out of their $62 life savings by con men who also take their car. The boys are sent on a treasure hunt and dig through to a federal bank, where they find loot. Says Larry: "There's enough here for Jimmy's operation." Curly: "There's enough here for all of us to have an operation." The boys are caught, but once their motive is clear, they're told they've been granted executive clemency. Curly: "No, not that!"

SLAP COUNT: 3
MEMORABLE LINE: Moe: "Remind me to kill you later." Curly: "I'll make a note of it."

Gold prospecting in Cash & Carry, 1937.

26.

Playing the Ponies,

1937. Screenplay by Al Giebler, Elwood Ullman, Charles Nielson. Associate producer, Jules White. Directed by Charles Lamont.

The boys run the Flounder Inn, and Curly's food preparation will become a staple of future Stooge restaurant gags. He pulls out the carcass of a chicken, pours water through it, and calls it chicken soup. Despite such possibilities, the boys leave the eatery business when they trade the Flounder Inn for a horse. Called Thunderbolt, the filly looks more like a camel than a thoroughbred, with its concave back. "He must have slept under a lumber pile," says Curly as the Stooges quickly try to get their horse ready to race. After Moe tells Curly to race the horse around the track, Curly comes back, winded, and says, "You told me to race him around the track and I did, and I beat him." Larry enlists as the jockey, and though Fine takes out the top of the stable with his head as they lead the horse to the starting line, he winds up winning the $5,000 Benson County Sweepstakes. A fun smattering of sight gags ends with the boys strapping on the feed bag at a banquet, right alongside the horse.

SLAP COUNT: 8
CONKING HEADS: 1

27.

The Sitter-Downers,

1937. Story and screenplay by Ewart Adamson. Associate producer, Jules White. Directed by Del Lord.

It's spring and the boys are in love. When the father of the girls spurns their wedding proposals, the boys stage a strike, carrying signs that read "This place unfair to union suitors." After they get newspaper attention, Dad relents and the boys get their girls. They decide the love pairings by putting their names in a hat. Out comes

Persistent suitors in The Sitter-Downers, 1937.

Florabelle and Corabelle for Moe and Larry. Curly chooses his from the hat and says, "I get Stetson, which one is she?" The lovebirds are given a free house; unfortunately, it's in the form of a kit that needs assembly. This gives the boys the chance to once again show their carpentry prowess, or lack of it. The short is unusual because the plot goes beyond a single thought and because Larry gives Moe a rare beating and Curly abuses his heavyset lovemate, Dorabelle. She pulls him out of a tree by whacking him with a board, and he cushions his fall by landing on her, knocking the oversize wife out cold. To revive her, he throws a pail of water. Unfortunately, the large lump of hardened cement that is also in the bucket crowns her and doesn't help much. When the lopsided house is completed, the now con-scious Dorabelle pulls out one seemingly mis-placed beam, which causes the entire house to tumble down.

SLAP COUNT: 3

Termites of 1938,

1938. Story and screenplay by Elwood Ullman, Al Giebler. Associate producers, Charles Chase, Hugh McCollum. Directed by Del Lord.

An escort is needed by a wealthy matron whose husband is skipping her big bash to go fishing. A friend tells her about the Acme Escort Bureau, a totally reliable place where the dates are from Harvard and Yale. She tells her black maid to call Acme, and as the woman flips through the pages of a phone book, the matron says, "I hope they're discriminating," with the black maid looking up, slightly rattled, and saying, "Discriminating?" Per-haps appropriately, the maid accidentally calls Acme Exterminator Co., a totally unreliable pest prevention service whose slogan is "If you got 'em, we'll get 'em." Moe is showing Larry and Curly his latest invention, the Simplex Rodent Exterminator, in which a fairly large cannon is pointed at the wall. Right away, you know there's going to be plaster damage. After Larry hooks a mouse with a fishing pole, only to be pulled head-first into the wall, Curly tries his own method, playing the flute. Showing Moe a copy of "The Pied Piper of Hamelin," by Robert Browning, Curly reasons: "If a pie-eyed piper can call them out, I guess I can sober." When the mouse comes out of the hole and the cannon won't go off, the boys bend down to tighten the trigger strings. The mouse walks up the string leading to the trigger, setting off the charge that catapults the boys through the wall.

Now hard of hearing, they take the phone call from the matron, thinking they're going to kill pests. Soon they're guests at a mansion, their tuxes belying the fact they're about to destroy the place. The guests mimic the Stooges' bad table manners, including the difficult-to-execute arcing olive toss into the mouth, and the efficient practice of smearing mashed potatoes on a knife and then dipping it into the bowl of peas, which traps the vegetables like flypaper. They then serenade the dinner crowd by playing a marching band tune, with Moe manically plucking the bass fiddle until he accidentally uses a saw instead of a bow and halves the instrument. Mice appear, and the boys get busy. They give one guest an eyeful of pesticide as he gazes through a hole in the wall they've just drilled. Another female guest gets a broom in the butt from Moe. The matron retreats to a phone in a room below the staircase to call Acme. She's promptly drilled in the tail, driving her head through the steps above. Her husband returns, then chases the boys out of the house. As they drive away in their car, the guy tosses a gopher bomb they left behind. It's a bull's-eye, which totals the car and destroys their tuxes, a hilarious ending to a hysterical short.

SLAP COUNT: 7
EYE POKES: 1
CONKING HEADS: 1

Wee Wee Monsieur, 1938.

29.

Wee Wee Monsieur,

1938. Story and screenplay by Searle Kramer. Associate producer, Jules White. Directed by Del Lord.

Opens with a sign: "Paris, Somewhere in France." The Stooges are struggling artists in Paris, with Curly painting and Moe chiseling as Larry accompanies on piano. The boys jabber in French, and after Moe drives his chisel into Curly's cranium, Curly says, "Oui, oui, oui, oui, oui." Moe: "Oui what?" "We should be more careful what we do around here. Chiseler." Pan to Larry, who fusses with his music, as we hear the distinctive sound of Curly's head being pounded again. They're eight months behind on the rent, and Curly uses his fishing pole to find food as a ped-dler walks by with a fresh-fish cart. The first cast hooks a fish, the second the uniform of a police-man, who runs off in his underwear. The landlord knocks down the door and Curly tells him he'll have the money when he sells his painting. It's an abstract, which Curly calls "A maid on her night out winding her grandfather's clock with her left hand." When the landlord says "phooey," Curly smashes the painting over his head. They escape out the window, as good a time as any to join the foreign legion.

Thinking the French foreign legion is the equiv-alent of the American Legion they belong to, the boys enlist enthusiastically, thinking they're signing an IOU for passage on a homebound ship. Soon they're in the desert, guarding Captain Gorgonzola, who's promptly captured. They're facing the firing squad, but talk the commanding officer out of it. "Remember, your mother and my mother are both mothers," says Curly. "On his father's side," Moe adds helpfully. Since no white man has ever entered the domain of Simis, Curly has a brainstorm: go undercover as three Santa Clauses.

Once in the castle, they wander into a harem. When Curly asks an exotic blonde where she's been all his life, she answers, "Down at Toidy-toid and Toid Avenue. I just got ova." The boys dress as harem girls and rescue the captain when they run right into a lion's cage. Curly tames the lion, and it drags their wagon to safety.

SLAP COUNT: 5
EYE POKES: 1

30.

Tassels in the Air,

1938. Story and screenplay by Al Giebler and Elwood Ullman. Associate producers, Charley Chase, Hugh McCollum. Directed by Charley Chase.

Omay, the famous interior decorator, has opened an office in town, and a wealthy woman pesters her husband—a former letter carrier who came into money—to have the house decorated as a political move to get them into *Who's Who*. The boys are painting outside Omay's office, and when the pretentious decorator asks how it's possible to

Larry gets a facial in *Tassels in the Air*, 1938.

Varnishing Curly's noggin in Tassels in the Air.

becomes clear that one of the society women is dropping Omay's name to get a cut of his business. As the three women leave—chairs stuck to their rumps—the boys try to douse them with buckets of paint. They jump on planks which send the buckets airborne—straight up and straight back down.

SLAP COUNT: 4
EYE POKES: 1

31.

Flat Foot Stooges,

1938. With Dick Curtis, Chester Conklin, Lola Jensen.
Associate producers, Charley Chase, Hugh McCollum.
Directed by Charley Chase.

make so much noise painting, Curly spies tassels about his waist and goes into his familiar tizzy. Moe, while calming the frenzied Curly by tickling his chin with a paintbrush, explains he was tickled as a youth with a pussy willow. The boys are given stencils to put up on the office doors and screw them up so that their closet becomes the office of Omay. The woman thinks Moe is the decorator, by merit of the sign on the door. The super fires them, and when he opens his door to give them severance, he steps into the elevator shaft, the result of the Stooges' stenciling. Down he goes. "When did he move his office to the basement?" Curly asks. They take the decorating job and we're off to the races. After painting a table that's an antique once owned by Louis XVI, the boys first-coat chairs and the stairs. When Curly sees tassels, a resourceful Moe uses a torn chunk of Larry's hair to chin-tickle his manic partner. Sitting in wet paint, the card-playing women get stuck to the chairs, when Omay shows up. It

The fire chief argues over the merits of a motorized or horse-drawn fire truck. The boys are firemen, and when told there will be a prize for the best-looking horses at the picnic, they take the ponies to a Turkish bath for a massage. The salesman trying to sell motorized fire trucks dumps gunpowder into the horse-drawn truck. The chief's daughter sees him and he chases her into the firehouse, accidentally setting it ablaze. Then it becomes a race to put the house out, as the Stooges blow up the fire truck but eventually save the girl.

SLAP COUNT: 10
EYE POKES: 1
CONKING HEADS: 2

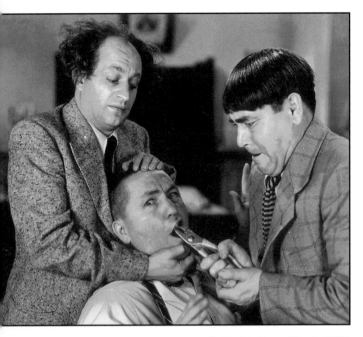

Healthy, Wealthy, and Dumb, 1938.

Swept off their feet in Healthy, Wealthy, and Dumb.

32.

Healthy, Wealthy, and Dumb,

1938. Story and screenplay by Searle Kramer. Associate producer, Jules White. Directed by Del Lord.

The boys start out in a card game at breakfast, betting pancakes for poker chips. Curly cooks while he works on his slogan for a radio contest: "Roses are red, violets are blue, try Stickfast glue, and you'll be stuck too." After Moe mistakes Curly's can of glue for syrup, Larry discovers that scalding-hot water opens a freshly glued mouth just fine, even though it seems to burn. Moe employs a pair of pliers to unglue a spoon from Curly's mouth but pulls a tooth instead. Curly wins $50,000 from the Coffin Nail Cigarette Co., and the promise of riches beckons the boys: "Pie a la mode with beer chasers, three times a day," promises Curly. Next we see them in tuxes, staying at the Hotel Costa Plente to celebrate. Three gold diggers try to siphon the money from the trio, until the check comes. After taxes, all that's left is $4.85.

SLAP COUNT: 5
CONKING HEADS: 3

Violent Is the Word for Curly, 1938.

33.

Violent Is the Word for Curly,

1938. Story and screenplay by Al Giebler, Elwood Ullman. Associate producers, Charley Chase, Hugh McCollum. Directed by Charley Chase.

Short, whose title is a play on words for *Valiant Is the Word for Carrie,* a feature that was popular that year, opens at Mildew College, est. 1885. The coeds play sports while we cut to a gas station where the Stooges are attendants. They wash the car of visiting scholarly-looking college professors, destroying it and ruining their lunches. After blowing up the car by putting gas in the radiator and water in the gas tank, the trio escapes in an ice cream truck (Curly in the icebox). After they thaw a frozen Curly out by roasting him over a spit, the boys are soon mistaken for the missing professors. In the short's most memorable gag, the boys teach their students the rhyming song "Swingin' the Alphabet."

SLAP COUNT: 22
CONKING HEADS: 5

Three Missing Links,

1938. With Monty Collins, Jane Hamilton, Naba. Story and screenplay by Searle Kramer. Associate producer and director, Jules White.

The boys are maintenance men, cleaning up the Hollywood office of Super Terrific Productions president B. O. Botswaddle. After witnessing their incompetence as cleaning men—Curly cleans his desk with a rake, a battle between the trio ends with a bucket crashing through the exec's glass door—they're fired. But when Curly does a spot-on impression of a chicken with his head cut off—spinning around on the floor in trademark style—the exec immediately sees his potential. "Do you see the same thing I do? He's the dead image of the missing link." "Thank you," says Curly. And the other two? "Neanderthal men, straight from the Stone Age."

The actors are soon off to the jungle, where Curly's hired to play a gorilla in a movie. They're lost (Curly navigates, wearing snowshoes), but find the hut of Dr. Ba Loni Sulami, Medicine Man (Naba), a dark-skinned savage with a ring through his nose, a cannibal who, curiously, dispenses love candy. The Stooges escape, pound each other silly setting up a tent, and get menaced by a feet-licking lion. Of course, when they make the movie, a real gorilla shows up. Curly eats love candy, falls in love with the gorilla, and chases him into the jungle.

SLAP COUNT: 11
EYE POKES: 1
CONKING HEADS: 4

Mutts to You,

1938. With Bess Flowers. Story and screenplay by Al Giebler, Elwood Ullman. Associate producers, Charley Chase, Hugh McCollum. Directed by Charley Chase.

Before heading on vacation with wife and child, a man takes his dog to be washed. Cut to a sign reading "K-9 Dog Laundry. Dogs Washed While U Wate 50 cents Clipping Curling Simonizing $1.00." The Stooges operate the automated washer, with a conveyer belt and six hands, which not only soap up the dog but flip him over and scrub his belly. Sporting raincoat and umbrella, Curly supplies the water, pedaling a bike to produce the rinse. The boys wind up finding a baby on a doorstep (the mother, the wife of the dog owner, is locked out and leaves the tot on the doorstep while she runs to open the back door). They decide to take the kid to a police station but first sneak it into their rooming house, which does not allow children. Naturally, the headlines declare the kid has been kidnapped.

Curly dresses in drag—his hilariously skinny legs require Moe and Larry to stuff his stockings with sponges. Suddenly, he's Mrs. Dennis O'Toole from Ireland. Introduced to an Irish cop who calls the kid "a fine brat of a lad," the cop asks if he's on the bottle yet. "I should say not, he don't drink, smoke, or chew," says his sponge-legged mom. Curly gets soaked with a hose, and his legs swell, giving away his disguise. Then the chase is on. Moe and Larry disguise themselves as Chinese laundrymen, wheeling Curly and the kid in a laundry cart. Once the baby's recovered, the mother realizes what happened and the boys are

Automated dog washer in *Mutts to You*, 1938.

cleared. But the kid's filthy, and he's taken to the automated washing center. Curly pulls an extra handle, and the six scrubbing hands begin spanking the tot.

SLAP COUNT: 7
CONKING HEADS: 3

Three Little Sew and Sews,

1939. With Phyllis Barry and Harry Semels. Story and screenplay by Ewart Adamson. Associate producer, Jules White. Directed by Del Lord.

Opens with a sign: "Republic of Telvana—Naval Base." Admiral H. S. Taylor is invited to a lunch with Count Alfred Gehrol, a suspected spy. "Take my uniform to be pressed, and tell those dumb tailors not to burn holes in them this time." So you know right away the Stooges are bumbling sailors/tailors. Moe burns the captain's pants as Larry looks forward to a date with the bearded lady—"Is she a beaut when she gets a shave," he reasons. Curly finds the telegram and, figuring a tailor has been invited to lunch, dons Admiral Taylor's uniform. Moe and Larry get locked up for hitting an officer (Curly). Curly offers to spring Moe and Larry for five dollars each, and soon the trio is pretending to be the admiral and lunching with the spy. A gorgeous spy pumps Curly for info about a sub. Next they're on board, fighting over a gun as the sub sinks to the bottom. The navy drops torpedoes, and after the Stooges get control of the craft and Curly opens the hatch to take a look, he's ducking mortar shells and catches a torpedo. When the admiral asks how they captured the spies, Curly demonstrates by hitting the torpedo with a hammer. After a large explosion, the Stooges are wearing wings and trying to outrun the winged admiral, who's right behind them. The second death for the Stooges onscreen.

SLAP COUNT: 11
EYE POKES: 2
CONKING HEADS: 2
MEMORABLE LINE: Moe: "We'll be shot at sunrise tomorrow." Curly: "Maybe the sun won't be out tomorrow. It might rain."

We Want Our Mummy,

1939. Starts with a different intro logo. Directed by Del Lord.

Opens with a sign: "Museum of Ancient History, Hours 10 to 5." The boys step backward into the Egyptian room, wearing Sherlock Holmes masks—on their backs. "At your service night and day. If we don't get 'em, you don't pay. Excelsior!" The boys are offered a job to travel to Cairo to pick up the cursed mummy of Rootentooten. "Say I've got an uncle in Cairo. He's a chiropractor," says Curly. Offered a $5,000 reward for the mummy, they take a cab to Egypt, incurring a fare of $2,198.55. Curly sees a mirage of a ship on water, and when the boys dive in, they land in the mummy's tomb. Curly finds a mummy, then falls on it as it disintegrates. Curly dresses in mummy rags, and when a bad guy roots around his body for jewels, he finds a newspaper which discloses that the Yanks won the Series. The other guy said he had the Cubs, leading to a short baseball discussion between the two, until the guy realizes

We Want Our Mummy, 1939.

Curly's not a mummy. Turns out the mummy Curly vaporized was Rootentooten's wife, Queen Hotsy Totsy. He's a midget in a small coffin. Curly then sees an alligator, and thinking it's a mummy, wants it as a souvenir. It's real, and chases the trio back into the taxi and away they go.

SLAP COUNT: 3
EYE POKES: 1
CONKING HEADS: 1

38.

A Ducking They Did Go,

1939. Original screenplay by Andrew Bennison.
Associate producer, Jules White. Directed by Del Lord.

The boys start as beggars, eventually stealing a watermelon which ends up on the head of a cop. They escape into a building and into a sales office for memberships to the Canvas Back Duck Club. Proclaiming themselves "three of the best salesmen that ever saled," they apply. "Ever sold anything?" Curly's asked. "Just about everything we could lay our hands on." Moe: "That's stole, not sold." Curly: "Sorry, I misunderstood." Curly brags further: "Canvas back! That's what they used to call me when I was a fighter, I was on the canvas so much." Told they'll get 10 percent of each fifty-dollar membership they sell, the trio winds up in the office of the chief of police and sells him and the mayor a membership. That's a problem, since the whole club is a con. The boys slingshot decoy ducks across the pond as the mayor and cops shoot. Curly, playing a kazoo, brings a whole flock of ducks. Asked how, he replies, "You've heard of the pie-eyed piper of Hamelin, ain't you? Well, I figure if he could pipe brats pie-eyed, then I could pipe ducks sober." The boys wind up in a boat trying to get a few birds for themselves, until Curly shoots out the bottom. They become the targets of the hunt when the cops find out the ducks were stolen. They leap over bushes and land on a cow and head off, woop-wooping.

SLAP COUNT: 3
EYE POKES: 1 (another 1 blocked)
CONKING HEADS: 1

Advertisement for Yes, We Have No Bonanza, 1939.

39.

Yes, We Have No Bonanza,

1939. With Dick Curtis, Lynton Brent. Original screenplay by Elwood Ullman, Searle Kramer. Associate producer, Jules White. Directed by Del Lord.

Begins with a sign: "Maxey's Place." Mustached Moe and Larry frolic with three cowgirls. Curly appears to be a cowboy riding a horse, but a cutaway shows him aboard a scooter. He's the bartender. Turns out the boss stole $40,000 and wants to bury it. The boys, looking for money to marry the girls, become gold prospectors. They find a

gold tooth, right where the bad guys buried the cash, and discover the money. They don't suspect anything, even though they find the money in sacks, with dollar bills and even bond certificates. The bad guys steal the money and the chase is on, the Stooges atop a cigar store horse lassoed to the bad guy's getaway car. They crash into a jail and knock out Curly with a brick.

SLAP COUNT: 12
EYE POKES: 4
CONKING HEADS: 2

Saved by the Belle, 1939.

40.

Saved by the Belle,

1939. With LeRoy Mason and Carmen LaRoux. Story by Searle Kramer, Elwood Ullman. Associate producers, Charley Chase, Hugh McCollum. Directed by Charley Chase.

Starts with a sign: "Valeska: A thriving kingdom in the tropics." The boys are tossed out of a rooming house where they stay while on business with the King Winter Outfitting Co. Presented with a bill that features a long beer tab, they think they're getting money from their company, but receive a telegram that reads, "No passage money until you get rid of present wardrobe." They bail on the bill and are imprisoned. They're drafted to help Rita, a revolutionary, get a map to the troops. They lose the map under a couch and mistakenly pull out a rolled calendar that sits next to the map. The revolutionary leader turns out to be the hotel owner. The boys almost die on the firing squad but escape in an ammo truck, which explodes, landing them on the back of a concave horse in the conclusion of this convoluted short.

SLAP COUNT: 7
EYE POKES: 2

Chow time at the animal hospital in <u>Calling All Curs</u>, 1939.

41.

Calling All Curs,

1939. Screenplay by Elwood Ullman, Searle Kramer. Story by Thea Goodan. Associate producer and director, Jules White.

Called the world's greatest specialists, the boys appear to be prestigious surgeons, but are animal docs. As they remove a thorn from the paw of a rich woman's dog, they're interviewed by two suspicious-looking newspaper reporters. The thug-sized scribes tour the hospital, where beds are filled with dogs and cats. One feline suffers operatic tendencies, a St. Bernard suffers from acute alcoholism. "He's a lapdog, he lapped up two cases of beer," says Curly. Another is a GCM—garbage can moocher—suffering from scavengitis. "Call-

ing all curs," the loudspeaker beckons. "Lunch is served, that is all." As the boys rush to eat with the animals, the reporters, or should we say dognappers, make off with the prized pooch and leave a ransom demand. The boys take a mutt and glue horsehair from a mattress to make him look like Garcon, the woman's prize pooch. When a maid vacuums off the hair, the ruse is up and the boys must recover the dog. They find the baddies, and in a gag that's repeated in at least half a dozen Stooge shorts, Curly gets his arm into the jacket of one guy's sleeve, turns in a circle, and punches the other guy, who then clocks his accomplice as he comes around in the other sleeve of the jacket.

SLAP COUNT: 38
EYE POKES: 2
CONKING HEADS: 1

42.

Oily to Bed, Oily to Rise,

1939. Original screenplay by Andrew Bennison, Mauri Grashin. Associate producer and director, Jules White.

This is a perfect example of a Jules White–style short, with the boys braining each other silly from start to finish. Three shady guys buy land from poor farmers who don't know their land sits on oil. The boys work for food on a farm. They saw wood, an excuse for Moe to run a saw across Curly's head, ruining the blade. There's a funny scene as they try to load wood into a wagon, with the bottom dropping out and logs crushing Curly. The bad guys leave one farmland deed in the car. Curly steps out into mud, wiping his foot with a poster that reads "Free Auto Given Away Every Saturday. Fairport Theatre." When he folds it and leaves it on the car running board, it reads "Free Auto." Which the Stooges see just after Curly wishes for a car. As they drive off, Curly wishes for a cigar and finds three in the glove box. The three puff away and discover nobody is driving. "Hey, don't look now, but we're about to be killed," says Curly as the car heads toward a cliff. The boys careen toward a farm, and when Curly wishes for roast chicken and dumplings, the matronly farm owner serves them just that.

Curly wishes for three girls to marry, and suddenly appear her daughters, April, May, and June ("three of the prettiest months of the year," says Curly). Finding that the drinking water tastes like coal oil, the boys agree to fix the well pump. Soon oil is gushing from the pump, and the boys have to stop the bad guys from filing that land deed, which they don't know is in the car's glove box. The boys confront the bad guys in drag, knock them out of the car, and, once again, relax as the driverless car heads for a cliff. They save the farm and Curly wishes for a justice of the peace. He gets one, dips his girl—and kisses Moe.

SLAP COUNT: 5
CONKING HEADS: 1

43.

Three Sappy People,

1939. With Lorna Gray, Don Beddoe, Bud Jamison. Original screenplay by Clyde Bruckman. Associate producer and director, Jules White.

A high-society party is under way, and the husband of the birthday girl is distraught because she's not there. She makes an entrance, driving the car right into the living room. Cut to the office of Dr. Z.

Three Sappy People, 1939.

Ziller, X. Zeller, and Y. Zoller. The Stooges are phone repairmen, and Curly smashes the door with his ladder, along with the water cooler, then brains Moe. "Remind me to tear your Adam's apple out," says Moe. "I'll make a note of it," says Curly. Each time he pulls out a longer and longer pencil, Moe rips it away. "You'll break my pencil." "I'll break your head," says Moe. They wind up taking the call to cure the eccentric birthday girl and drive up on a bicycle built for three. They join a formal dinner, with the usual upsetting of dignity, culminating in a colorful food fight. Cream puffs are tossed, and the husband comes out with the birthday cake. "Oh, darling, in all my life, I've never had so much fun," she says. He dumps the cake over her head. It's actually the closest thing the Stooges have had to a pie fight so far.

SLAP COUNT: 14
EYE POKES: 1
PIES THROWN: 32 (actually cream puffs) PLUS 1 LARGE BIRTHDAY CAKE

You Nazty Spy!, 1940.

44.
You Nazty Spy!,
1940. Story and screenplay by Clyde Bruckman, Felix Adler. Produced and directed by Jules White.

Opens with a warning: "Any resemblance between the characters in this picture and any persons, living or dead, is a miracle." This was the first of a two-part episode. Though it was slapstick fun, the short was courageous in lacerating Adolf Hitler before it was fashionable. Moe, with the stunted mustache, is a dead ringer for Hitler and used the look numerous times while World War Two raged on. This one is set in the kingdom of Moronica, with Mr. Ixnay, Onay, and Amscray plotting an overthrow of the king. "There's no money in peace. If the king wants peace, we'll have to oust him and put in a dictator." Enter Moe Hailstone, Curly Gallstone, and Larry Pebble. Told that as dictator of Moronica he'd "make love to beautiful women, drink champagne, enjoy life, and never work," Moe warms to the job. "He makes speeches to the people, promising them plenty. He gives them nothing and then he takes everything," Moe is told. While Moe ponders, he slaps on the Hitler mustache. Next, he's giving speeches, promising "to make the country safe for hypocrisy . . . We will extend two helping hands,

You Nazty Spy!

and help ourselves to our neighbors." Soon the flag has snakes in the shape of a swastika, Hailstone is barking jibberish in that clipped Hitler speaking style, they're burning books and putting the poor in "a concentrated camp." After more barbed political commentary, the Stooges are appropriately fed to the lions.

SLAP COUNT: 12
EYE POKES: 3

Rockin' Through the Rockies,

1940. With Linda Winters, Lorna Gray, Dorothy Appleby, Kathryn Sheldon. Story and screenplay by Clyde Bruckman. Produced and directed by Jules White.

Opens with a sign: "Nells Bells Direct from Three Hot Weeks in Kansas." A wagon train full of showbiz gals tours the West, and the Stooges are assigned to protect them from Indians, even though the group matriarch says, "Those three wouldn't know a redskin from a sunburn." They run into a hostile chief who warns them to be gone. "Two sundowns, 23 skidoo, take 'em scalp." From there, the boys get into a variety of misadventures, the highlight of which is an ice fishing episode where Curly and Larry hook Moe, pull him through his hole into the water, and out through their hole. "Hey, this fish looks like Moe," Curly says as those familiar slapping sound effects follow closely. When they return, the girls have been kidnapped by the Indians. They escape, run back, and the Stooges get the wagon under way by rigging a sail in a stiff wind.

SLAP COUNT: 19
CONKING HEADS: 1

46.
A Plumbing We Will Go,
1940. Story and screenplay by Elwood Ullman. Produced by Del Lord, Hugh McCollum. Directed by Del Lord.

The trio begins down-and-out once again, but this is no run-of-the-mill Stooge short. It's one of the best they did at Columbia. Curly's acquitted in court of stealing chickens but then is caught fishing—in a pet store tank. Chased by a cop, he hides, as a magician works a disappearing act with a beautiful woman in the street. When the wand waver opens the door, Houdini and the cop discover Curly making time with the magician's assistant. The boys flee, steal a plumber's truck, and wind up as leak pluggers in a ritzy house. Curly takes to the bathroom, connecting pipe lengths to stop a leak. By the time he's finished, he hasn't stopped the leak, but has encased himself in a pipe

A Plumbing We Will Go, 1940.

prison. His solution, of course, is to saw through the floor. Soon the lady of the house is in the drawing room showing a crowd her new television set, which will show footage of Niagara Falls. When it starts, real water crashes through the screen and floods the room. Turns out it's the home of the judge who acquitted Curly. Soon the Stooges are being chased by the judge, cops, and houseguests. The short ends with them escaping through the same box the magician used earlier.

SLAP COUNT: 4
CONKING HEADS: 1

The boys dress as girls to cheer up a sad child in Nutty but Nice, 1940.

47.

Nutty but Nice,

1940. Story and screenplay by Clyde Bruckman, Felix Adler. Produced and directed by Jules White.

Starts with a sign: "Ye Colonial Inn presents those Hilarious Hash Slingers, America's Gift to Indigestion." They operate a restaurant but are soon enlisted to help cheer up a little girl, despondent because her bank cashier father disappeared with $300,000 worth of bonds. They are unable to make her laugh, even after dressing up as little girls and doing a lollipop routine. The Stooges decide to locate the guy, armed only with the following information: he's forty years old, 5' 10", and has a bald spot and an anchor tattoo, and is a capable yodeler. After measuring most of the men in the neighborhood, they find the guy, who's been kidnapped. They escape down a dumbwaiter, then elude the bad guys in a humorous scene in which the lights are turned off and on, with different guys getting bashed each time the lights go on. The trio winds up back in the restaurant, singing and engaging in a pie fight.

SLAP COUNT: 18
EYE POKES: 2
CONKING HEADS: 1
PIES THROWN: 2

48.

How High Is Up,

1940. Story and screenplay by Elwood Ullman. Produced by Del Lord, Hugh McCollum. Directed by Del Lord.

The boys, sleeping under a car, are washed down the street by a broken hydrant and awaken when they're about to be run over. From the car, they run the Minute Menders Inc. service. After braining each other with such noisy weapons as anchors, the boys go through the amusing chore of helping Curly remove his sweater—he didn't have any trouble putting it on but "might have put on a couple of pounds since then." Chisels and hammers are used, and the resourcefulness is hilar-

ious. Finally, they cut it off with a scissor. The boys wind up working as riveters—"three of the best riveters that ever riveted," Curly boasts as they volunteer for the job. It's on the ninety-seventh floor of a building under construction. Curly (who has a parachute, just in case) finds the hot rivets are tasty, eating them as quickly as Larry cooks them ("A weenie, but it's kind of tough," Curly says). After making an awfully crooked structure, the boys fall off the building, parachuting into a car and driving away, the parachute covering the car as they speed onto the concourse.

SLAP COUNT: 10
EYE POKES: 1

From Nurse to Worse, 1940.

From Nurse to Worse,

1940. Story by Charles L. Kimball. Screenplay by Clyde Bruckman. Produced and directed by Jules White.

The boys, working as wallpaperers, are convinced to buy an insurance policy worth $500 a month if they claim Curly's crazy. Soon they're in the offices of Dr. D. Lerious, M.D., CCC, FHA, WPA, AWOL, Colossal Insurance Examiner. Curly pretends he's a dog, brought in on a leash.

The doc wants to operate and the boys hide out in a dog catcher's truck, leading to a humorous scratching scene after they're infested with fleas. The boys are chased through a hospital, repeatedly knocking down an orderly in the way, and throw the pal who sold them the insurance policy into a paint trough.

SLAP COUNT: 14
EYE POKES: 1
CONKING HEADS: 4

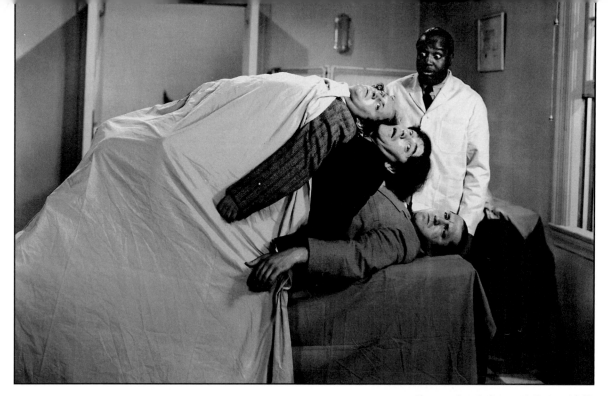

50.

No Census, No Feeling,

1940. Story and screenplay by Harry Edwards, Elwood Ullman. Produced by Del Lord, Hugh McCollum. Directed by Del Lord.

Short opens at the Square Deal Swap Shop. If you think the boys own it, you're wrong. The owner unrolls the outside awning, which the sleeping Stooges fall out of. After breaking his stuff, they flee to City Hall, and exit as census takers who'll make four cents a survey. Moe rings a doorbell, asks a man, "Are you married or happy?" On cue, the guy ducks, a pot hits Moe in the head, and he falls off the stoop. Curly tries to get a survey done by making time with a housemaid, who agrees to participate if he mixes the punch. Moe enters the kitchen and unwittingly takes Curly's census.

Moe: "What was your family decomposed of?" Curly: "Well, I'll tell you. There was a litter of three, and I was the one they kept." Moe, realizing it's Curly, works a cheese grater across his jowls. Then Moe fights Larry for the homeowner. "Hey," Larry says, "he was mine. You owe me four cents." "Will you take five?" asks Moe. "Oh, a bonus," says Larry. Five hard ones follow, in the form of a slap, with Moe closing Larry's head in an armoir for good measure. Curly, trying to sweeten the punch, dumps alum, a mouth-narrowing compound that ruins the bridge game, with no one able to speak. The scene is hilarious. The census takers, unable to make any cents, head for a football stadium full of people. They end up trying to take the census of the players on the field. The Stooges are soon in the center of the action, then flee out of the stadium with the ball, the players in hot pursuit.

No Census, No Feeling, 1940.

ice on the fish (to save money) and have been trying for thirty days to unload their catch. They try to better their lot by getting into the salon business but are persuaded to buy a salon in Cucaracha, Mexico. Four beauties come in to be bleached blond, and things don't go well. One gets curlers glued to her head, another gets a cement facial, a third gets her nails sprayed with paint. The quartet end up balder than Curly, then close the short using the fleeing Stooges for firearm target practice.

SLAP COUNT: 15
EYE POKES: 3 (another 1 blocked)

SLAP COUNT: 18
EYE POKES: 1
CONKING HEADS: 2
MEMORABLE LINE: Stooges, trying to sneak onto the football field, don uniforms and parade past the guard. "Quarterback," says Moe. "Halfback," says Larry. "Hunchback," says Curly, pointing to a hump on his back.

51.
Cookoo Cavaliers,
1940. Story and screenplay by Ewart Adamson. Produced and directed by Jules White.

Another short that begins with a sign: "Larry Hook, Moe Line & Curly Sinker." The boys sell fresh fish from a truck. Trouble is, they didn't use

Cookoo Cavaliers, 1940.

Boobs in Arms, 1940.

Boobs in Arms,

1940. With Richard Fiske, Evelyn Young. Story and screenplay by Felix Adler. Produced and directed by Jules White.

The boys sell greeting cards for all occasions. Sample: "Greetings, little shut-in, don't you weep or sigh, if you're not out by Christmas, you'll be out the Fourth of July." They help a woman who wants to make her husband jealous. Told by Moe to "get some guy to make love to ya, and make 'im jealous," she uses the Stooges, who then get chased by the burly husband. They wind up in army recruiting headquarters, where the motto is "Join the Army and see the world or what's left of it." Of course, their sergeant turns out to be the jealous hubby, who informs the Stooges, "I'm gonna make soldiers out of you if I have to kill you, and I hope I do." After a variety of mishaps, all at the expense of the sarge, the Stooges find themselves in battle, sleeping while mortars blast all around them. The Stooges detonate a laughing-gas bomb, get captured in a laughing fit, disarm the enemy, and fly off into the air, laughing, aboard an artillery shell.

SLAP COUNT: 16
EYE POKES: 2

53.

So Long, Mr. Chumps,

1941. Story and screenplay by Clyde Bruckman, Felix Adler. Produced and directed by Jules White.

The Stooges are unsuccessful street cleaners, as Larry attempts to spear a piece of paper and harpoons Moe's can instead. Curly sweeps while doing the shuffle. The boys find war bonds and return them to their owner, B. O. Davis. He promptly hires them to find an honest man of executive abilities and promises a $5,000 reward. The boys find out that man is Percy Conroy, wrongfully in jail for stealing. After several failed attempts, they get arrested in hopes of finding the guy. Curly's prison pinstripes say H_2O, Larry is $6\frac{7}{8}$, and Moe is +4. The boys find black paint and color their uniforms and Percy's to look like guard outfits. They attempt to escape but run into the guy who hired them, who's really Lone Wolf Louie, the biggest bond swindler in America. The short ends with the Stooges still in prison, Curly cracking rocks on his head with Moe splitting them with a hammer. On the third rock, Curly says, "Hey wait a minute, that's a real one, I'm no fool, nyuk, nyuk, nyuk." Both Larry and Moe break into spontaneous smiles, and it seems a rare moment of breaking out of character.

SLAP COUNT: 12
EYE POKES: 2
CONKING HEADS: 2

So Long, Mr. Chumps, 1941.

54.

Dutiful but Dumb,

1941. Story and screenplay by Elwood Ullman. Produced by Del Lord, Hugh McCollum. Directed by Del Lord.

Short begins with a photo of the front page of the *Star Dispatch,* with the headline "Percival De Puyster Elopes. Movie Star and Bride Elude Photographers." Cut to door bearing the sign "WHACK The Illustrated Magazine If It's a Good Picture. It's Out of WHACK." The Stooges are photographers, and after they get a picture of the movie star and bride, only to have it destroyed, they are sent on assignment to Vulgaria. Since photographers face the death penalty if they shoot pictures, the Stooges are soon hunted for the firing squad. Citing rule 27 of international law, Curly asks for a last smoke, then pulls out a submarine-sandwich-sized stogie. The delay allows for escape, and the Stooges spend the rest of the short fleeing. Solid gags include Curly crawling into a large radio and broadcasting the news. And the portly one engages in a battle with an oyster that fights back in his oyster soup and eats Curly's crackers. That gag Del Lord took from an old Mack Sennett short that Lord directed in the twenties, and the Stooges would reuse it numerous times. The boys wind up getting caught, carried away impaled on bayonets.

SLAP COUNT: 6
EYE POKES: 1

Moonlighting as dentists in *All the World's a Stooge*, 1941.

55.

All the World's a Stooge,

1941. Story and screenplay by John Grey. Produced by Del Lord, Hugh McCollum. Directed by Del Lord.

The boys clean windows outside the office of Dr. I Yankum, Dentist. Soon they're practicing tooth pulling after the doc walks out of the office and a patient in pain walks in. They fill his mouth with cement, which is great until it hardens. Next the boys are hired to pose as children so they'll be adopted by a wealthy woman. After destroying her house, they're chased into the sunset by an ax-wielding husband.

SLAP COUNT: 7
EYE POKES: 1

56.

I'll Never Heil Again,

1941. Story and screenplay by Felix Adler, Clyde Bruckman. Produced and directed by Jules White.

The second Jules White–directed short that lacerates the Third Reich opens with the message "The characters in this picture are all ficticious. Anyone resembling them is better off dead." This is the sequel to the 1940 short *You Nazty Spy!* Though that one ended with the Stooges getting killed, the boys are back and running Moronica. Amscray, Ixnay, and Umpchay, who last time unseated the King of Moronica, Herman of 6⅞, now want to put Hailstone the dictator (Moe) out of business. The Hitler look-alike is bent on world dominance, and the Stooges have a pow-wow with a Mussolini look-alike named Chissolini and a Japanese leader who insists on taking photographs. They fight over who will control the world and get into a football game, using the globe as the ball. Eventually, the trio is blown up by a pool ball rigged with explosives, their heads mounted to the wall.

SLAP COUNT: 3
EYE POKES: 1 (another 1 blocked)

Plotting world takeover in *I'll Never Heil Again*, 1941.

The trio ends up mounted in *I'll Never Heil Again.*

57.

An Ache in Every Stake,

1941. Story and screenplay by Lloyd A. French. Produced by Del Lord, Hugh McCollum. Directed by Del Lord.

The boys are ice salesmen. Curly falls asleep in the truck and has to be thawed out. This is a fairly violent short, with braining done by ice tongs and hammers. When Curly bowls an ice block that knocks down some milk bottles in front of a house, he says, "I got a perfect score." Moe, before slapping him, says, "No you don't, you need another strike." That leads to a timeless gag in which Curly runs up a long concrete stairway to deliver a block of ice to a woman, only to have it shrink to an ice cube by the time he gets there. Somehow the boys prompt the cook to quit. Soon they're preparing a birthday dinner for a man they've already twice knocked into his own birthday cake in earlier meetings on the street. Kitchen antics culminate in the Stooges filling a deflated cake with gas. It explodes, sending them flying down the long stairs.

SLAP COUNT: 11

58.

In the Sweet Pie and Pie,

1941. Story by Ewart Adamson. Screenplay by Clyde Bruckman. Produced and directed by Jules White.

When three women need to marry to inherit a fortune, their lawyer recommends the Mushroom Murder Gang, a trio headed for execution. Of

In the Sweet Pie and Pie, 1941

course, it's the Stooges. Larry's pinstripes read O-K–67, Moe is B-K–68, and Curly is A-K–70. The women show up, ask if the boys will marry them, and then quickly exit before the boys even get a kiss. Great move, until Mickey Finn and his gang confess, and the Stooges are free. Now the reluctant brides conspire to bump off the boys. There's a recycling of dependable Stooge gags here, including Curly vaulting up onto the top of a triple-decker bunk bed and falling through. And the Stooges taking dancing lessons from a woman who gets a bee in her dress and flails about wildly, the boys trying to keep up with her herky-jerky moves. The highlight comes when the girls give a party, which leads to the first really good pie fight in a Stooge short. Though the Stooges are renowned for pie throwing, it took seven years and fifty-eight shorts before the first truly sustained meringue-topped battle.

SLAP COUNT: 27
EYE POKES: 1
CONKING HEADS: 1
PIES THROWN: 35

59.

Some More of Samoa,

1941. Story and screenplay by Harry Edwards, Elwood Ullman. Produced by Del Lord, Hugh McCollum. Directed by Del Lord.

A wealthy and crusty old man suffers a nervous breakdown caused by his worrying about the deteriorating condition of his rare puglis persimmon tree. Enter the Elite Painless Tree Surgeons, the Biggest Grafters in Town. At Elite headquarters, Curly is giving a vitamin injection to a tree but is injected with the needle and grows like a weed. Summoned by the traumatized tree owner, the boys tell him the only remedy is to find a mate for the ailing plant, found only on the Isle of Rhum Boogie. From there, the short is a matter of the boys eluding savages. Curly's forced to marry the chief's homely sister in order to get the tree. The Stooges are faced with being eaten but manage to flee with the tree, only to have their boat sink.

SLAP COUNT: 8

Some More of Samoa, 1941.

60.

Loco Boy Makes Good,

1942. With Dorothy Appleby, John Tyrrell. Story and screenplay by Felix Adler, Clyde Bruckman. Produced and directed by Jules White.

Opens with a sign: "Happy Haven Hotel. Room $1 a Month. Free Showers When It Rains." The boys are tossed from the premises, by way of the stairs, and hatch a scheme for Curly to slip on a bar of soap at a hotel. A lawsuit will put them on easy street. They find a hotel and Curly makes a deal with the soap bar: "Now, you work with me and I'll see that you're put in a tub and that nobody uses you." Just as they're about to run the scam, they hear the old female owner threatened by a debtor, who promises to take her hotel and kick her out. Rather than sue her, the Stooges vow to help her keep the place. They headline the show "Nill, Null and Void, 3 Hams who lay their own eggs, appearing in The Kokonuts Grove." A Walter Winchell–like columnist named Waldo Twitchell is in the crowd, and a good write-up will save the hotel. After singing the old Stooge standby "She Was Bred in Old Kentucky, but She's Just a Crumb Up Here," the boys engage in slapstick, highlighted by Curly mistakenly donning a magician's jacket and pulling animals from every pocket. Twitchell is in stitches until Curly pulls a skunk.

SLAP COUNT: 2
EYE POKES: 1

Loco Boy Makes Good, 1942.

Cactus Makes Perfect,

1942. Story and screenplay by Elwood Ullman, Monty Collins. Produced by Del Lord, Hugh McCollum. Directed by Del Lord.

The boys live poor in a farmhouse, working on inventions. Kicked out of the house, they step right into busy traffic and are soon scammed out of their savings by a con man who sells them a map to a lost mine. Soon Curly is using his invention (the collar button locator) to find fortune. The short is incredibly violent as the boys brain each other with assorted digging instruments. Sure enough, they find the lost mine and all the riches but are pursued by desperadoes. They lock themselves in a vault and wind up getting blown up.

SLAP COUNT: 11
EYE POKES: 1
CONKING HEADS: 3

What's the Matador,

1942. With Suzanne Kaaren, Harry Burns, Dorothy Appleby. Story by Jack White. Screenplay by Jack White, Saul Ward. Produced and directed by Jules White.

The Stooges are vying for a stage gig at a Latin American talent agency. They hurry to Mexico, only to have their suitcase mistakenly taken by the husband of a beautiful woman the boys have been sweet-talking. She tells them her hubby's incredibly jealous, and soon they're sneaking around her apartment trying to get the luggage while he's taking a siesta. He winds up chasing all three out of the apartment, vowing revenge. He gets his chance when they entertain at the bullfight, with Curly a matador and Larry and Moe in a bull costume. The jealous husband releases a real bull, leading to a mano a bullo battle with Curly, who ultimately charges and knocks the bull cold.

SLAP COUNT: 10
EYE POKES: 3 (another 1 blocked)

Matri-Phony,

1942. With Marjorie Deanne, Vernon Dent. Story and screenplay by Elwood Ullman, Monty Collins. Produced by Del Lord, Hugh McCollum. Directed by Harry Edwards.

Opening titles reveal that the short is set in Ancient Erysipelas, in the reign of the rash. The emperor is Octopus Grabus. The boys run Ye Olde Pottery and Stone Works, with Mohicus, Larrycus, and Curleycue the proprietors, proudly known as "The Biggest Chiselers in Town." The emperor, a terrible womanizer who might have been the precursor to Bill Clinton, is looking for another addition to his harem, and the Stooges wind up hiding

a beauty. They're taken to the palace in chains. Soon Curly is in drag, seducing the emperor. Short ends with the boys escaping out a window and landing on the spears of the emperor's guards.

SLAP COUNT: 3

Three Smart Saps,

1942. With Bud Jamison, Barbara Slater, John Tyrrell. Story and screenplay by Clyde Bruckman. Produced and directed by Jules White.

When the boys show up with flowers for their girlfriends, the girls tell them their father, a prison warden, has been wrongfully put behind bars by a crooked colleague who's taken over the warden job and turned the prison into a haven for other crooks. The boys vow to get arrested to help spring their future father-in-law. Told they don't arrest ordinary people, Curly assures the girls, "We're not ordinary people, we're morons." After several botched attempts to assault a cop and break an unbreakable glass window, the Stooges find their way behind bars. Indeed, they uncover a full-fledged party, and the Stooges mix until they figure a way to spring the warden by getting a picture of the hijinks.

SLAP COUNT: 14
CONKING HEADS: 5
MEMORABLE LINE: Told he's a graceful dancer, Curly replies, "I come from a family of dancers. My father died dancing, on the end of a rope."

Matri-Phony, 1942.

Even as I O U, 1942.

Horse-racing handicappers in Even as I O U.

65.

Even as I O U,

1942. With Ruth Skinner, Stanley Blystone. Story and screenplay by Felix Adler. Produced by Del Lord, Hugh McCollum. Directed by Del Lord.

The boys start out as con men, giving racing tips. But soon they're trying to help a woman and her young daughter who've been dispossessed. They win at the track, only to be coaxed by con artists to invest the $500 winnings in a horse. Moe realizes the mistake when they meet Sea Biscuit, which he describes as "a refugee from a glue factory." The convoluted plot ends with the horse bearing a foal.

SLAP COUNT: 3

MEMORABLE LINE: Stooges pose as journalists flashing with phony badges as a way to get into the horse track without paying. Moe: "Press." Larry: "Press." Curly: "Pull."

Sock-a-Bye Baby, 1942.

66.
Sock-a-Bye Baby,

1942. Story and screenplay by Clyde Bruckman.
Produced and directed by Jules White.

A woman leaves a baby in a basket on their doorstep, and the Stooges warm to the child, whom they call Jimmy. Soon the mother reports the child missing and the Stooges are on the run, and the cop in pursuit is the baby's father. By the time the wife tells her husband she left the baby, the Stooges are making their escape under a haystack. Some good hijinks, if slight on plot.

SLAP COUNT: 10

They Stooge to Conga,

1943. Story and screenplay by Elwood Ullman, Monty Collins. Produced by Del Lord, Hugh McCollum. Directed by Del Lord.

This time the boys are hapless handymen, hawking their services on the sidewalk, with Larry wearing a sandwich board that reads "Fix-All Fixers, Ink. General Handiwork Our Speshalty." They wander into a home, where they're hired to fix a doorbell. Turns out they're in spy headquarters of Nazi and Japanese conspirators. The boys tear up all the wiring in the home and engage in some violent mishaps: Curly's nose is run across a grinder, and the climbing spikes on his shoes are driven into Moe's eye and ear; and, oh, yeah, Curly is electrocuted. From there, the boys settle down and direct the nasty business toward the saboteurs, giving bad coordinates to a Nazi sub which leaves the vessel flopping around the water (stock footage from *Three Little Sew and Sews*). Once again the forces of evil are thwarted by the Three Stooges.

SLAP COUNT: 9
EYE POKES: 1 (Moe does it to Hitler poster)
CONKING HEADS: 1

Dizzy Detectives,

1943. Story and screenplay by Felix Adler. Produced and directed by Jules White.

Again the Stooges are handymen and start with a line that dates back to the early Ted Healy shorts. "Get the tools," Moe barks. "What tools?" says Larry. "The tools we been usin' for the last ten years." "Oh, those tools." Of course, Moe takes the line Healy used, as he essentially took Healy's controlling role. This leads to a classic sequence in which Moe stands atop a table, and Curly saws it, dropping Moe in a mishap that looks like it really hurt. Undaunted, Curly and Larry drop a door on Moe, crushing him, and power-saw the floor beneath him to get him out. When he falls to the floor below, Curly says, "Hey, whatcha doin' down there?" "Cmere," Moe beckons. "He wants you," Curly says to Larry. "Both of you," says Moe. After a proper braining, Moe leads them to join the police force, where the real plot begins.

They're assigned to solve the Ape Man burglaries and wind up at the Gypsom Good Inc. Antique shop, where the monkey is looting the place. A frightened Curly sits in a rocking chair, rocking back and forth over a cat's tail, with the cat pulling its tail back each time. Once it doesn't, and the cat shriek causes Curly to swallow his cigar. "Moe, Larry, a woman, she screamed and clawed me on the leg," Curly shrieks. "Is that bad?" Larry asks. Another priceless gag has Curly hiding under a rug, with a hat falling on his foot. Each time he peeks out, he sees the hat and thinks it's a man. Finally, he shoots, injuring his foot. When Moe and Larry pepper him with questions about the injury, Curly says, "I'm dyin' and you're startin' a quiz program." Finally, they solve the crime. The culprit is the city advocate, who earlier had complained about the crime spree. Short ends with the thieving gorilla drinking nitro, and Curly doing a header into his stomach, causing an explosion.

SLAP COUNT: 25
CONKING HEADS: 1

69.

Back from the Front,

1943. Story and screenplay by Jack White, Ewart Adamson. Produced and directed by Jules White.

Back from the Front, 1943.

You know it's another White-fueled propaganda short, with the opening frame featuring a disclaimer: "Any resemblance between the characters in this picture and other human beings is a dirty shame." The boys start off as sailors on a warship, seasick and swabbing decks. Turns out the bosun they've been abusing is a spy who signals coordinates to a Nazi sub, which torpedoes the boat. Curly catches the salvo and identifies it as a whale. When he tries to kill it with a hammer, the ship explodes. Soon the boys stow away aboard the S.S. *Schickelgruber,* a Nazi freighter, and find out the bosun is actually a Nazi officer. It comes down to a battle between good and evil, with the Stooges luring each Nazi to the deck and braining each with a club. Then they sneak into a meeting of officers, where Moe does his dead-on Hitler impersonation and tells the officers that unless they catch the spies, they are to blow their own brains out. "But, mein führer, we are Nazis, we have no brains," says the captain. Moe's plan nearly works, until he sneezes off his mustache.

SLAP COUNT: 6
CONKING HEADS: 2

70.

Spook Louder,

1943. With Stanley Blystone, Lew Kelly. Story and screenplay by Clyde Bruckman. Produced by Del Lord, Hugh McCollum. Directed by Del Lord.

Short opens in the office of J. O. Dunkfeather, special investigator. Eyeing a skull, the sleuth tells a reporter, "Just as I suspected, she had dandruff, which proves it was suicide." Dunkfeather recounts a case involving three stooges, "jap" spies, and the invention of a "death ray machine that will destroy millions." The Stooges, not having much luck selling the Miracle Reducing Machine, go door-to-door until they get to the home of Graves, the inventor. They're hired as caretakers, getting $100 a month and room and board. "I want you to look out for spies—especially jap spies," says Graves. "You're not a jap, are you?" he asks Curly, who's indignant. Sure enough, the spies show up, dressed as goblins.

When the Stooges lampooned the Nazis, their targets were always veiled, but in this short and several others that go after the Japanese—with whom the United States was also at war when the short was filmed—the attack is squarely ethnic and racist, with the Japanese always depicted as long-toothed morons. Today, these shorts are a bit uncomfortable to watch.

SLAP COUNT: 9
CONKING HEADS: 3
PIES THROWN: 6

Spook Louder, 1943.

Three Little Twirps, 1943.

77.

Three Little Twirps,

1943. With Chester Conklin, Stanley Blystone. Story and screenplay by Monty Collins, Elwood Ullman. Produced by Del Lord, Hugh McCollum. Directed by Harry Edwards.

The boys are papering the town with circus posters but get caught by the circus owner when Moe knocks Curly through one of the posters. When they find their payment is tickets to Herman's Great Show Combined, the boys hit the circus, find a roll of tickets, which they try to sell.

Soon they're being chased through the circus by angry owners. Curly winds up in the tent of the bearded lady, who thinks he's a blind date, her "bald eagle." He shaves the hairy babe bald and knocks her cold. The boys then climb into a horse costume to hide, not knowing the horse is about to become lion meat. Caught and forced to be used as targets for the spear-throwing exploits of the Sultan of Abudaba, Curly returns fire and is chased by the wild man across the tightrope. When Curly falls and causes a huge hole in the ground, the boys jump in after him and escape.

SLAP COUNT: 5
EYE POKES: 2

Higher Than a Kite, 1943.

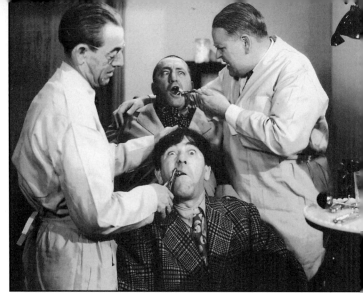

Higher Than a Kite.

72.

Higher Than a Kite,

1943. Story and screenplay by Elwood Ullman, Monty Collins. Produced by Del Lord, Hugh McCollum. Directed by Del Lord.

Opens with a sign: "A Flying Field Somewhere in Somewhere." The boys appear to be aviators for the military but are actually car cleaners, the best job they could find after joining the RAF and failing the intelligence test. When the colonel's car develops a squeak, the Stooges are put on the case. After Moe is shot out from under the car by the engine backfire, his head gets stuck in a pipe, leading to a prolonged and rather. brutal attempt to free him. He's burned, stretched, assaulted with a crowbar and a hammer, then nearly drowned in water and, boy, it's nice to see him take some abuse for a change. Once freed, an angry Moe flings a hammer at his rescuers, which shatters the car's windshield. That's nothing compared to what happens when the boys are through fixing the car. Curly winds up with a pile of parts on the floor and returns them to the engine with a shovel. In one of the awkwardest of plot transitions even for a Stooge short, the boys hide in a sewer pipe, only to find it's a bombshell. They wind up right in Nazi headquarters and are soon thwarting the bad guys. Short ends with a hilarious gag where Curly has a photo of Hitler stuck to his derriere. Each time he faces the Nazis, they attack. When he turns to run, they see the photo, halt, and salute, "Heil, Hitler." His foolproof escape plan backfires when a bulldog wearing a U.S. Marines helmet and coat sees the photo and attaches itself to Curly's butt.

SLAP COUNT: 19
CONKING HEADS: 2

I Can Hardly Wait,

1943. Story and screenplay by Clyde Bruckman.
Produced and directed by Jules White.

Dizzy Pilots,

1943. Story and screenplay by Clyde Bruckman.
Produced and directed by Jules White.

The boys are airplane builders. Once again the Japanese take it on the chin, with lines like "If those japs ever knew how many planes we turned out today, their yellow jaundice would turn green." The Stooges try to eat, without much luck, and Curly fills in the lyrics to what's becoming a familiar song for him: "She was bred in Ole Kentucky, but she's just a crumb up here. She's knock-kneed and double-jointed, with a cauliflower ear. Someday we shall be married, and if vegetables get too dear, I'll cut myself a nice big slice of her cauliflower ear. 'Cause that ain't rationsssss." Curly gets a toothache and is dragged to dentist Y. Tug and A. Yank Dentists, DDS, PHD, COD, FOB, PDQ. Curly is nervous, especially when a patient storms out and tells the doc, "What did you do before you became a dentist?" "Why, I was a butcher," says the dentist. "As far as I'm concerned, you still are." Moe, demonstrating to Curly how easy it is to sit in the chair, is mistakenly doped by the doc and has his tooth pulled. Turns out Curly has been dreaming in his bed. After he falls through to the bottom of three bunks, Moe socks him, knocking out Curly's bad tooth.

SLAP COUNT: 14

Short begins with a telegram from Republic of Cannabeer, P.U., giving the Stooges a thirty-day deferment from military service because of their claim they've invented an airplane that will revolutionize flying. Cut to the Stooges, who are working in the shop on a plane they'll coat with rubber so that it won't melt or freeze. Moe falls in the vat of hot rubber and is covered with the black skin of self-sealing rubber. Curly and Larry

Dizzy Pilots, 1943.

fill him with hydrogen gas, and Moe flies off like a balloon. Curly uses the shotgun, exploding Moe and dropping him in a well. Later the Stooges have another problem. They can't get the plane out of the hangar, and after Curly tries to saw the wings to make it fit, Moe tells him, "Don't saw the wings, you saw the garage." "I see the garage, but I don't saw the garage," says Curly, adding, "You are speaking incorrectly. You are moidering the king's English." Soon Moe tries to spin the prop and is propelled back into the vat of rubber, with Larry pulling him out with a pair of ice tongs. After a test flight ends with the Stooges losing the rudder and Curly taking literally an order by Moe to throw out the clutch, the plane nose-dives into a well. The Stooges are then sent to the army. In the Stooge version of déjà vu, we're suddenly given boot camp footage from the earlier short *Boobs in Arms,* in which they throw their guns at the drill instructor, then dash out of what appears to be a side gate of the Columbia studio.

SLAP COUNT: 9
EYE POKES: 1
CONKING HEADS: 1

Phoney Express,

1943. With Shirley Patterson, Bud Jamison. Story and screenplay by Elwood Ullman, Monty Collins. Produced by Del Lord, Hugh McCollum. Directed by Del Lord.

Opens with the sign "Peaceful Gulch" and cuts to an Old West town with bullets flying everywhere. The boys are featured on a poster, "Wanted for Vagrancy, Reward 50 cents or 3 for $1." Sheriff Hogwaller puts their photo in the paper, boasting that they're three famous marshals coming to town. After being chased out of town hawking snake oil, the boys saunter into the town's bar, wondering why they're getting so much respect. They're deputized to guard the First National Bank, which gets robbed under their noses. Curly becomes a bloodhound to find the loot, but locates a skunk instead. Finally, he finds the money under floorboards. Red's gang put the dough there and wants it back. The Stooges catch the bad guys in rather brutal-looking animal leg traps, and Curly hides with the money in a cookstove. When Red drops his lit cigar in with Curly, it sets afire his gun belt, with the stove spinning around and bullets spraying the bad guys. Not exactly their best effort.

SLAP COUNT: 9
EYE POKES: 1

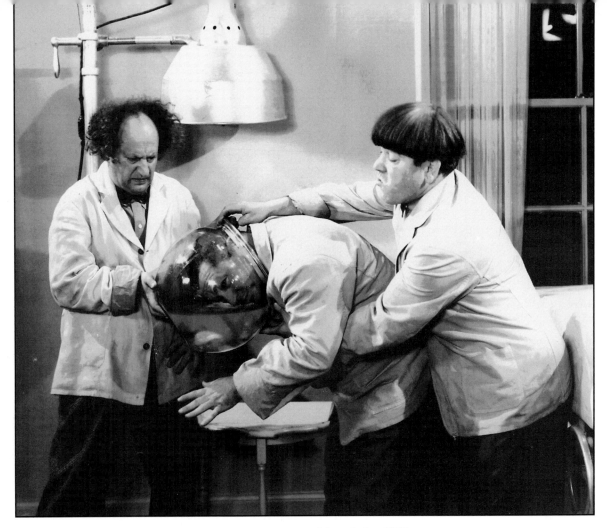

A Gem of a Jam, 1943.

76.

A Gem of a Jam,

1943. Produced by Hugh McCollum. Written and directed by Del Lord.

Opens with a sign: "Drs. Hart-Burns and Belcher." While the Stooges seem like they're doctors, the boys are actually office cleaners and begin with the obligatory mishaps. Moe is electrocuted. Curly swallows a goldfish, and Moe uses a drop line he feeds down Curly's gullet to pull the fish out. The trio winds up patching up a bad guy who's been shot in the arm. They drop him out of a gurney and into a cop car, then try to elude his partners.

SLAP COUNT: 17
EYE POKES: 1
CONKING HEADS: 2

77.
Crash Goes the Hash,

1944. With Dick Curtis, Bud Jamison, Vernon Dent. Story and screenplay by Felix Adler. Produced and directed by Jules White.

Opens with a sign: "Daily News Founded 1890." Fuller Bull, the managing editor, is angry because the *Daily Star Press* has gotten the scoop on Prince Shaam of Ubeedarn getting engaged to a widowed socialite. Bull's reporters came up empty. He peeks out the window and sees the Three Stooges in back of a truck which has two doors in the rear, one open. The closed door reads "Star Press," and Bull calls them up. Once he walks away, they close the other door, so now the message reads "Star Cleaning Pressing Co. Daily Delivery 'We Dye for You.'" They're ready to kill for the editor when he offers them a $100 bonus if they get a picture of the prince. They pose as a cook and two butlers, which leads to some fun in the kitchen. Asked if Moe is good with stews, Curly says, "Sure, he's always half stewed." Finally, the butler says, "Such levity, you remind me of the Three Stooges." Curly: "Hey, that's an insult." After the time-honored gag of a bird flying into the cooked turkey and bringing it to life, the Stooges discover the prince is a pauper and that he and the butler are con men swindling the dame. In another well-recycled gag, Moe brains the baddies by slipping his arm into one sleeve of the guy's coat and revolving in a circle. Moe punches his accomplice, and the accomplice punches the other bad guy until they both go down.

SLAP COUNT: 37
EYE POKES: 2
CONKING HEADS: 2

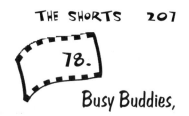

78.
Busy Buddies,

1944. Story and screenplay by Del Lord, Elwood Ullman. Produced by Hugh McCollum. Directed by Del Lord.

The Stooges operate a restaurant but aren't doing very well. When they're given a pastry bill of $97, Curly ties his apron, knotting it around the pastry shelves, knocking everything down. Told they have until Monday to pay the bill, the Stooges close up shop and take a job with Sellwell Advertising, getting a penny for every poster they hang. When they see a milking contest with a $100 prize, they enter Curly. He practices on a bull and is rewarded for his milking prowess by being gored over a fence. The contest begins and Curly's losing badly. Moe is in a cow suit and cheats by pouring milk out of a bottle. They're discovered, and the champ throws both Curly and the costumed cow out of the ring. They hobble away.

SLAP COUNT: 2
CONKING HEADS: 1
PIES THROWN: 1

Busy Buddies, 1944.

79.

The Yoke's on Me,

1944. Story and screenplay by Clyde Bruckman.
Produced and directed by Jules White.

Drummed out of the army, the Stooges buy a farm for $1,000 and a car. It's a disaster, but a good setting for yet another racist short against the Japanese. Turns out "some japs escaped from a relocation center and we're checking all cars," a cop says. The Stooges mess with some of the animals, and Curly feeds an ostrich blasting powder. On cue, here come several "japs" with buckteeth. The Stooges wind up throwing explosive ostrich eggs and kill the four Japanese villains. Knowing what we do now about how Japanese-born American citizens were mistreated and stripped of their belongings in relocation centers makes this as funny as a train wreck.

SLAP COUNT: 11

Idle Roomers, 1944.

80.

Idle Roomers,

1944. With Duke York, Christine McIntyre, Vernon Dent.
Story and screenplay by Del Lord, Elwood Ullman.
Produced by Hugh McCollum. Directed by Del Lord.

Short takes place in Hotel Snazzy Plaza, where the boys are incompetent bellhops. They get brained by the husband of a beautiful woman. He has smuggled in Lupe, the wolf man, whom the husband wants to use in a circus act. While cleaning the room, Curly frees the beast. The savage goes ballistic when he hears the radio. Though Curly and the beast do an amusing gag with a glassless mirror, this one leaves much to be desired as the Stooges wind up in an elevator that crashes through the ceiling, up into the clouds.

SLAP COUNT: 7
CONKING HEADS: 1

The Yoke's on Me, 1944.

81.
Gents Without Cents,

1944. With Lindsay, LaVerne, Betty. Story and screenplay by Felix Adler. Produced and directed by Jules White.

This short is almost like a sitcom, with more dialogue and acting than most, and best remembered by the famed Niagara Falls routine. Stooges rehearse that skit—"Slowly I turn, step by step, inch by inch, until . . ."—but they are interrupted by the sounds of hoofing coming from the apartment below. When they angrily arrive to complain, they discover the offenders are three leggy dancers, Flo, Mary, and Shirley. The boys are smitten. The ladies join the boys as they play a gig at the Noazark Shipbuilding Co. shipyard, with the act billed as "Moe, Larry & Curly in Two Souls and a Heel." They perform the entire Niagara Falls act, in which Moe recounts to Curly that he was dumped by a lover for another man (Larry) and what he'd do if he ran into him. Interestingly, the normally seamless Larry blows his line in the last act, as Larry, together with Moe, says, "Slowly I turn, step by step, step by step . . ." Moe, at the same time, says, "Slowly I turn, step by step, inch by inch . . ." They didn't reshoot much in those days and left it alone. After they take bows, the Stooges are told that Castor & Earl, the main attraction, are no-shows. Soon the girls are cartwheeling and jumping rope as they take the act's place. Another skit follows and the Stooges are headed to Niagara Falls, where they've all gotten hitched. When Curly gets out and reads the Niagara Falls sign, Moe and Larry recite the chant, as he inches the car into a fleeing Curly. One of the best remembered of the Curly shorts.

SLAP COUNT: 7
EYE POKES: 1
CONKING HEADS: 1
MEMORABLE LINE: "Slowly I turn, step by step, inch by inch."

82.
No Dough, Boys,

1944. With Vernon Dent, Christine McIntyre. Story and screenplay by Felix Adler. Produced and directed by Jules White.

Yet another short torturing the Japanese, who were still at war with the United States at the time. The Stooges are playing Japanese in a war scene. On break and in costume, they enter into a

No Dough, Boys, 1944.

luncheonette. The owner has just read a newspaper account with the headline "Jap Sub Blown Up Offshore, U.S. Coast Guard Deals Death Blow, 3 Japanese Soldiers Escape." He thinks the Stooges are the escapees, especially when they talk with mouths full. After being attacked, they knock the counter guy into a flame and flee. They run into a house, smack into a Nazi who's expecting the real trio, Nackie, Saki, and Wacky, a group of saboteurs. The bad guys figure out the Stooges are phonies, and when the real guys show up, the Nazi points to the Stooges and barks, "Grab them in the name of the new world order." The Stooges get the drop on the Nazi, and when they tear off his clothes, he's wearing swastika pajamas. They crush a globe on his noggin and once again have done their part for America and democracy.

SLAP COUNT: 18
EYE POKES: 1
CONKING HEADS: 4
PIES THROWN: 1

83.

Three Pests in a Mess,

1945. With Christine McIntyre, Brian O'Hara, Vernon Dent. Produced by Hugh McCollum. Written and directed by Del Lord.

Opens with a sign: "Cheatham Investment Co. I Cheatham Pres." Bad guys need to find three guys who've got a sweepstakes ticket worth $100,000. Stooges are across the hall, trying to patent a con-

voluted fly-catching invention. A female scam artist thinks they're the winners and she woos Curly until she finds he's not. The Stooges flee but accidentally shoot a mannequin and think they've killed a real guy. They head for a pet cemetery to bury him, and the owners show up dressed in scary costumes (they were going to a costume party). There's much hijinks, ending when the Stooges are scared out of their shoes and run off into the dark.

SLAP COUNT: 7

Moe and Christine McIntyre in *Three Pests in a Mess,* 1945.

Booby Dupes, 1945.

Booby Dupes,

1945. With Rebel Randall, Vernon Dent. Produced by Hugh McCollum. Written and directed by Del Lord.

Once again the Stooges are hawking fish, with Curly singing, "Don't chop the wood, Mother, Father's coming home with a load on." After they're asked for a catfish, the boys open the truck and see a slew of cats run out while they're left with just fish bones. Curly has the bright idea that if they catch their own fish, they'd cut out the middleman. They buy a boat for $300 and prove inept fishermen. Curly battles a fish, puts a hole in the boat when he tries to kill it with an ax. Curly then finds a "water letter outer," which is actually a hand drill, and he further ventilates the hull. In peril, they wave a white flag which just happens to have a large red dot on it. Soon U.S. bombers buzz overhead. "Yep, they're japs all right, let 'em have it," says a pilot, who drop bombs on the suspected Japanese vessel. Under heavy fire, the boys make their escape using a Victrola as a propeller.

SLAP COUNT: 4

Idiots DeLuxe, 1945.

85.

Idiots DeLuxe,

1945. Story and screenplay by Elwood Ullman. Produced and directed by Jules White.

Starts in a courtroom, where Moe defends himself of assaulting his two roommates with intent to commit mayhem. Moe tells the judge he's a sick man, having just had an operation for "crushed grape seeds." The judge says he's had the same operation, and they compare scars in the groin area. Cut to the past, as Moe takes nerve tonic, a shaky mess, while his roomies rehearse. They're the Original Two Man Quartet. Larry plays drums and clarinet, while Curly plays slide trombone and cymbals with his head. They're loud and Moe is frantic, wrapping the slide trombone around Curly's neck. They decide to go hunting, and once they see a sign that reads "Fine for Hunting," they figure they've arrived. Bulk of the short concerns a bear, which eats Moe's food and generally torments him. Short is not short on violence, as Curly falls into a bear trap, Moe is shot in the grape seeds by Larry. Moe ends up in the car with the bear and totals the car. Cut back to courtroom. Moe is acquitted and given his ax back. He uses it to brain Curly and Larry, chasing them from the courtroom.

SLAP COUNT: 12
EYE POKES: 1
CONKING HEADS: 1

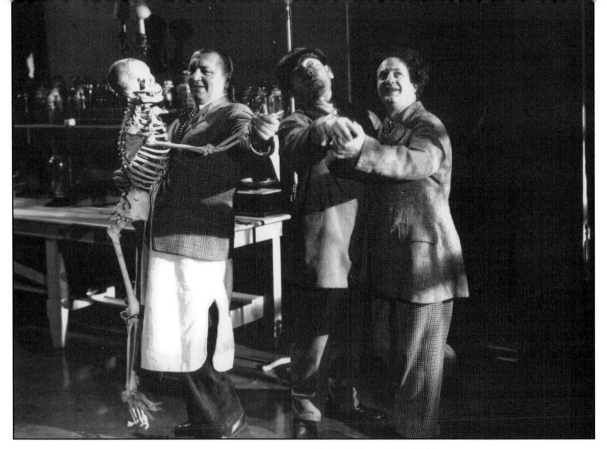

If a Body Meets a Body, 1945.

86.

If a Body Meets a Body,

1945. With Theodore Lorch, Fred Kelsey.
Story by Gil Pratt. Screenplay by Jack White.
Produced and directed by Jules White.

The boys are down on their luck again and evict Curly when he serves them horse soup and Moe gets a horseshoe in his bowl. They take Curly back when they read in the paper that Curly Q. Link is the missing heir to Professor Robert O. Link and that he's due a $3-million estate to be given away at his home on 111 Riverside Drive. When Curly announces himself as Curly Q. Link, the butler, Jerkington, replies, "Oh, you're the missing Link." It turns out the professor was murdered and there is no will. The rest of the short has the Stooges finding and running from a series of corpses, before they crash into a maid, who's really a male villain. When it comes time to read the will, Curly gets sixty-seven cents and Moe slaps Curly and tears out a chunk of Larry's hair. Short is kind of sad, because there's the first real evidence here from Curly's voice and mannerisms that he's beginning to slow down and slur his speech a bit. Edward Bernds said that though nobody knew it at the time, Curly had already had a small stroke, which would lead up to the debilitating one in 1946 which ended his career.

SLAP COUNT: 25

Micro-Phonies, 1945.

87.

Micro-Phonies,

1945. With Christine McIntyre, Symona Boniface, Gino Carrado. Produced by Hugh McCollum. Written and directed by Edward Bernds.

The boys are handymen, trying to fix a heating pipe at a radio station. Soon they are braining each other with pipes and playing around with the radio equipment. Curly dresses in drag and lip-synchs, "I hear the voice of spring is in the air." Turns out a wealthy woman named Mrs.

Bixby has come to hire the singer (who is really the daughter of a friend) for her radio program. Curly, now known as Señorita Cucaracha, accepts a $500 offer to sing the song at her party. Though Lady Cucaracha is accompanied by Señor Mucho (Larry) and Señor Gusto (Moe), the boys still show their rough edges at the upscale party. "Quite a shack, this Bixby joint." "Yes, it reminds me of reform school," says Larry. A tenor, whom the Stooges fought with at the radio station, destroying both his glasses and his violin, is the first to sing. The Stooges fire cherries into his mouth when he hits the high notes, choking him until he stops, especially after they give him a "salvo." He gets revenge while the Stooges are lip-

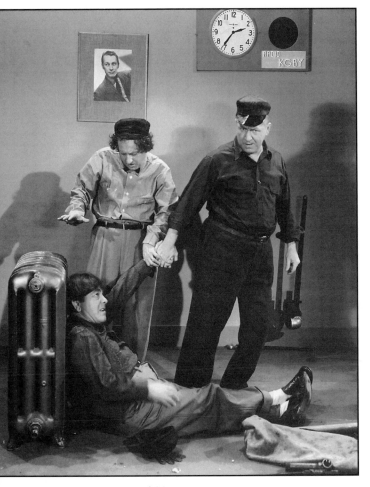

Micro-Phonies, 1945.

Bernds's first short was *A Bird in the Head,* but in that one, Curly began to show the debilitating effects of what would later be diagnosed as a stroke, and the short was subpar. Bernds said Columbia exec Hugh McCollum shuffled the order, because of the subpar short came first, Bernds might have been bounced as director by Jules White and Harry Cohn.

SLAP COUNT: 3
CONKING HEADS: 1

Beer Barrel Polecats,

1946. With Robert Williams, Vernon Dent. Story and screenplay by Gilbert W. Pratt. Produced and directed by Jules White.

synching when he pulls the plug on the record player. Finally, the real singer (the lovely Christine McIntyre) helps them by singing from behind a curtain. She's discovered and pleases her father, who'll let her be a singer. The Stooges, meanwhile, are pelted with phonograph records.

This short is remembered as one of the better-quality Curly shorts. Edward Bernds, longtime Stooge soundman, made his directorial debut on it, and proved that one could make humorous Stooge shorts without much violence. Actually,

When Prohibition prevents them from being able to get a beer, the Stooges decide to go into the brewing business. They get a book—*How to Make Panther Pilsner Beer,* by J. Panther Pilsner—and have soon bottled 185 brewskis. Some adherence to the formula would have been advisable, because the heat from the kitchen explodes the bottles, and the Stooges are jailed for eight months as bootleggers. Curly brings a keg under his coat to keep them from being thirsty, explaining satisfactorily to the jailer that he has a goiter. This leads into recycled prison footage from the 1941 short *In the Sweet Pie and Pie.* The footage essentially runs to the end of the old short, but this one ends with the Stooges being freed after forty years. The

Beer Barrel Polecats, 1946.

old men stagger out of the prison gates, but throw Curly back in after he suggests they get a beer. Larry and Moe walk off together, talking about seeing "a couple of blondes." Presumably, Curly was getting sicker and that's the reason the short relied mostly on the old footage; the story lines didn't really match up.

SLAP COUNT: 20
EYE POKES: 2 (another 1 blocked)
CONKING HEADS: 2

A Bird in the Head, 1946.

89.

A Bird in the Head,

1946. With Vernon Dent, Robert Williams, Frank Lackteen.
Produced by Hugh McCollum.
Written and directed by Edward Bernds.

The boys are wallpaper hangers, working across the hall from the mad scientist Professor Panzer. After they do an awful papering job, the Stooges are chased into his laboratory. The scientist is looking for a human brain small enough to be transplanted into the head of a gorilla. Panzer fixes on Curly's cranium. They run away as Larry says, "Maybe he's a headhunter." Replies Moe: "If he's a headhunter, he's hunting small game." Curly

bonds with the gorilla, and together they brain the scientist. Again Curly is hurting.

SLAP COUNT: 16

A Bird in the Head.

Uncivil Warbirds, 1946.

90.

Uncivil Warbirds,

1946. Story by Clyde Bruckman.
Produced and directed by Jules White.

Stooges are three Southern gents who ask their girls to marry them. Unfortunately, it's during the Civil War and the trio decides to join up. Trouble is, Curly's joined the Confederate army, while Moe and Larry show up in the uniform of the opposite team. They take turns locking each other in the smokehouse, depending on which side is winning. Next they don blackface and masquerade as slaves. After a few turns before a bumbling firing squad, including a spirited death scene by Curly even though he's not really shot, the boys give Northern maps to the Southern generals and marry their sweethearts.

SLAP COUNT: 2
EYE POKES: 2
CONKING HEADS: 1

The Three TroubleDoers, 1946.

91.

The Three TroubleDoers,

1946. With Christine McIntyre, Dick Curtis. Story and screenplay by Jack White. Produced by Hugh McCollum. Directed by Edward Bernds.

It's the Old West again, and as the Stooges arrive in Dead Man's Gulch, a guy sits before the town sign, crossing off the population sign each time gunfire rings out. The town count has gone from 216 to 199 when they enter, and the Stooges discover that six sheriffs in five months have been killed by Bad-

lands Blackie and his gang. He's kidnapped the father of a beautiful woman, and Blackie tells her that her dad will die unless she marries him. Curly, who also woos the lass, becomes a sheriff after she pledges she'll marry him if he can make Blackie fade to black. Cut to the finale, where the Stooges have freed her father, only to find he'd rather die than let her marry Curly. Curly hands him a stick of dynamite, and the Stooges run away before it goes off. A rather uninspired episode.

SLAP COUNT: 3
CONKING HEADS: 1

Monkey Businessmen, 1946.

guys, and Curly winds up curing a rich guy with a bum foot when he crashes into his wheelchair. Curly's given a $1,000 reward, then gets brained by his partners when he suggests going somewhere for a nice long rest.

SLAP COUNT: 19
EYE POKES: 1

92.

Monkey Businessmen,

1946. Story and screenplay by Edward Bernds.
Produced by Hugh McCollum. Directed by Edward Bernds.

The boss is complaining about his electricians: "The manpower shortage is supposed to be over!" Cut to the Stooges, where Curly is stuck in a ladder that has crashed to the floor. "You pebble brain," says Moe, "why don't you be more careful when you climb a ladder." Says Curly: "I only climbed seven steps." Moe: "Well, the ladder only had six." The Stooges decide they need a rest after being fired, and head for Mallards Rest Home. Dr. Mallard is a quack and the place is a scam. They're chased through the home by the bad

93.

Three Loan Wolves,

1946. With Beverly Warren, Harold Brauer.
Story and screenplay by Felix Adler.
Produced and directed by Jules White.

The Stooges operate the shop Here Today Pawn Tomorrow, and they are the fathers of a seven-year-old who wants to know how he got there. The Stooges tell him. After a mobster named Butch McGee tries to shake down the pawnshop, his moll, Molly the Glamour Girl, leaves the baby there with Larry. The Stooges try to care for it, with Curly giving the tot that time-honored Stooge alternative to the pacifier, the barrel of a loaded gun. The Stooges get in a fight with McGee's ruffians and beat them up. Once the kid hears the story, he leaves to find his real mother, and Curly and Moe work over Larry for bringing in the tot in the first place. Curly's physical condition and voice are worsening.

SLAP COUNT: 32
EYE POKES: 2 (another 1 blocked)

94.

G.I. Wanna Go Home,

1946. With Doris Houck, Judy Malcolm, Ethelreda Leopold.
Story and screenplay by Felix Adler.
Produced and directed by Jules White.

The boys head home from the war to see their sweethearts, Jessie, Tessie, and Bessie. They've been dispossessed and, with the war over, flats are scarce. They wind up living in a backyard. There's a recycled (for what seems like the thousandth time) gag where a bird flies into the carcass of a cooked goose, and just as they're about to eat, a bulldozer levels the fence and their makeshift kitchen. Finally, the boys and girls marry and get six bunk beds. Curly climbs to the top and, of course, falls right through to the bottom. "Oh, what do you know, I didn't get hurt," says Curly. Moe: "Oh, yes you did." He brains him. Edward Bernds said that Curly would be good on some weeks and almost not be able to work on others. This was a good week.

SLAP COUNT: 20
EYE POKES: 1

G.I. Wanna Go Home, 1946.

Rhythm and Weep.

Rhythm and Weep,

1946. With Gloria Patrice, Ruth Godfrey, Nita Bieber, Jack Norton. Story and screenplay by Felix Adler. Produced and directed by Jules White.

Begins with a sign: "Garden Theater, Stage Entrance." The Stooges fly out the door, thrown out of the twenty-sixth-straight theater. They decide to jump off a building and end it all, right after Curly has a piece of pie, "so I can die jest right." On the roof, they meet three other frustrated entertainers, Hilda, Wilda, and Tilda, also planning to jump. They meet a millionaire piano player up there who produces musicals and offers to pay them $100 a week to star in his. They stage the musical, and just when the millionaire doubles their salary, they find out he's actually a loony carted away by men with white coats.

SLAP COUNT: 16
EYE POKES: 3
PIES THROWN: 1

96.

Three Little Pirates,

1946. With Christine McIntyre, Robert Stevens, Vernon Dent, Dorothy De Haven. Story and screenplay by Clyde Bruckman. Produced by Hugh McCollum. Directed by Edward Bernds.

Stooges wash up on a garbage scow at a palace and are captured and given their choice of death sentence. Curly chooses being burned at the stake over having his head chopped off because, as hard-core Stooge fans well know by now, "a hot steak is better than a cold chop." Imprisoned, they're helped by a beautiful maiden, who shows them a slew of power tools to use to break through a wall in the closet. Of course, the Stooges choose the one wall that leads back into the cell. Though Curly is deteriorating, he does the memorable nearsighted Rajah of Canarsie (uttering jibberish, "Nah hah, rasbanyah"). Soon they're off to the island of Coney to bring back damsels, and wind up in a bar with Black Louis, who wants to kill them. There is a humorous knife-throwing contest (with Larry the target) and a major melee in which the Stooges clean house, though Moe is conked on the head by a large hammer at short's end.

SLAP COUNT: 12

Three Little Pirates.

job under severe adversity, even tossing in a pretty good pie fight.

SLAP COUNT: 9
PIES THROWN: 20

98.

Fright Night,

1947. With Dick Wessel, Claire Carleton. Story and screenplay by Clyde Bruckman. Produced by Hugh McCollum. Directed by Edward Bernds.

Opens with a sign: "Muscle Manor We Train the Fighters. The Three Stooges Props." Inside, Stooges root for their fighter, a heavyweight named Chopper, who relaxes in a chair reading *Love Tales* magazine and curling a small weight. They coax him to hit Oscar the dummy, but Chopper watches as the Stooges knock themselves silly hitting the dummy on a rocking base and getting brained by it. Finally, they suggest he spar Shemp. The reluctant new Stooge gets in the ring, and Larry laces his glove to the ring rope. Larry's girl, a gorgeous blonde named Kitty, comes in, and Chopper aims to impress her. He essentially hits Shemp about sixty times, leaving him in a crumpled heap. When Chopper heads for the showers, two mugs enter the ring and warn the Stooge that Big Mike says that Chopper has to lose to Gorilla Watson.

Larry decides they should soften up Chopper by feeding him sweets so he'll lose and they'll win. Sure enough, he sits at a table with Kitty, eating tarts and asking her, "Will you read me another

Half-Wits' Holiday, during which Curly suffered his debilitating stroke. Note his ragged appearance.

97.

Half-Wits' Holiday,

1947. With Vernon Dent, Barbara Slater, Ted Lorch. Story and screenplay by Zion Myers. Produced and directed by Jules White.

A remake of one of the best early Stooge shorts, *Hoi Polloi,* in which two upper-crusters bet $1,000 on whether gentlemen are molded by heredity or environment. This short is memorable for two reasons. It's Curly's last, as he suffered a stroke partway through the short. Save for a cameo in *Hold That Lion,* it's his final act of stoogery. It's also the first appearance of longtime Stooge actor Emil Sitka, who plays Sappington the butler. Considering the turmoil of having to finish the short after Curly was rushed to the hospital, a heartbroken Jules White did a pretty good poem about love?" Cut to fight night and Chopper is mad. Kitty has left him for Gorilla and he's ready to rumble. Moe tosses a cream puff that hits Gorilla, and the boxer breaks his fist against a brick wall after narrowly missing Moe's mug. The fight's canceled, and an angry Big Mike takes the boys for a one-way ride. In a warehouse, Shemp shows his stuff as he begs for mercy, leading to a long chase around crates. Shemp's head is used for a battering ram, but, through a combination of mothballs and an ax, he brains the bad guys. One fires a shot and hits a red paint can, spilling paint on Shemp, who goes through an impassioned death scene.

Considering how quickly Shemp was pressed into duty for his ailing younger brother Curly, he fit in with the boys rather seamlessly after all those early years of working together. The studio expected Curly to return to work, so Shemp figured this gig would be temporary. While measuring up to his younger brother's physical prowess was an unfair burden, Shemp more than holds his own, with a distinctly different character creation.

SLAP COUNT: 69
CONKING HEADS: 3
PIES THROWN: 3

99.

Out West,

1947. With Christine McIntyre, Jack Norman, Jacques O'Mahoney. Story and screenplay by Clyde Bruckman. Produced by Hugh McCollum. Directed by Edward Bernds.

Short starts with Shemp on a doctor's table, told he's got an enlarged vein in his leg. The doc draws

a picture of it. "I don't want to lose the leg, Doc, I've had it since I was a little kid," Shemp says. He's told to head out west for a few weeks to heal it. Cut to a frontier town, with the Stooges dressed as cowboys, heading into the Red Dog Saloon. The bad guy, Doc Barker, mistakes Shemp's drawing of his shin vein for a map of a gold vein. The Stooges try to help a barmaid whose boyfriend, the Arizona Kid, has been imprisoned by Barker and will be killed unless she marries the bad guy. Kid is sprung and fetches the cavalry to save the Stooges. "Sir, I hope you're not too late," says the strapping Kid. "Son, never in the history of motion pictures has the United States cavalry been too late," says the commanding officer. Of course, they are, and the Stooges get the best of the bad guys by the time the cavalry arrives. Told by Moe that "the Stooges have landed and have the situation well in hand," the cavalry rides back from where it came—in reverse. A fairly clever effort.

SLAP COUNT: 9
CONKING HEADS: 1

Moe demonstrates how to mix a cocktail in Out West, *1947.*

Tying up Emil Sitka in <u>Hold That Lion</u>, 1947.

A final moment for Curly in <u>Hold That Lion</u>.

100.

Hold That Lion,

1947. With Kenneth MacDonald, Emil Sitka, Dudley Dickerson. Story and screenplay by Felix Adler. Produced and directed by Jules White.

Opens with a sign: "Cess, Poole & Drayne Attorneys at Law." The boys are appealing to their lawyer to get the inheritance left them by Ambrose Rose, the millionaire junk dealer. Told that the executor, Icabod Slipp, has the money and that he's likely trying to give the boys the slip and keep it for himself, they show up to his office, each armed with a subpoena to serve him. Cut to another door sign: "Slipp, Tripp & Skipp," where Slipp indeed plans his getaway. Slipp is played by the oily, silver-tongued Kenneth MacDonald, a venerable villain in Stooge shorts. Hearing the boys outside the door voicing their plan to serve him and knowing they don't know what he looks

like, Slipp accuses each of them of being Slipp and brains them one by one, tearing up their subpoenas when they're knocked cold. Shemp goes down after doing a rope-a-dope dance that the fight fan would make one of his staple comic mannerisms. The Stooges track him to the Cannonball Express, a railway train. As they walk up an aisle searching for him, they lift a hat off a sleeping man, who wears a clothespin on his nose to keep him from snoring. Despite the full head of dark hair, it's Curly, who doesn't wake up. The cameo was done at a time when Curly was still fully expected to come back, with Shemp still viewed as a temporary troupe member. Soon after, it was evident that the debilitating stroke had taken too much of a toll on one of the century's great physical comics, and this cameo would serve as his screen farewell. The rest of the short goes downhill, as the boys find Slipp, let a lion out of a cage, destroy the slumber of the sleeping compartment, and finally brain Slipp with a hammer. Shemp gets an egg facial before the close. If you're still in withdrawal over Curly, this short demonstrates how much the Stooges miss his ability to make even the blandest scene interesting with his innate physical talent.

SLAP COUNT: 28
EYE POKES: 3
CONKING HEADS: 1

101.

Brideless Groom,

1947. With Dee Green, Christine McIntyre, Doris Colleen. Story and screenplay by Clyde Bruckman. Produced by Hugh McCollum. Directed by Edward Bernds.

Begins with a sign—"Professor Shemp Howard Teacher of Voice"—and a recording, "The Voices of Spring," originally sung by Christine McIntyre in the Bernds-directed short *Micro-Phonies.* Here Shemp is teaching an awful songstress, who attempts to copy the tune but does a better rendition of a cat being strangled. "You're supposed to be singing about the voices of spring, not about the eruption of a volcano," Shemp chides. "Gargle with old razor blades," he advises his charge, who chirps, "Oh, Professor, I know you wouldn't want anything to happen to my throat." Once he lets her out and closes the door, Shemp retorts, "Except to have somebody cut it."

Cut to the real story behind the short, that Shemp has been left $500,000 by his uncle Caleb, contingent upon his getting married—in seven hours. After an amusing attempt in a pay phone in which Shemp calls up all his old girlfriends, then drops his nickel and gets entwined with Moe in phone cable that leaves them bursting out of the booth, Shemp proposes to his student songstress and appears before Justice of the Peace J. M. Benton. He's played by Emil Sitka, who would emerge as by far the funniest recurring nonregular performer in the Stooge short series. "Hold hands, you lovebirds," warbles Benton, a line that can be heard in Quentin Tarantino's *Pulp Fiction* in the scene in which John Travolta plunges a needle full of Adrenalin into the heart of Uma Thurman after her ticker quits from an overdose of heroin. A newspaper account of Shemp's pending fortune herds all of the former girlfriends Shemp called earlier, and a major bout breaks out. Larry loses more hair, torn out in tufts by one catfighting female Shemp suitor, and another puts the squeeze on Shemp with the help of a large table vise that might have inspired a similar eye-popping torture scene in the Martin Scorsese film *Casino.* The ladies battle to the credits, driving up the slap count to acceptable levels.

SLAP COUNT: 20
MEMORABLE LINE: "Hold hands, you lovebirds."

Shemp and Emil Sitka are woman-handled by one of several Shemp suitors wanting to marry him for his money in Brideless Groom, 1947. The short is best remembered for Sitka's line "Hold hands, you lovebirds," which Quentin Tarantino used in Pulp Fiction.

102.

Sing a Song of Six Pants,

1947. With Virginia Hunter, Harold Brainer, Vernon Dent.
Story and screenplay by Felix Adler.
Produced and directed by Jules White.

Opens with a sign: "Pip Boys Lary, Moe & Shemp. Unaccustomed Tailor's Men's Furnishings New and 2nd Hand Clothes Cheep. Cleaning, Pressing, Altercations." The boys get a bill demanding $321.86 in overdue payment for cleaning equipment from the Skin & Flint Finance Corp., I. Fleecem, President. After some dry-cleaning hijinks—Larry, pressing a pair of pants, mistakes a spot of sunlight peeking through a window shade for a stain and rubs a hole in the garment in a gag that'll be reused in future shorts; Moe uses a dry-cleaning press to make pancakes; a pants-pressing Shemp picks a fight with a fold-out wall ironing board and loses decisively—the short gets down to business. Terry "Slippery Fingers" Hargan has robbed his eighteenth safe in nine days, and there's a reward for his capture. Sure enough, he's on the run and ducks into the shop, posing among a group of clothes-modeling mannequins. Soon the Stooges have stripped him of his suit, which contains the combination of another safe. Efforts to recover it lead to a battle between the bad guys and Stooges, with Hargan getting knocked out. The cop takes the reward and gives the Stooges tickets to the policemen's ball. But they find cash in Hargan's coat, and Moe counts it out: "One hundred, two hundred, three hundred, four hundred, five hundred, fifty . . . how'd that get in there?" Moe tosses the fifty on the floor, and the Stooges dive on it, fighting for the bill, a clever bit we'll see again.

SLAP COUNT: 12
EYE POKES: 1

103.

All Gummed Up,

1947. With Christine McIntyre, Emil Sitka.
Story and screenplay by Felix Adler.
Produced and directed by Jules White.

Opens on a store window: "Cut Throat Drug Store Everything from a Needle to a Battleship." The boys run the store, and Shemp's trying to hook a customer to buy a fishing pole. Demonstrating a cast, Shemp reels in a skirt, looking up to see the silk-slipped bottom of a shocked woman. "Is that lady bowlegged?" asks Shemp. "That's no lady, that's my mother-in-law," replies an indignant customer, who huffs out the door. Another customer comes in with a prescription written hastily on his shirt for his ailing wife. Saying they need to record it, they tear the shirt off his back. The Stooges are told by their cranky landlord (Sitka) that they're being kicked out after ten years, with the Pinchpenny Market taking over the site. He's got lumbago, and the Stooges soon have him hunched over, with their heat therapies merely leaving tattoo burns of the words "mustard" and "Horse radish" on his back. His

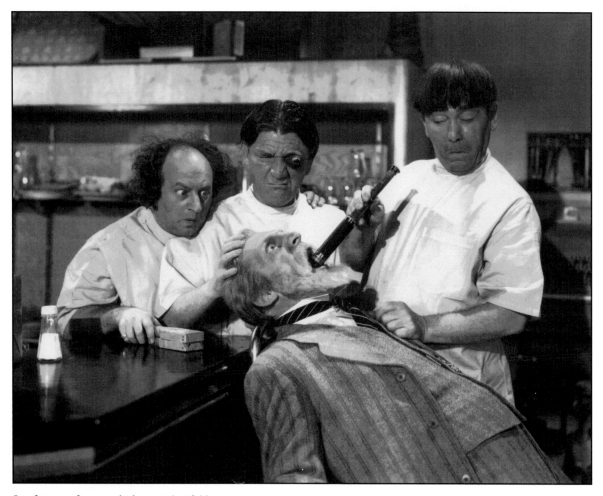

Emil Sitka with Stooges in All Gummed Up, 1947.

wife comes in and the landlord says he's tossing out the old bag.

Shemp comes up with the idea to create a vitamin that will restore her youth. Sure enough, one dose turns the old Mrs. Flint into the lovely Christine McIntyre. The boys give it to the landlord in exchange for tearing up the lease, but it doesn't quite work as well on him—he remains old, but shrinks in his suit. Short ends with Christine baking a celebration cake, frosting with bubble gum instead of marshmallows and making for a bubbly close. Much of this footage will be reused in the 1953 short *Bubble Trouble.*

SLAP COUNT: 76 (65 of them come as Moe and Larry coax the youth vitamin idea out of Shemp by braining him in a stereo-head-pounding flurry)

PIES THROWN: 6

Shivering Sherlocks, 1948.

they do their familiar kitchen wizardry, such as the well-worn chicken soup trip in which boiling water is poured through the carcass of a bird into a bowl below, only to be spilled on Moe's back. Moe gets an egg facial and then steals the famous Curly clam chowder eating scene which Del Lord in turn lifted from the old Mack Sennett shorts of the twenties. Moe even borrows Curly's bark as he battles the cracker-eating mollusk. Finally, the Stooges spot one of the robbers and wind up in a deserted house, being pursued by a hairy, humped, cleaver-wielding freak-killer named Angel. In a storage room the size of a warehouse (doesn't every house have one), Shemp drops tall barrels on the bad guys, leading to their arrest. Much of the footage from the short will be repeated in the 1955 short *Of Cash and Hash*.

SLAP COUNT: 15

104.

Shivering Sherlocks,

1948. With Christine McIntyre, Vernon Dent, Kenneth MacDonald, Frank Lackteen, Duke York. Story and screenplay by Del Lord, Elwood Ullman. Produced by Hugh McCollum. Directed by Del Lord.

In an opening that could have come out of *The Untouchables*, cops are called to the scene of an armed heist. The crooks are gone, but they find the Stooges battling it out in a trash can, and the boys are hauled in as prime suspects. Vernon Dent questions them with a lie detector, a most hilarious scene when he himself is proved to be lying about his whereabouts owing to late night cavorting. Still suspects, they retreat to the Elite Cafe, where the owner is going under and the boys agree to help her out and work for her. There

105.

Pardon My Clutch,

1948. With Matt McHugh. Story and screenplay by Clyde Bruckman. Produced by Hugh McCollum. Directed by Edward Bernds.

The boys pace back and forth, waiting for a diagnosis for their ailing pal Shemp. Turns out a friend's doing the doctoring to save them money and tells them to give him sleeping pills and follow the directions. They interpret giving pills and then skipping an hour to mean rope skipping, and Shemp complies. Turns out he's got a bad tooth, and the friend pulls it and recommends a trip to the country. Turns out, too, he's got a car he'll sell for $900, and he'll throw in the camping equipment as well. After pitching the tent in the living room and destroying the furniture, they come out to see their new vehicle. It's a heap of a jalopy called a Columbus ("I thought he came over in a boat," Moe retorts). They wind up changing a flat, crushing Moe's toes on the axle, and rolling the spare into a garage, where they fight the mechanic for it. As they tie their payload to the vehicle, the rope they toss over the top strangles Larry, who gets a nice beating for being in the way. All the while, Emil Sitka spies from the bushes and rushes them after they start the lemon and it literally falls apart. He's a talent scout and wants to buy the car for a movie for $2,000. The lemon-selling friend steps in to take the cash, voiding his earlier sale. The joke's on him when white-coated men take away Sitka, who's a babbling mental patient. That joke was lifted from the 1946 Curly short *Rhythm and Weep*.

SLAP COUNT: 7

MEMORABLE LINE: Moe: "Remind me to kill you later." Shemp: "Sure, I'll make a note of it." First used in early Curly *Cash & Carry*, but still a gem.

106.

Squareheads of the Round Table,

1948. With Christine McIntyre, Phil Van Zandt, Jacques O'Mahoney, Vernon Dent. Produced by Hugh McCollum. Written and directed by Edward Bernds.

Opens with a legend: "In Days of Old, When Knights Were Bold, and Suits Were Made of Iron." It's the Middle Ages, and the Stooges are trying to get the armor off Shemp. "How'd you get into that thing?" groans Moe. "I was always popping rivets so I had my tailor spot-weld me," Shemp replies. Guards enter saying they're looking to behead Cedric the Blacksmith. After the Stooges convince the guards they're only troubadours on the way to the court of King Arthur, out steps the muscle-bound and valiant Cedric. He enlists the help of the Stooges for the hand of Princess Elaine, whom the king's promised to the Black Prince. The troubadours serenade under her window, singing the escape plans, but are caught. The king is played by Vernon Dent, who sleeps in his daughter's room. Though punishment is usually the Stooges' domain, Vernon gets dented mightily; he's conked with a rock, has a bed land on him, and falls from a trellis outside the window. The troubadours are caught and placed in the dungeon, which they break out of when served bread baked by the princess. It has a high iron content—as in escape tools. The Stooges uncover the Black Prince's plot—to kill the king the moment the marriage takes place. Cedric's to be beheaded when the wedding horns blow, so the Stooges, disguised as knights, hurl fruit into the horns to stuff them up. The plot's uncovered, and as the king declares his daughter will marry the worthy blacksmith, the horns indeed blow—jettisoning the fruit into the faces of the Stooges.

SLAP COUNT: 12

CONKING HEADS: 1

MEMORABLE QUOTE: Larry, told he's going to be executed: "I can't die, I haven't seen *The Jolson Story*."

Fiddlers Three,

1948. With Vernon Dent, Virginia Hunter, Phil Van Zandt. Story and screenplay by Felix Adler. Produced and directed by Jules White.

Opens with a legend: "Coleslaw-Vania, A Small Kingdom in Ye Old Country, Where Ye Men Are Men and Ye Women Are Glad of It." Dent is king again, this time Old King Cole, and the boys are jesters. They make the king laugh, with Larry showing off his violin prowess. The boys ask the king for his blessing to marry and he agrees—but not until his daughter, Princess Alicia, reaches an altared state first with Prince Gallant III of Rhododendron. The boys do some skits, such as Jack Be Nimble (Shemp depicted sitting on a candle), Little Miss Muffet (Larry in drag, menaced by a spider), and Simple Simon (Moe and Shemp in pie mishap). Suddenly, a minion tells the king his daughter's been kidnapped. "Call out the guards, telephone the newspapers, and notify the FBI—Flanagan, Branagan, and Iskovitch, they're detectives," says Dent. The boys pledge to solve the crime and prepare to do it on horseback, leading to this memorable tongue twister. Moe: "Our steed is not shod. Sue has not a shoe." Shemp: "Then we will shoe Sue. For if Sue has no shoe, a shoeing Sue we must do."

After multiple mishaps in the blacksmithing shop used in the preceding short, the boys are mule-kicked into a basement, leading to the room in which the princess is held captive by rogue guards who plan to return her as part of a magician's trick. Upstairs, the magician Murgatroyd

gets the king to agree to let him wed the princess if he makes her reappear. Down comes the magician's sexy assistant, and the guards follow her, allowing the princess to escape. The boys materialize in the box, and the magician plunges swords and saws into various parts of their anatomies. The scam is uncovered, and Murgatroyd is caught—until his assistant walks by. All the men follow except Shemp, who drinks water and turns into a human sprinkler from the earlier sword trick. In prose that would make Shakespeare cringe, Shemp says, "Moeth, Larryeth, get a plumber. I think I sprungeth a leak."

SLAP COUNT: 11
EYE POKES: 1
PIES THROWN: 7

The Hot Scots,

1948. With Herbert Evans, Christine McIntyre, Charles Knight, Ted Lorch. Story and screenplay by Elwood Ullman. Produced by Hugh McCollum. Directed by Edward Bernds.

Opens with a legend, "Scotland Yard," then cut to the desk of Inspector McCormick, who meets with the beard-sporting Stooges. After tearing off the hair to show their ability for disguises, the Stooges say they're answering the ad for "experienced yard men." A smirking McCormick indeed asserts he can give them a job locating missing papers—which turns out to be trash they're

The Hot Scots, 1948.

assigned to pick up in the yard outside. This vintage scene would be used in two future shorts. The boys retrieve a case blown off McCormick's desk and set out to prove their gumshoe abilities. They head off to Glenheather Castle on the bonny banks of Scotland, though Shemp reminds, "'Tis late and the bonny banks are closed." They dress as Scots and introduce themselves as McLarry, McShemp, and McMoe. An earl wants them to guard his valuables while he's off to meet his clan ("Oh, a clan bake"), and the thieves help themselves to all the loot they can carry while the Stooges doze. Given a wiff of old Scotch when they meet the earl, he offers them a taste when they figure out his butlers and maiden, Lorna Doone, are the culprits. In what gives new meaning to skeleton in the closet, a bony bagpipe-playing corpse appears from the Scotch closet, sending them running. If it seems like coincidence that three straight Stooge shorts were set in a castle, think again. Jules White got permission to borrow the set of the Columbia feature *Lorna Doone,* and he took full advantage.

SLAP COUNT: 10

MEMORABLE LINE: Shemp, introduced to Lorna Doone: "Hi, Lorna, how ya doin'."

Shemp and Moe in Heavenly Daze, 1948.

Heavenly Daze.

109.

Heavenly Daze,

1948. With Vernon Dent, Sam McDaniel. Story and
screenplay by Zion Myers. Produced and
directed by Jules White.

Moe is Mortimer, the keeper of the Pearly Gates,
reviewing the afterlife prospects of nephew
Shemp. After suggesting Shemp get an asbestos
suit, Shemp replies, "Get me a pitchfork and a red
union suit and I'll go." He's given an alternative:
return to earth and reform corrupt cousins Moe

and Larry. Shemp takes the Heavenly Express
train back, materializing in the law offices of I.
Fleecem, who reads Shemp's will. His pals are left
his fortune of $140, stuck in an old sock. Moe
divvies it up. "A hundred and forty smackers, that
makes seventy for you, Larry, one, two, three,
four—say, at what age did you graduate from
grammar school?" Larry: "Eighteen." Moe: "Oh,
eighteen, nineteen, twenty. Say, tell me, how old
do you have to be to collect your old-age pen-
sion?" Larry: "Sixty-five." Moe: "Sixty-five, sixty-
six, sixty-seven, sixty-eight, sixty-nine, seventy."
After Fleecem takes all the money for his legal fee,
telling the boys, "Any other lawyer would have
taken the case for twenty dollars," Shemp swipes
the dough and puts it back in his pal's pockets. At

this time, they realize they're being haunted by their pal. Despite this, they use the money to rent a room, hoping to scam an investor out of $50,000 for the coveted invention of a fountain pen that writes under whipped cream. Shemp sabotages the showing, leading to cream facials all around and Shemp waking up in bed on fire. He's been dreaming, and the bed catches fire while he's smoking. Moe and Larry extinguish him in one of the more bizarre endings to a Stooge short. Larry got an actual fountain pen stuck in his forehead in a mishap.

SLAP COUNT: 14
PIES THROWN: 10 (really whipped cream)

I'm a Monkey's Uncle,

1948. With Dee Green, Virginia Hunter, Nancy Saunders. Story and screenplay by Zion Myers. Produced and directed by Jules White.

Starts with an inscription: "According to Darwin, our ancestors hung from trees by their tails and thereby hangs our tale." Then it's followed by a disclaimer: "Any similarity between the characters in this picture and real monkeys is definitely unfair to the monkeys." It's the Stone Age, where the Stooges sleep under a large fur blanket. Shemp is "geeb-geeb-geebing" as Moe talks in his sleep about his girl Aggie and plays "she loves me, she loves me not" with chunks of Larry's already sparse hair. Then it's on to hunting and cooking,

with the expected mishaps, as Moe prepares to introduce the boys to Aggie and her sisters, Maggie and Baggy. The first two are beauties, the latter might be called Haggy, prompting Shemp to ask her, "Did you come from behind that rock or from under it?" After asking her, "What would you charge to haunt a cave?" Shemp flees, but Baggy makes an open field tackle that Dick Butkus would envy and claims Shemp. Suddenly, three irate cavemen appear and want their girls back. Using a branch, the boys slingshot rocks, eggs, and what look like dinosaur turds into the faces of the bad guys. Finally, a skunk salvo drives the ruffians away and the boys get the girls.

SLAP COUNT: 6
EYE POKES: 1

Mummy's Dummies,

1948. With Vernon Dent, Ralph Dunn, Phil Van Zandt, Dee Green. Story and screenplay by Elwood Ullman. Produced by Hugh McCollum. Directed by Edward Bernds.

Set in ancient Egypt, "in the reign of the great King Rootentooten." Cut to sign: "The Smiling Egyptians. Used Chariots." Boys are painting a beat-up chariot, which they con a guy to pay four hundred shekels for. When he steps right through it outside their gates, he tracks them down. Turns out he's chief of the palace guards, and the salesmen are in trouble. Brought to Rootentooten's palace, they try to endear themselves to the king, who's cranky from a royally bad toothache. In a rip-off of Curly's classic (the further you go into the later shorts, the more classic everything Curly did becomes) Rasbanyah routine, Shemp puts on Coke-bottle glasses, calls himself Painless Papyrus, and pulls the tooth. Suddenly, they're royal chamberlains and uncover a plot by the guard captain and tax collector to do some unauthorized withholding. The boys uncover the ruse and the king rewards them. "One of you will have my daughter's hand in marriage." She appears, a toothless hag. "Let the lucky man take one step forward," he says as Larry and Moe take one step back. As the hag grabs Shemp, he bellows, "Moe, Larry, do something!" They pelt him with rice and shoes, the traditional wedding blessing.

SLAP COUNT: 4

The boys grill Christine McIntyre in Crime on Their Hands, 1948.

112.

Crime on Their Hands,

1948. With Kenneth MacDonald, Christine McIntyre, Charles C. Wilson, Lester Allen. Story and screenplay by Elwood Ullman. Produced by Hugh McCollum. Directed by Edward Bernds.

A gangster (MacDonald) holds the Punjab diamond. Cut to newsroom, where J. L. Cameron, managing editor, growls, "Well, men, this is a tough assignment. Do you think you can cover it?" He's talking to the boys, who are upholsterers working on his chair. Reporter wanna-bes, they take a tip that the stolen gem is at McGuffy's Cafe.

When the boys show up, they canvass the bar, then head upstairs. Christine McIntyre, playing the moll, hides the rock in a candy dish, thinking the boys are cops.

Shemp eats the diamond with some candy, and when the boys tell her they're cub reporters, the bad guys invite them to get Shemp to cough up the gem before they operate. After turning their mate upside down and employing ice tongs to no avail, Moe and Larry get locked in a closet while the thugs plan to cut Shemp open. Fortunately, a gorilla is next door, and after getting drilled in the butt by Larry and Moe as they break through the wall, the gorilla saves the day for Shemp. Cops come, and when they ask if Shemp knocked out the bad guys by themselves, the gorilla jumps up and says, "I helped."

SLAP COUNT: 10

Skulduggery in The Ghost Talks, 1949.

113.

The Ghost Talks,

1949. Story and screenplay by Felix Adler.
Produced and directed by Jules White.

Opens in a castle on a stormy night. Stooges are movers from the A to Z Express Co. Shemp sets the mood doing his best radio voice, "This is Desmond of the Outer Sanctum. Strange things will happen in this mysterious castle. Who could get along without a nice bloody murder?" Shemp is then brained with a medieval shield hanging on a wall, Larry gets shot by an arrow from a crossbow, and a suit of armor begins talking. It tells the boys the story of how it is the spirit of Peeping Tom, accused of peeping at Lady Godiva. Beheaded, he's waited a thousand years for her ghost and begs the Stooges not to move him. "If you take me, bad luck will follow." After a parade of skeletons (one's named Red Skeleton), Godiva enters on horseback and rides away with the knight.

SLAP COUNT: 7
EYE POKES: 1
PIES THROWN: 4

114.

Who Done It?,

1949. With Christine McIntyre, Ralph Dunn, Charles Knight, Emil Sitka, Duke York, Dudley Dickerson. Story and screenplay by Edward Bernds. Produced by Hugh McCollum. Directed by Edward Bernds.

The Phantom Gang is bumping off rich guys, and Mr. Goodrich (Sitka) is next. He frets over why the detectives he's hired haven't shown up. He calls the Alert Detective Agency, where the Stooges are tied up—literally. Goodrich, sure enough, is attacked, and the butler is in on it. The boys arrive, and Shemp is promptly fed a rat poison cocktail by a beautiful girl and does some admirable floor work reminiscent of brother Curly. After much running through hallways and being chased by the goons—Moe limps noticeably, which Bernds said came in an accident from an earlier scene—they escape the bad guys, with Goodrich falling from a closet. "I'm not dead," he says. "I'm a lover of fine music. They tied me up and made me listen to singing commercials. I thought I'd go mad." Shemp wipes out the bad guys with a fireplace shovel, then, after braining Goodrich and the Stooges, knocks himself out.

SLAP COUNT: 26
CONKING HEADS: 5

115.

Hokus Pokus,

1949. With Marty Ainslee, Vernon Dent, Jimmy Lloyd. Story and screenplay by Felix Adler. Produced and directed by Jules White.

Boys wait hand and foot on Mary, a blonde in a wheelchair running a scam to get an insurance check for $25,000. She reveals her plans over the phone to her partner, calling the boys the "three saps who will be my witnesses." The boys shave one another, make breakfast, with Shemp engaging in a frustrating attempt to open the legs of a folding table, which is textbook Curly, even to the point where Shemp cries for Moe. After letting in the insurance adjuster, the boys go to work as poster hangers, unfurling one for "The Great Hypnotist Svengarlic," who just happens to be walking out with the circus owner, who tells him business is lagging. The boys want him to hypnotize Mary to walk, but instead he transfixes them, coaxing them out on a flagpole jutting from the side of a building. A crowd watches below, and a bicyclist looking up knocks Svengarlic unconscious, breaking his spell. The boys hang terrified from the pole, and when it breaks, they swing down through a window, where Mary's taking her insurance check. She jumps up to get out of the way, and the adjuster tears up the check.

SLAP COUNT: 16
EYE POKES: 1
CONKING HEADS: 2

kidnapped, flown and taken by train to the State of Anemia, where they're told to mix their magic. Larry takes the initiative in a lab that looks like it came from the short *All Gummed Up*. By the time they've mixed a batch, the real prof and his daughter have been captured and are placed in the cell directly below. Larry gets the unusually bright idea to pour the acidic formula on the floor to get down to the cell (Moe: "You know, he's the most intelligent imbecile I ever saw"), but Larry's not smart enough to do it while he's not standing on the spot. After a tug-of-war between the Anemic troops upstairs and the Stooges below, which stretches Shemp to hysterical lengths with an obviously fake head, the Stooges and the prof escape to a car. Shemp pours the formula into the gas tank and they take off as the backfire strips the pursuing troops of their uniforms. One of the most violent of recent episodes and also one of the funnier ones.

SLAP COUNT: 29
CONKING HEADS: 4

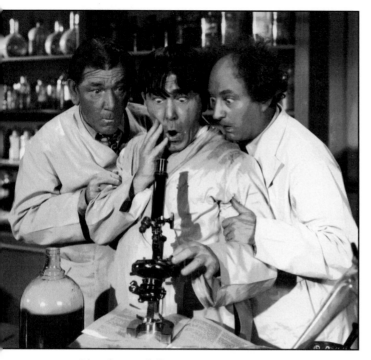

Fuelin' Around, 1949.

116.

Fuelin' Around,

1949. With Christine McIntyre, Emil Sitka, Vernon Dent, Philip Van Zandt, Andres Peta, Jacques O'Mahoney. Produced by Hugh McCollum. Directed by Edward Bernds.

Short opens in front of the home of Professor Sneed (Sitka), as three bad guys want the formula for a super rocket fuel. They mistake Larry for the prof, but he and his mates are carpet layers. There are some inspired moments of how not to lay carpet, such as when Moe crawls under to remove a lump and Larry and Shemp tack him in and try to pound him even with the floor with hammers and carpet stretchers. Once they're finished, the boys are

117.

Malice in the Palace,

1949. With Vernon Dent, George Lewis, Frank Lackteen. Story and screenplay by Felix Adler. Produced and directed by Jules White.

Opens with a legend: "Somewhere in the Orient." Cut to "Cafe Casbah Bah. Meeting Place of Black Sheep Bah-Bah-Bah." Two men talk in

hushed tones. "What delays Hafadollah? We'll get the map by hook or crook, as sure as my name is Gin-a Rummy." Stooges are waiters, and quickly empty full trays of food all over the two men, Gin-a Rummy and Hassan Ben Sober (get it?). Larry works in the kitchen, cooking for the two men before they head off to find the tomb of Rootentooten. In one of the more clever plotlines lately, Larry chases a cat around the kitchen noisily, then, cleaver in hand, pursues it into the dining room and carries it back with him. He does the same with a small dog, and when the men are served their food, they think they're dining on the pets—particularly because the real cat and dog are under the table making noises.

Hafadollah shows up and reminds his coconspirators they should send someone into the tomb, since the first to touch the hundred-carat diamond suffers the curse of a thousand deaths. Their plan to get the Stooges to search for the gem is over when a note is thrown through the window affixed to a rock. It reads: "You are late. I got the diamond, you got the gate. Omigosh Emir of Shmow."

The men begin to cry. "With that diamond, I could have quit my job as doorman at the Oasis Hotel," says one, who gets kicked in the tail by Shemp. The other, seemingly about to attack with his giant curved knife, tries to sell it to the boys for five dollars. Moe offers two—as in fingers to the eye sockets. The boys decide to get the gem and return it for the $50,000 reward, which Larry feels will be enough for a one-room flat in Hollywood. For what seems like a minute, they study a map of Starvania—bearing such geographical landmarks as Great Mitten, Hot Sea Tot Sea, Rubid-Din, Slap Happia, Bay of Window, I Ran, He-Ran, She-Ran, They-Ran, Also-Ran, Isle Asker. You get the idea. Moe plots a course: "We start here at Jerkola. Down the Insane River, over the Giva Dam, through Pushover, across Shmowland to the stronghold of Shmow." The boys arrive dressed as Santas and meet Shmow as he reads the funnies, the giant diamond the centerpiece of his turban. They totemize into a giant spirit and escape with the jewel until Shemp hits a low ceiling and they fall to the floor. After Shemp gives a guard a fruit facial, they get the gem.

SLAP COUNT: 12
EYE POKES: 1
CONKING HEADS: 10

118.

Vagabond Loafers,

1949. With Christine McIntyre, Kenneth MacDonald, Symona Boniface, Emil Sitka, Dudley Dickerson, Herbert Evans. Written by Elwood Ullman. Produced by Hugh McCollum. Directed by Edward Bernds.

Couple admires the Van Brocklin painting they just bought for $50,000, with the griping husband (Sitka) saying, "He only had to die in poverty, now I have to live in it." Planning a showing, the couple calls plumbers to fix a leak. At Day and Nite Plumbers headquarters, Moe (reading the book *How to Be a Plumber*) answers the call and pledges to be there in "two shakes of a martini." He rolls Larry and Shemp out of bed, with Moe and Larry driving away before Shemp drops down the fire pole. "We got to get a bigger jeep," Shemp moans from the garage floor. In what's a pretty good rip-off of the seminal Curly short *A Plumbing We Will Go,* they make a mess of the house with plumber pipes, with Shemp encasing himself in pipes as he floods the bathroom. Shemp falls through to the basement, cushioning the impact by landing on Moe. They tear out electrical pipe to use for plumbing. Sitka's gentle clipped delivery makes him the perfect comic foil, as he's pulled through a wall, saying, "Short circuit, no doubt."

While later Stooge shorts would routinely recycle earlier Stooge footage and could not be called remakes as much as rip-offs, this one embellishes the original Curly short plot with Kenneth MacDonald and Christine McIntyre's plan to steal the Van Brocklin. Sure, they use the gag where the homeowner shows her guests her TV, with footage of Niagara Falls followed by water that crashes through the TV set and floods the room. Now the painting is missing, and the bad guys are scared by a flour-covered Larry and are caught. Perhaps the best of the remakes.

SLAP COUNT: 5
MEMORABLE LINE: Moe, seeing the flour-covered ghostlike Larry: "What would you charge to haunt a house?" Larry: "How many rooms?"

Dunked in the Deep, 1949.

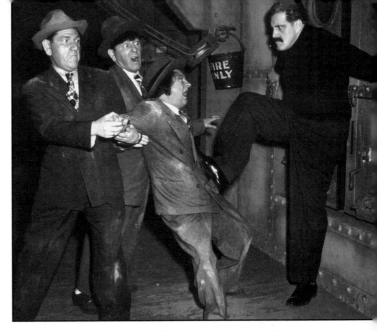

Battling Gene Roth in Dunked in the Deep.

119.

Dunked in the Deep,

1949. With Gene Roth. Written by Felix Adler.
Produced and directed by Jules White.

As a radio crackles that "foreign elements stole secret documents," a spy stuffs microfilm into watermelons. The Stooges are his neighbors and enter his apartment dressed as children giving out handbills for Old Holland Cheese (five delicious flavors—Amsterdam, Rotterdam, Beaver Dam, Boulder Dam, and Giva-Dam). Spy pal Borscht asks the Stooges to carry the melons to Pier 7, where he'll leave the country. They arrive early for some dockside stoogery, with Moe swatting flies on his face and having an egg land in his hand,

which leads to the familiar egg facial. The boys meet their pal on the ship, and when it begins moving, he informs them he's a stowaway and they are his guests. After stealing his salami, the trio gets seasick, and Shemp, wearing a pasty white makeup, continues to show his own ability for slapstick. A battle with a porthole gets him buckets of water in the kisser, and his attempt to sleep in a hammock once again ends with him lighting himself on fire while smoking, ending with his butt in a fiery barrel. The boys finally decide to eat the melons, find the film, and discover their pal is indeed a spy. From there they fight the much larger Borscht, who chases Shemp while the Stooge dons melons on each foot like shoes. A large winch hook on a rope brains Borscht. They plan to turn him in at the first port, and when Shemp is sent back to the porthole to locate land, he gets a mud facial. "Land ho," he says.

SLAP COUNT: 6
EYE POKES: 1
CONKING HEADS: 1

120.

Punchy Cowpunchers,

1950. With Jock O'Mahoney, Christine McIntyre, Kenneth MacDonald, Dick Wessel, Vernon Dent, Emil Sitka. Produced by Hugh McCollum. Written and directed by Edward Bernds.

Short starts with gunfighting stock footage from old westerns. Cut to "Fort Scott, Kansas 1868. The Heroic Men of the U.S. Cavalry." Next we see the Stooges in F Troop outfits trying to saddle a horse. After nailing the sarge with the saddle, then several horseshoes, the sarge retaliates but brains the captain (Sitka) and gets bucked down to private. When the sarge is told to choose a group of men for a dangerous job—"the men you choose will probably never come back"—he knows just whom to choose. "I have just the men," he says. Enough foreplay, at this point the short gets down to business. The Stooges are sent undercover to the Red Dog Saloon to bring down the Killer Dillons. They meet up with the gunslingers at the saloon, with the familiar macho one-upmanship. Shemp orders a milk shake, quickly asking for sour milk. They have allies in the beautiful barmaid Nell and the bumbling cowboy Elmer, whose gun skills make the Stooges look like marksmen. As the Stooges flee the gunmen, Elmer heads off to get the cavalry, much the way the same actor, playing the Arizona Kid, fetched the cavalry in the 1947 short *Out West*. This time the result is different. Elmer's told there is no one around because yesterday was payday. While Elmer heads back, Shemp hides in a safe the Dillons want to blow up. Nell takes matters in her own hands, decking three villains and Elmer in the best punches landed in the short.

SLAP COUNT: 9
CONKING HEADS: 1

121.

Hugs and Mugs,

1950. With Nanette Bordeaux, Christine McIntyre, Kathleen O'Malley. Written by Clyde Bruckman. Produced and directed by Jules White.

Three conniving women have checked a necklace into National Express Storage before doing a year for shoplifting, and they're back for the goods. Unfortunately, they learn the lot was sold to the Shangri-La Upholstery Co., a biz run by the boys. Off they go to woo the boys out of the necklace. One coos with Larry, commenting on his "beau-

Hugs and Mugs, 1950.

tiful head of skin" ("I polish it with floor wax," he brags), but soon the ladies are tearing out the few chunks of Larry's remaining hair as the cat-fighting commences. Meanwhile, three mobsters have tailed the dames. From here, the short grows so violent it would get four stars from the Marquis de Sade. The Stooges battle the bad guys in a fabric-filled bin, and Shemp goes to work on everyone with a hot iron. The boys recover the necklace. The women, now hooked on the valiant but bumbling upholsterers, pledge to return the necklace to its rightful owner. Shemp sits upon an iron, cools his tail in a water-filled bucket. Unfortunately, an electric fan has fallen in, and it chews his tail to ribbons.

SLAP COUNT: 17
EYE POKES: 4
CONKING HEADS: 1

Dopey Dicks, 1950.

122.

Dopey Dicks,

1950. With Christine McIntyre, Philip Van Zandt, Stanley Price. Written by Elwood Ullman. Produced by Hugh McCollum. Directed by Edward Bernds.

Opens with a door sign: "Sam Shovel Private Investigator." The boys are assigned to shovel Sam's belongings into another office, and while Shemp sits and romanticizes what it'd be like to be a private eye, in walks a beautiful woman. "Strange men are following me," she says. "They'd be strange if they didn't," Shemp replies. She's immediately nabbed but has left her address, and the Stooges are off in hot pursuit. An evil scientist, frustrated in another botched attempt to make a mechanical man that ends with the dummy losing its head, says he needs a human head and a brain small enough to put in the dummy. Enter the Stooges, and after Moe tells the doc he's the brains of the outfit, he flees while Shemp unties the girl. From there, it's a nonstop chase to keep their heads, ending when they escape, hitch and catch a ride in a car driven by the headless dummy. "Safe at last," says the woman.

SLAP COUNT: 8
CONKING HEADS: 2

Pie facial for Shemp in <u>Love at First Bite</u>, 1950.

Love at First Bite,

1950. With Christine McIntyre, Yvette Raynard, Maris Monteil. Story and screenplay by Felix Adler. Produced and directed by Jules White.

The boys are getting married and reminiscing how they met their brides-to-be, with accompanying flashbacks. Larry recalls: "I was stationed in Italy eating bread and hot dogs and waiting to be mustered out." Moe's shown in Vienna, where he meets a blonde mopping the floors and slips in her mess, falling to the floor with the beauty. "She literally swept me off my feet," he says. Shemp's flashback is on the Rue de Schmeil in Paris. A sailor, he sits with a beauty drinking beer at a table. "I left my heart with her on Rue de Pew," he sighs. The boys toast their luck with Old Panther (bottled yesterday). Stewed, they insult each other, brawl, and, thinking they've killed Shemp, give him cement shoes for a proper watery burial. He revives, and the repentant boys try to help him get rid of those heavy shoes with a dynamite blast. It sends the trio flying, right to the docks where the ladies are waiting. A classic White effort; fewer blows are struck at prizefights than were landed in this short.

SLAP COUNT: 35
EYE POKES: 4 (another 1 blocked)

124.

Self-Made Maids,

1950. Written by Felix Adler. Produced and directed by Jules White.

Short opens with the advisory (or is it a warning?) that "all parts in this picture are played by the Three Stooges." That is instantly apparent as the opening scene shows three of the most god-awfully ugly women imaginable. It's Moe, Larry, and Shemp primping for their big dates. Moe looks like Joan Crawford, Larry like Bette Davis in *Whatever Happened to Baby Jane?* Shemp—well, it's hard to describe how bad Shemp looks as a

femme. They wax on about their boyfriends, who happen to be artists named Moe, Larry, and Shemp. The beaux deface a statue, a painting, and a clay sculpture Larry works on (he crashes into it, ending up with a Durante nose and doing a passable impression—"I'm mortified, it's sabotoogee, that's what it is"). The boys, after engaging in a clay fight, sit the girls for portraits. The femmes hold ant-infested flowers to their faces, and much scratching ensues. The boys propose to the girls, and they plan to marry. The father of the girls (Moe) is hesitant to bless the wedding and wants to meet the boys. He does, unbeknownst to all of them, when they collide in the lobby and the boys give him the business. Topped by a cake and ice cream facial. Dad returns to the apartment, and the short becomes a rather clever chase sequence in which shots are fired, lumps are raised, and Dad is tied to the couch, his feet tickled until he gives in. Next we see the children of these unfortunate couplings—the Stooges, fighting over milk.

SLAP COUNT: 3
EYE POKES: 1
PIES THROWN: 1 (actually a cake)

Three Hams on Rye,

1950. With Nanette Bordeaux, Christine McIntyre, Emil Sitka. Written by Clyde Bruckman. Produced and directed by Jules White.

Short opens with a glimpse of the Theater Chit-Chat column by Nick Barker. Under the headline "Another Broadway Turkey All Set to Lay an Egg, B.K. Doaks, Producer of 10 Flop Shows, to Open Latest Can of Corn Tonight . . . 'The Bride Wore Spurs,'" the Walter Winchell–like columnist is brutal, reporting that "smart boys along the Gay White Way predict that the odor coming from the Mason Theatre will smell up Broadway for miles. The betting is one hundred to one that 'The Bride Wore Spurs' will fold after the first performance." Cut to Doaks, who flings the paper. The boys, meanwhile, are painting props and are soon in full blackface as they get most of the paint on each other. Ridiculed by the chorus girls because they only have a small part at the end, the boys are assigned by Doaks to keep Barker from showing up. Naturally, they blow the assignment and are

soon making a cake for the final scene. As has happened with most cakes prepared by the Stooges, dating back to the 1935 short *Uncivil Warriors,* a pot holder finds its way into the recipe. When Janiebelle orders the boys to engage in a cake-eating contest to see who will marry her, the cast is spitting and coughing up feathers all over the stage, the crowd roaring. Doaks screams that he's finished, but the columnist comes back and calls the act a sensation.

SLAP COUNT: 22
EYE POKES: 1 (another 1 blocked)
PIES THROWN: 1

Studio Stoops,

1950. With Christine McIntyre, Kenneth MacDonald, Vernon Dent. Written by Elwood Ullman. Produced by Hugh McCollum. Directed by Edward Bernds.

Opens with B.O. Pictures Corp., in the publicity department, where the Stooges are killing termites and need to do it before the publicity guys come back from location. The boys are mistaken for movie execs—"I understand you boys have been knocking them dead lately," says the studio chief, the boys thinking he means bugs. He's brought new star Dolly Duvall, wants a publicity stunt to make her famous, and promises a big bonus. Suddenly, they're publicists. The Stooges propose making her disappear as a kidnap victim, with pics in the paper, while she hides out at Clinton Arms Hotel. A couple of thugs overhear and take the idea literally. Moe tells Shemp to take a letter, and he sits fetchingly on Moe's lap with a stenography pad. Some fun misadventures follow with the typewriter, as Larry's carriage flies off and hits Moe in the head. Newspaper guys don't believe them and won't publish their story. The starlet's ransomed for $10,000. The boys locate her, stuck in a zippered garment bag in the closet. Shemp takes her place and, still in the bag, tries to escape and promptly finds his way onto a window ledge, about ten stories above the street. Shemp falls ("and he had his good suit on, too," Larry mourns). He hangs from the sill and manages to make a phone call—to Moe and Larry, asking for a rope. "Say, we'd better hurry before our adversaries come back," says Larry, stopping Moe in his tracks. "Since when did you get to be so smart?" They give Shemp the rope, but the Stooge disembarks on the balcony where a fetching femme sunbathes. The sudden slack sends Moe and Larry flying across into a full bathtub. "Hey, this ain't Saturday night," Larry complains. "What have we got to lose," says Moe. "Where's the soap?" They suds up.

SLAP COUNT: 9
PIES THROWN: 1

127.
Slaphappy Sleuths,
1950. With Stanley Blystone, Emil Sitka, Gene Roth. Written by Felix Adler. Produced and directed by Jules White.

Opens with a sign: "Onion Oil Co. Established 1904. I. M. Greecy Pres." Cut to Fuller Grime,

the general manager, complaining that with a string of gas station robberies, they need three "brainy but stupid-looking private detectives who can pose as gas station attendants." The three have eyes painted on the lids of their actual closed eyes, a joke cribbed from the 1935 short *Horses' Collars.* Grime pumps the boys to see if they can handle the job. He asks Moe if he got a commission while in the service, only to be told, "No, just straight salary." Asking Shemp if he's a good detective, he's told, "See that heel, I ran that down"—another gag originated in the Curly era. After some violent hijinks with a knife that ends up embedded in Grime's behind, the boys are off to a filling station with three pumps—Ethel thirty cents a gallon, Becky twenty-six cents a gallon, Hazel twenty-two cents a gallon. A customer enters with an overheated engine, and by the time he leaves, the boys have shaved him, popped corn in his radiator, and brained him with the hood of his own car. Enter the robbers, who show up for an oil change, clean out the register, and head off, leaving a trail of oil that leads right to an office door. Inside, the boys find the car and the villains, mixing it up with 'em. Shemp does the Curly routine where he sticks one arm into the coat of one bad guy and wheels in a circle while he punches one guy and that guy punches the pal sharing the coat. Another baddie gets his head crushed in a vise—a favorite White torture. After Shemp cleans house, he knocks Moe and Larry out, then himself.

SLAP COUNT: 54
EYE POKES: 2
CONKING HEADS: 1

A Snitch in Time,

1950. With Jean Willes. Written by Elwood Ullman. Produced by Hugh McCollum. Directed by Edward Bernds.

Opens with a sign: "Ye Olde Furniture Shoppe, Antiques Made While U-Waite." The Stooges are furniture makers, and in an opening scene that seems more appropriate to Jules White than Bernds (who eschewed the violence), Shemp holds a beam while answering a phone, turning it to conk Moe and hurtling him face-first into the moving blade of a table saw. Then Larry uses a door plane on Moe's head, with Moe returning the favor with interest (Moe tears out chunks of Larry's hair, tells him, "Here, go stuff a mattress"). Shemp gets a glob of glue in Moe's eye, sealing it shut. The boys remedy that with the help of a hammer and chisel, a stunt that sends Moe back into the saw blade, this time posterior-first. Hired by a woman to do work, they meet boarders Jerry

A Snitch in Time, 1950.

and Steve, who, as most boarders in Stooge shorts happen to be, are bank robbers. After numerous mishaps mixing furniture stain with lunch, the boys turn on the radio and get the description of the robbers who stole $50,000 from Hendrick Jewelry, with a $5,000 reward offered. Of course, the mugs are right behind them, and the rest of the short is a dizzying battle, ending with the woman burning her bank robber boarders with a hot iron.

SLAP COUNT: 19

Three Arabian Nuts,

1951. With Philip Van Zandt, Vernon Dent, Dick Curtis, Wesley Bly. Written by Elwood Ullman. Produced by Hugh McCollum. Directed by Edward Bernds.

Opens with a sign: "Superior Warehouse and Storage Co." The Stooges take inventory of precious dishes, with the expected disastrous results. After breaking most of the items, burning themselves with coffee and a hot iron, Shemp finds a lamp with a genie inside and wishes for "a new suit, something sharp." Two killers want the lamp, and when the Stooges drop off the stuff at the home of John Bradley (Dent), the expected battle ensues. The Stooges win, and end up being fed grapes by beautiful women while the bad guys sit tied up, thanks to the dark-skinned genie the Stooges condescendingly call "Amos."

SLAP COUNT: 3
CONKING HEADS: 1

while the boys sleep, and the trio is dispatched to get him back from the Folger Apts. on 212 10th Street. Turns out the father's not such a bad guy, and after the boys get their toes hammered by the tot, the husband and wife see each other and immediately hug. As they cry happily, Junior does a headstand to make them stop.

SLAP COUNT: 23
EYE POKES: 2 (another 1 blocked)
MEMORABLE LINE: Shemp: "Eureka!" Moe: "You don't smell so good either."

Baby Sitters Jitters, 1951.

130.

Baby Sitters Jitters,

1951. With Lynn Davis, David Windsor, Myron Healey, Margie Liszt. Story and screenplay by Felix Adler. Produced and directed by Jules White.

The boys, in an effort to stave off eviction, learn to become baby-sitters. First job, they enter the woman's home and find the baby sucking on the barrel of a loaded handgun, a gag that doesn't age as well over time as say, the eye poke. Shemp fires the gun, creating a new hair part for Moe. The woman fears Junior will be kidnapped by her estranged husband. One wonders why anyone would want Junior, other than to check his scalp for the inscription "666." The little brat is a ton of trouble and only calms down when Shemp stands on his head. The kid does indeed get swiped

131.

Don't Throw That Knife,

1951. With Jean Willes, Dick Curtis. Written by Felix Adler. Produced and directed by Jules White.

Opens with the familiar disclaimer "Any Resemblance Between the Three Stooges and Regular Human Beings, Whether Living or Dead, Is a Dirty Shame." Actually, the disclaimer might have read: "It's downhill from here." Because from this point on, we see a steady regurgitation of material that begins with borrowed concepts refilmed with Shemp in the role Curly played. As the short subjects department continued to operate on tighter and tighter margins, whole filmed scenes from earlier shorts turn up in later ones, with the flimsiest of plots to explain the old footage.

Here the boys are census takers who find their way into the home of a woman with a husband who's a prestidigitator ("someone who makes things disappear"). "I got an uncle who makes things disappear," says Shemp. "Is he a magician?" "No, a kleptomanic." Shemp is whacked and falls through one of three fun-house mirrors. After about a solid minute spent as Moe and Larry size themselves up in the mirrors, the wife reveals that her husband is insanely jealous, and if he finds them, he'll kill them. From here, the short borrows gags and story lines from the 1942 short *What's the Matador*. Shemp, hiding under a bed, is mistaken by the man for his wife, who has left the room. That's until he works his way up her forearm and finds a preponderance of manly hair. Then it becomes the Stooges fleeing the knife-throwing guy. He winds up pulling out an machine-gun-like device that fires eggs. After getting pelted with the hen fruit, the Stooges flee down a hallway. Stopping to grab scooters, they escape.

SLAP COUNT: 9
CONKING HEADS: 1

With wide-eyed Emil Sitka in Scrambled Brains, 1951.

Scrambled Brains,

1951. With Babe London, Emil Sitka, Vernon Dent. Story and screenplay by Felix Adler. Produced and directed by Jules White.

Opens with a sign: "Croackers Sanitarium Under Management of Doctors—Hart-Burns and Belcher." Moe and Larry pace worriedly as Shemp is about to be discharged, free of halluci-

nations. He's hardly cured, as he introduces them to Nurse Nora, a woman he describes as having "eyes like stars, a shape like Venus, and teeth like pearls." She's an oversize toothless hag, and Moe and Larry cringe. "Hey, you know, I think she's uglier than you," Larry tells Moe. Before they can throw a net over Shemp, he asks the hag to marry him. They go through a humorous checkup from Dr. Gezundheit (Sitka in Coke-bottle glasses). Shemp's advised to take piano lessons, and plays very well, because there are four hands playing the keys in his hallucinatory state. They take him back to the loony bin and make a call from the lobby. The trio crowds into the booth with Vernon Dent, who holds a sack of groceries. It's a hysterical sight, trying to make a phone call in the overstuffed booth, with the boys ending up in a fight with the guy. Moe unscrews the overhead lightbulb, sticks it in Dent's mouth, and hits him from above and below to break it. The booth tips over, and the boys get ready for Shemp's wedding to Nora. She enters, absolutely putrid in her wedding dress, and in walks her father (Dent). The

Stooges are pummeled, and when Dent looks to finish them off, Nora intercedes. "Hold it, Pa, I'm savin' this one for me." She carries Shemp like a sack of flour over her shoulder and out the door. He hits his head and apparently comes to his senses, because he cries out for Moe and Larry to rescue him from the hag.

SLAP COUNT: 58 (42 come in one Shemp frenzy)
EYE POKES: 1

Merry Mavericks,

1951. With Don Harvey, Marian Martin, Paul Campbell.
Produced by Hugh McCollum.
Written and directed by Edward Bernds.

Short opens with Wanted poster of the Stooges, but typical of their low ambitions, the crime is vagrancy, with a reward posted of fifty cents, or three for a dollar. After seeing the poster, Shemp asks what vagrancy is. Larry: "Take a flower that smells nice, that's vagrancy." The boys bail and head to Peaceful Gulch, a town blazing with cowboys and gunfire. The stock footage is most reminiscent of *Punchy Cowpunchers,* but the story line is a direct lift from the 1943 Curly short *Phony Express,* where the Wanted for Vagrancy bit was first used. A couple of nervous bankers hoping to scare off the bad guys and save the contents of their bank safe take the Stooge photo and put it in the paper, explaining that the three are famous marshals arriving to clean up the town. Actually,

the Stooges hope to do just that—but want janitor jobs. Shemp's boast that "we aim to do a little cleaning up around here" is misinterpreted, and the boys are soon dodging lead volleys. Soon we meet Clarence Cassidy, an aw-shucks kind of clumsy cowboy hero (once again *Punchy Cowpunchers* is the inspiration). The Stooges hide out, and once the bad guys enter costumed to exploit a legend about the ghost of a scalped Indian chief, Shemp brains them with an ax. The bold Clarence enters when the deed is done and promptly faints when he sees a trickle of blood on the mouth of one of the bad guys. Though it's necessary for the bit, it's unusual to see blood, since it goes against Stooge policy that despite the life-threatening violence that happens in every minute of every short, no one sustains any permanent injuries.

SLAP COUNT: 5

The Tooth Will Out,

1951. With Margie Liszt, Vernon Dent. Produced by Hugh McCollum. Written and directed by Edward Bernds.

The Stooges are having trouble holding down jobs again, and open the short being tossed out of the Dainty Dolly Dish Co. A second job as dishwashers at the Vesuvius Ravioli Co. leads to an equally spirited firing, as the restaurateur chases them down the block. They duck into an office and are faced with Vernon Dent, who thinks they're enrolling in his dental school, which turns out practitioners in one week for a four-dollar tuition. The boys, after manufacturing a set of choppers appropriate for a werewolf, graduate but are encouraged to head west—far west. They wind up in Coyote Pass, where the short strays into territory later mined for terror in the Dustin Hoffman movie *Marathon Man*. As Shemp puts on his now familiar Coke-bottle lenses to drill a cavity, he grinds the drill into a patient's skull and jackhammers his dental work until smoke pours out of the poor guy's head. Then they go to work on the sheriff, who killed the last dentist for sub-par service. The boys are using a *Practical Dentistry* handbook, but Shemp mistakenly gets his instruction from an amateur carpentry book and the sheriff has his chest sanded and his head varnished. He's not happy, and when they pull the wrong tooth, he fills them with lead.

SLAP COUNT: 8

Hula-La-La,

1951. With Jean Willes, Kenneth MacDonald, Emil Sitka, Joy Windsor. Written by Edward Bernds. Produced and directed by Hugh McCollum.

Opens with a shot of the gate for the B.O. Pictures Corp., Stage 19. Three dancing girls are hoofing it up, with Larry on piano. Shemp is a dance instructor. "Hit it, egghead," he barks as Larry leads him into a god-awful number. In comes studio head Baines (Sitka), whose company

Hula-La-La, 1951.

is failing. For reasons that aren't clear, the boys are sent to the South Seas to get the cooperation of the natives for a film that will save the studio. There they meet a witch doctor. In a case of miscasting, the silver-tongued Kenneth MacDonald is the shrunken-head-collecting savage witch doctor, and he has designs on the craniums of the boys. He also has designs on marrying the chief's daughter. After some clever shenanigans involving Shemp hiding under a bed and being attacked by alligators, the boys have a lengthy encounter with a four-armed Asian statue which guards a crate of hand grenades and slaps the boys silly until a well-placed eye poke thwarts her. The doc, practicing his head-chopping abilities, pounds the crate and is blown to bits, the short ending as Shemp teaches the natives to dance in his odd manner.

SLAP COUNT: 52
EYE POKES: 1

Pest Man Wins,

1951. With Margie Liszt, Nanette Bordeaux, Vernon Dent, Emil Sitka. Written by Felix Adler. Produced and directed by Jules White.

Essentially a remake of the classic Curly short *Ants in the Pantry*, a woman pastry maker who is out to impress the restaurant owners' association with a dinner party is suddenly plagued by pests—planted by the Stooges. The boys aren't doing well in their pest removal service and plant ants, mice, and other critters in the house, showing up just as the pests are discovered by the horrified homeowner. The boys are dressed in tuxes so they won't be detected by guests. "They must not know what you're doing," she warns. "That's a cinch, lady, we don't know what we're doing either," Larry assures her. From there, the short builds nicely as cats are caught in the piano, a guest with a mouse down his back does a spirited dance, and the butler (Sitka) admonishes the boys not to steal the silver, then drops the pieces he himself has pilfered. White added about the only thing missing from the earlier classic—a massive pie fight which ends when the homeowner brains the boys with Ruthian swings of a baseball bat, then watches as the cats lick pie off their unconscious faces.

SLAP COUNT: 11
EYE POKES: 2
CONKING HEADS: 1
PIES THROWN: 31

A Missed Fortune, 1952.

A Missed Fortune,

1952. With Nanette Bordeaux, Vivian Mason, Vernon Dent. Story by Searle Kramer. Screenplay by Jack White. Produced and directed by Jules White.

Another remake, this time of the 1938 short *Healthy, Wealthy, and Dumb*. Shemp works on entries for a slogan contest that could win him $10,000. It leads to an amusing bit in which Moe confuses glue for syrup on his hotcakes—Larry finds that boiling water works wonders in unsealing a glued mouth. Shemp accidentally wins the Mystery Motor Jackpot Contest. Asked to name the mystery motorcar engine, Shemp responds that his "bunion aches," and it's close enough to the Bunyan Eight answer to land the boys $50,000. They're next seen at the Hotel Costa Plente, where the manager is admonishing them not to mess up the Henry VIII bed or the delicate vase. The bed is destroyed when Shemp mistakes the canopy for a bunk. As happened in the first short, three ladies next door plan to fleece the boys of their money but don't get too far. After Moe destroys the Ming vase, the boys get a telegram describing their prize money. Minus the regular deductions—$30,000 for federal tax, $15,000 for state tax, $3,000 for unemployment, $1,900 for Social Security, and $95.15 for city tax—the boys are left with $4.85 in a letter signed by A. Gyper. The boys try not to let the manager know they're broke. "These figures stagger me," says Moe, and the manager replies, "So will my bill." The girls come calling and the boys think they're the hotel private investigators. After getting doused twice with water, the girls drop the decorum and brain the Stooges with champagne bottles. Blaming Shemp for their woes, Moe and Larry come up with their own slogan: "Roses are red, violets are blue, you crush his skull, I'll break him in two." Shemp ducks, and they brain each other with the bottles.

SLAP COUNT: 21
EYE POKES: 5 (another 1 blocked)
CONKING HEADS: 2

138.

Listen, Judge,

1952. With Kitty McHugh, Vernon Dent, Emil Sitka. Written by Elwood Ullman. Produced by Hugh McCollum. Directed by Edward Bernds.

Short opens in the courtroom, with a judge (Dent) reprimanding two cops for holding the Stooges on vagrancy charges (the boys certainly are recidivists, since those charges keep cropping up). The reason? Moe wears a sign: "Jiffy Fix. We repare everything, it's done in a flash for very small cash." The judge feels they have visible means of support, though he is concerned about Shemp's belief that he is a chicken. The boys then find work fixing a doorbell, with the usual results:

Listen, Judge, 1952.

Larry locates a wire, tears it through the wall of a posh home, and Moe, tugging on the other side, gets pulled completely through from one room to the other by Larry and Shemp. This time they think he's a gopher and brain him with hammers. Punishment follows. After moving a bookcase to cover the damage, the boys fill the homeowner's sudden need for a butler, cook, and waiter (the real ones have quit because of the Stooges' misdeeds). Shemp does things with a turkey that would make Julia Child cringe, and Larry passes out hors d'oeuvres, tipping guests to the ongoing kitchen carnage, "I just got a flash from the kitchen. You better stock up on these." Turns out they're working at the home of the judge who freed them. He doesn't remember until a deflated cake the Stooges have pumped up with gas explodes, and his wife pulls out the Jiffy Fixers sign from behind a curtain. The judge pulls a gun off the wall and fills them full of lead as the boys dive out the window.

SLAP COUNT: 5

MEMORABLE LINE: When the judge suggests institutionalizing Shemp because he thinks he's a chicken, Larry answers: "We can't, we need the eggs."

Corny Casanovas,

1952. With Connie Cezan. Written by Felix Adler. Produced and directed by Jules White.

The boys do housework and muse that their days doing chores will end once they get hitched. It's just as well, because Shemp's decision to pound a nail into the wall using the butt of a loaded handgun gives Moe a new hair part, and an attempt to reupholster a couch ends with Moe's butt full of tacks. He then swallows a bunch more. "The tacks won't come out," says Larry. "The taxes went in, maybe they're income taxes." Larry uses a magnet to extract them. Soon we get to the point of the short. The boys are in love with the same gold-digging blonde, who gets visited by each, takes a ring, and pits the boys against one another for her affections. There is spirited battle between the boys as the woman leaves after being nailed with a cake, with Shemp playing "she loves me, she loves me not" with chunks of hair from Larry's oft-abused scalp.

SLAP COUNT: 15
EYE POKES: 3
MEMORABLE LINE: Shemp, after braining Moe, poetically asks forgiveness: "Gee, Moe, I'm sorry, Moe, what mo' can a fellow say, that's all there is, there ain't no mo'." Moe, unmoved, uses a bucket to exact revenge.

He Cooked His Goose, 1952.

asking for a date, even though she's engaged to Shemp. After Larry eats a golf ball he's mistaken for an egg and then breaks his nose on the carpet slipping on it, Larry plans his revenge from his office in a pet shop. Moe surfaces, pummeling Larry because his wife had the Christmas card "Merry Xmas, Larry, Your Pet Man." He convinces Moe he's innocent and gets a brainstorm. When Shemp visits to tell Larry to stay away from his girl, Larry gets him a job modeling underwear—sending him to Moe's wife's house. Larry sends Shemp's girl to find him two-timing, but the ruse backfires and Larry winds up getting shot by Moe in a fairly clever switcheroo.

SLAP COUNT: 8
EYE POKES: 1
CONKING HEADS: 1

141.

Gents in a Jam,
1952. With Kitty McHugh, Emil Sitka, Dani Sue Nolan,
Mickey Simpson. Produced by Hugh McCollum.
Written and directed by Edward Bernds.

140.

He Cooked His Goose,
1952. With Mary Ainslee, Angela Stevens, Theila Darin.
Written by Felix Adler. Produced and
directed by Jules White.

A gorgeous blonde named Millie eats hard-boiled eggs as Larry enters, clearly on the prowl. He's

The boys are painters, and as soon as the landlady who hired them says, "These furnishings are worth a pretty penny, I wouldn't want anything to happen to them," you know what's coming. Massive destruction and an electrocution involving a radio result. The landlady's about to evict them. She hesitates when they mention that their uncle Finius is visiting and that Shemp is the sole heir to his $6-million fortune. A neighbor comes to borrow a cup of sugar. She's the wife of Rocky Duncan, world's strongest man. Naturally, they accidentally tear her dress off, putting her in their pajamas and incurring the wrath of Rocky. Originally offering to tear their telephone book in half, he wants to do the same to them once he discovers his wife in a state of undress. When Rocky gives Shemp a backbreaking hold that no chiropractor would recommend, the landlady drops the tough guy with a right hook, knocking out his teeth. Then she goes in to visit Finius, who, it turns out, is her long-lost love. So the Stooges lose the fortune and get chased by Rocky, who plows over Uncle Finius, who muses, "All I wanted was a quiet visit."

SLAP COUNT: 12

Three Dark Horses,

1952. With Kenneth MacDonald, Ben Welden.
Story and screenplay by Felix Adler.
Produced and directed by Jules White.

Opens with sign at campaign headquarters: "Hammond Egger for President." (Not to be confused with Mrs. Hammond Eggerly, who ran the Theatrical Apts. and rented a room to the Stooges in the 1936 short *A Pain in the Pullman.*) Crooked campaign manager Bill Wick has a problem: three delegates know that the candidate is a bad egger,

and they need three replacements, "three delegates who are too dumb to think and who'll do what we tell them. Now, where do we find such guys?" On cue, the Stooges enter to clean up the office. After they destroy it, vacuum up campaign literature and the tupe of Wick's assistant, the boys are designated delegates. Once there, the boys change their vote. "Good thing we found out that Hammond Egger is a crook. Wait'll they find out we're not voting for him," says Moe. Instead, they're behind Abel Lamb Stewer, who's a real lamb, sporting the slogan "Don't Be a Muttonhead! Vote

Three Dark Horses, 1952.

for Abel for President." After yet another episode in which a parrot flies into the carcass of a bird they're about to eat, the boys indeed turn the election by changing horses in favor of the lamb. They are attacked by the campaign managers. The Stooges end up knocking them unconscious into a partly filled bathtub and decide to bathe as long as they're in there.

SLAP COUNT: 9
EYE POKES: 5 (another 1 blocked)
CONKING HEADS: 1
PIES THROWN: 1

143.

Cuckoo on a Choo Choo,

1952. With Patricia Wright, Victoria Horne. Written by
Felix Adler. Produced and directed by Jules White.

Opens with a shot of the side of a railroad car, the Penciltucky RR Co. Shemp and Larry are inside, and a radio report that a railroad car has been stolen can be heard (it's obviously Moe's voice). Inside, Larry wants to marry a woman, who won't "I do" until her older sister marries Shemp, a drunk who sleeps with a Do Not Disturb sign on him. Shemp would rather drink than romance, and each time he takes a belt, we hear a noise similar to the one Larry heard each time he thought of his romantic nemesis Shemp in *He Cooked His Goose.* Moe's a railroad investigator about to bust them all, but he has eyes for Roberta, the girl who wants to marry Shemp. This is one of the oddest Stooge shorts in the bunch, with Shemp hallucinating about a large woman dressed in a canary outfit, and Moe and Shemp getting into a tremendous battle. Shemp gets Moe's electric razor down his back, and it renders him an electric kisser, making the girls want him more than ever. Shemp only has eyes for his imaginary canary and follows her out a closed door which she disappears through. He, of course, walks right into the door.

SLAP COUNT: 25
EYE POKES: 2
CONKING HEADS: 7

Up in Daisy's Penthouse, 1953.

144.

Up in Daisy's Penthouse,

1953. With Connie Cezan, John Merton, Jack Kenny.
Story by Clyde Bruckman. Screenplay by Jack White.
Produced and directed by Jules White.

This is essentially a remake of the 1937 Curly short *Three Dumb Clucks,* in which the Stooges are dispatched by their mother to stop their rich father's plans to wed a chippie. Last time it was Curly who played a dual role as son and dad. Shemp takes double duty here. Mom wakes the boys to show them the newspaper headline about the pending wedding. "Now that I'm old, your father has divorced me," she says. Cut to Shemp, with gray hair and sideburns, cooing with his young bride-to-be. She's the former chorus girl Daisy Flowers, who calls him Popsy Wopsy and is obviously after his newfound fortune garnered when he struck oil on his old farm. Aside from recycling the theme, the Stooges repeat some vintage bits, like when their father lends them clothes to watch him get hitched. Shemp, mistaking a spot of sunlight on his pants for a stain, wears a hole right through with cleaning fluid. Larry, trying to remove a thread from Moe's jacket, unravels all the stitching, shredding his coat. The boys overhear Daisy's real boyfriend go over a plan to bump off the old man Shemp as soon as he's hitched, leading to an amusing bit in which they drop Shemp down an elevator shaft, only to run into his father—a virtual clone once he shaves the sideburns and gets his hair dyed black. The comedy is essentially a direct lift from the original. The boys end up shimmying up a flagpole on the penthouse and are dropped off, bouncing off an awning and dropping onto a guy stuck in wet cement. It's the elder Shemp, who has Durante's nose and says, "I'm mortified."

SLAP COUNT: 15
EYE POKES: 2

145.

Booty and the Beast,

1953. With Kenneth MacDonald, Vernon Dent. Story by Felix Adler. Screenplay by Jack White. Produced and directed by Jules White.

This is a most interesting short, in that it shows a marked decline in originality and an increasing reliance on scenes plucked right from the old shorts. Jules White was faced with tightening margins as theaters became reluctant to feature the shorts, but he still had to crank out his quotas. With a growing reliance on his brother Jack as screenwriter, he did it by rehashing old shorts. At the time, who'd have known the original shorts would hold up so well in history and invite comparison? When White began pillaging the old shorts for minutes of vintage footage, it's likely that movie audiences didn't even realize that they were seeing recycled footage.

The short begins as a burglar trying to enter a house is interrupted by the backfiring car of the Stooges. They're conned by the thief (MacDonald) and not only break into the house but actually blow the safe for him. He leaves, but they know he's getting on a train. They board one, and suddenly it's like they've gone back six years. They walk up a row of seats, looking for the guy, and happen upon a man sleeping with a hat over his face. They pull it up, and it's Curly. Now, this short was released a year after Curly died. It's stock footage from *Hold That Lion,* the 1947 short that was the second made by Shemp at a time when Columbia execs were still hopeful that Curly would recover enough from his stroke to return to the shorts. In that short, the boys pursued Icabod Slipp, the executor of their estate who ran off with their funds. It's not even the only time the Slipp footage will be reused. In fact, the front end of that short will be used in the very next short. Here the boys recover the loot, with fresh footage shot and inserted to imply the boys will return the money. Then they get egg facials, giving Shemp a hen-fruit bath.

SLAP COUNT: 17
EYE POKES: 2
CONKING HEADS: 2

146.

Loose Loot,

1953. With Kenneth MacDonald, Tom Kennedy. Story by Felix Adler. Screenplay by Jack White. Produced and directed by Jules White.

The short opens with the door reading "Cess, Poole & Drayne Attorneys at Law." It's footage lifted directly from *Hold That Lion,* when the boys are told that their inheritance from the Ambrose Rose estate is in the hands of Icabod Slipp of Slipp, Tripp & Skipp Investment Brokers. The old footage continues as the boys head for Slipp's offices with subpoenas to get their money back, but not knowing what he looks like. He beats the daylights out of each and tears up their documents. Except this time, instead of heading for a train, he's off to the theater, where he's a producer. The boys find a poster, "Honest Icabod Slipp Theatrical Enterprises," at 412 Knish Bldg. There the boys engage in a hallway chase, then Slipp's head crashes through a door, with the boys keeping him there by placing a chair back over his head, which keeps him from moving. They brain him in a variety of ways. A sword fight ends with Shemp stabbing him in the butt. When he tosses his satchel in the air, a painting of Napoleon comes to life. The Frenchman grabs the satchel and tries to run, but the Stooges enter the frame like they're storming the Bastille. They flatten the Frenchie and recover their loot.

SLAP COUNT: 26
EYE POKES: 1
CONKING HEADS: 1

147.

Tricky Dicks,

1953. With Benny Rubin, Connie Cezan, Ferris Taylor, Phil Arnold, Murray Alper. Story and screenplay by Felix Adler. Produced and directed by Jules White.

Opens at a police station, where Larry and Moe are detectives answering phones. "You say you don't know what to do about a woman being annoyed by a man with a wooden leg by the name of Smith? Well, find out the name of his other leg," Moe barks. "My sister was engaged to a guy with a wooden leg," Larry says helpfully. "What happened?" "She broke it off." "The engagement?" Moe asks. "Nah, the leg," says Larry. "Some sister," Moe understates. Shemp brings in a female suspect who immediately glares at Larry, giving him a face slap worthy of Moe. "How dare you look like someone I hate," she shouts. Shemp gives her the third degree: "Where were you born?" "In bed. I wanted to be near my mother," she replies, pulling a line delivered in the 1951

Tricky Dicks, 1953.

short *Don't Throw That Knife,* when the boys were census takers.

The boys are drafted into solving the Ambrose Rose murder case, and they've got twenty-four hours to find the killer. They've got two major suspects, and the short from here has some clever lines. Moe: "You found a dead horse on Ticonderoga Street. How do you spell Ticonderoga? You don't know either? Well, drag him over to First Street." Shemp: "Release that guy that stole eleven bottles of whiskey. I know he's guilty but the DA says we can't make a case out of eleven bottles." As they continue grilling suspects, a guy Moe keeps kicking out finally establishes himself as the killer, and he begins shooting up the police station. It's a heckuva pistol, because he fires off eighty-two shots without reloading. Finally, the killer's conked by a bowling ball, and a monkey takes over the shooting. Shemp, thinking he's been shot, hams it up with a dramatic death scene. He takes a belt of Old Panther and springs a leak.

SLAP COUNT: 29
EYE POKES: 1 (another 1 blocked)

Spooks!,

1953. This features a new opening with the silhouetted heads of the Stooges. With Philip Van Zandt, Tom Kennedy, Norma Randall. Story and screenplay by Felix Adler. Produced and directed by Jules White.

It's the Stooges' first 3-D film and one of the earlier efforts in the genre. While it seems unusual

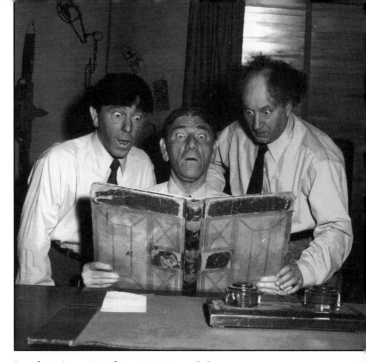

From *Spooks!,* one of two Stooge shorts done in 3-D.

that Columbia would invest in 3-D when it was clear they were tightening budgets on the short, the result here is a memorable batch of sight gags and a lot of fun. Opens on the door (with a typo) "Super Slueth Detective Agency. Divorce Evidence Manufactured to Your Order Don't Knock Walk In (Also Trap Criminals)." A guy walks in as the boys sleep. He introduces himself as George B. Bopper, which leads Shemp into a jive-talking riff about being a bebopper, ending when Moe bops him with the point of a fountain pen. The boys agree to help find Bopper's daughter and come up with an unusual cover: they give away pie samples at night. Turns out they find their way into an eerie house, where the girl is about to have her brain transplanted into the head of a gorilla. All of the camera techniques are done head-on to exploit the 3-D aspects, including an eye poke (with the fingers poking into the camera) and a doctor shooting a hypodermic needle into the screen. After much chasing around the haunted house, there is a nine-pie salvo (straight at the camera), and the bad guys get brained by the gorilla, who ends the short by pelting the Stooges with pies.

SLAP COUNT: 12
EYE POKES: 2
CONKING HEADS: 2
PIES THROWN: 13

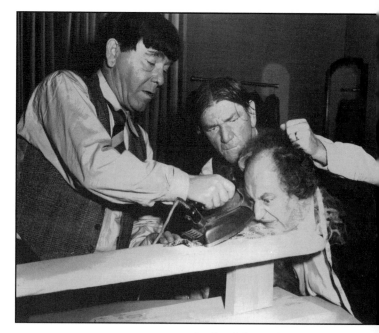

Rip, Sew & Stitch, 1953.

149.

Pardon My Backfire,

1953. With Benny Rubin, Frank Sully, Phil Arnold. Story and screenplay by Felix Adler. Produced and directed by Jules White.

The second and final 3-D effort begins with a tenth-anniversary celebration, of the engagement variety. Just as in the last short, the Stooges use every opportunity for straight-at-the-camera gags. During dinner, Moe tells Shemp: "Do you like asparagus?" "Love 'em." "Well, here's a couple of tips." Two fingers close in toward the camera. Followed by a meat fork, flames, oil, knives, and other projectiles in a story line about the Stooges operating a gas station and being menaced by escaped convicts who stole a car and need to be corralled. A humorous effort, even if watched without those goofy red-and-blue-framed 3-D glasses.

SLAP COUNT: 8
EYE POKES: 1
PIES THROWN: 1

150.

Rip, Sew & Stitch,

1953. Story by Felix Adler. Screenplay by Jack White. Produced and directed by Jules White.

Opens with the storefront "Pip Boys Larry Moe & Shemp. Unaccustomed Tailors. Men's Furnishings. New and Second Hand Clothes Cheep. Cleaning Pressing Altercations." If you're keeping score at home, you'll recall this is the opening of the 1947 short *Sing a Song of Six Pants*. Once again the boys are behind in payments and have a creditor's letter for the overdue amount of $321.86 from the Skin & Flint Finance Corp., I. Fleecem, President. The bank robber Terry Hargan's on the loose and the boys want the reward.

When a cop-fleeing Hargan sneaks in and hides among the mannequins, he leaves behind the combination to a safe. Most of the short is the old footage, but there are some fairly clever and gloriously violent scenes in the insert shots. Larry looks the same, as does Shemp, but Moe's getting bags under his eyes big enough to have Samsonite labels on them. We then return to the old footage, for the same ending.

SLAP COUNT: 26
EYE POKES: 2

Bubble Trouble,

1953. With Emil Sitka, Christine McIntyre. Story by Felix Adler. Screenplay by Jack White. Produced and directed by Jules White.

From now on, when Jack White is the writer and a story credit goes to another scribe, you can bet there is recycled footage involved. Here the short opens with a drugstore window: "Cut Throat Drug Store Everything from a Needle to a Battleship." It's footage taken directly from the 1947 short *All Gummed Up,* and the boys are told by their cranky old landlord that they're being tossed out to accommodate the Pinchpenny Market. The boys once again conjure up a vitamin that turns his old hag of a wife into Christine McIntyre (my, she is aging wonderfully), and once again she bakes a celebration cake in which gum is mistaken for marshmallows, making them tough to swallow. The only original footage comes when the landlord takes his share of the medicine. In the original, he shrank. Here he turns into a talking gorilla. And he's not happy about it. In fact, he grabs Moe, pounds his head into the ground, and spins his foot around in circles in moves that will be later duplicated in Steven Seagal films. Larry hits the chimp with chloroform and the gorilla pounds Moe's head, giving the head Stooge a Frankenstein-like flattop skull. Luckily, Shemp is able to pound it back to normal shape with a hammer. Shemp has the idea to keep the talking gorilla in a cage to make them rich, but Larry and Moe agree he needs a mate. While Shemp is the intended target of the medicine, Moe gets it, and ends the short in a close-up, mugging for the camera with his best chimp impression.

SLAP COUNT: 4
EYE POKES: 1
CONKING HEADS: 1
PIES THROWN: 1

Goof on the Roof,

1953. With Frank Mitchell, Maxine Gates. Story and screenplay by Clyde Bruckman. Produced and directed by Jules White.

The Stooges wear kiddie pajamas with bunnies on them in a bizarre opening to the short. Their pal Bill is getting married and they're going to have to move. He's having a TV delivered, and the boys decide to install the antenna as a gift. Big mistake.

Goof on the Roof, 1953.

Income Tax Sappy,

1954. With Margie Liszt, Benny Rubin, Nanette Bordeaux.
Story and screenplay by Felix Adler.
Produced and directed by Jules White.

This short is unusual in that most feature a series of mishaps in the kitchen or on an installation and repair job and then veer off in another direction. Here the boys are content to just destroy Bill's place. As well as his television, which they manage to completely gut. After Moe starts a fire within the wall and gets electrocuted in the process, Shemp gets on the roof with the antenna. His decision to nail it into the chimney leads to crumbled bricks. Undaunted, he nails it directly to the roof, collapsing the ceiling below him. Just in time for Bill to be carried over the threshold by his oversize bride, who tosses him off when she sees the mess she's supposed to live in. Bill responds by getting his gun and shooting his former pals, who end the short by dragging their smoking butts along the floor.

SLAP COUNT: 7
CONKING HEADS: 1

The boys argue with their sister over how to get money to buy a house. They decide that cheating on their income tax is most expedient. After mastering a formula in which Shemp claims eleven dependents—an ex-wife and ten bartenders—the boys go into the tax preparation business. After numerous mishaps, the boys are living the life of luxury, residing in a mansion, dapperly dressed in tuxedos. At a dinner party, they brag of making $100,000 last year, paying no taxes. When Moe counts his money, he crumbles up a fifty-dollar bill and tosses it. "Say, who put this measly fifty in with my thousands?" As they entertain, their clientele seem appreciative. "Not only are you good at evading taxes, you are wonderful hosts,"

Income Tax Sappy, 1954.

Larry battles a lobster bisque in Income Tax Sappy.

says an odd bearded man. After some fun at the dinner table—Larry does a variation on the Curly clam chowder routine when he attempts to eat lobster gumbo and loses a fight with a lobster claw—the bearded guy turns out to be an under-cover IRS agent. The Stooges are knocked onto burning cooktops and led away, their butts ablaze.

SLAP COUNT: 11
EYE POKES: 1
PIES THROWN: 1

Musty Musketeers,

1954. With Vernon Dent, Philip Van Zandt.
Story by Felix Adler. Screenplay by Jack White.
Produced and directed by Jules White.

A familiar opening establishes that the short is set in "Coleslaw-Vania, A Small Kingdom in Ye Old Country, Where Ye Men Are Men and Ye Women Are Glad of It." The boys are here to court maidens and go to the king for a blessing to marry. Suddenly, we're back in the 1948 short *Fiddlers Three,* where the boys are court jesters entertaining Old King Cole, whose daughter is kidnapped. The short is almost identical to the original, which makes one wonder why they'd bother to repackage it under another title. At least the ending is different. In the original, Murgatroyd the magician is thwarted in his plans to wed the princess after making her materialize in the magic box that he has skewered with swords. Once again he finds the Stooges inside. Last time the short ended when Murgatroyd's sexy assistant walked by and the entire group of men followed in her wake, entranced. Here the climax is a sword fight, with Shemp skewering fruit and giving the magician a fruity facial.

SLAP COUNT: 10
EYE POKES: 1
CONKING HEADS: 4

with Shemp on an examination table, the doctor telling him his bad leg is due to an enlarged vein. He draws a diagram of it and recommends they head on vacation out west. Then the villains believe the drawing is the map for a gold vein. Here we break into new footage when Nell, the buxom barmaid, enlists the boys to help her. In the original, her beau, the Arizona Kid, was imprisoned and set to be executed unless she married the evil Doc Barker. Now her sisters have been locked up. From there, the boys poison Doc Barker (fatally) and spring the girls. As they make their escape in a wagon, we cut to chase footage from the 1937 *Goofs & Saddles,* when Curly tossed pots to thwart the oncoming riders, whose mounts stepped in the pots and couldn't run. The boys escape when they feed bullets through a meat grinder, with a monkey taking over and blasting them (a gag also originated in *Goofs & Saddles,* though that earlier footage wasn't used here).

EYE POKES: 1

Pals and Gals,

1954. With Christine McIntyre, George Chesebro, Norman Willes. Story by Clyde Bruckman. Screenplay by Jack White. Produced and directed by Jules White.

The major innovation here is to marry footage from two older Stooge shorts and create a flimsy updated plot to bridge them. We begin with a straight pull from *Out West,* one of the more cleverly plotted Shemp shorts from 1947. It begins

Pals and Gals, 1954.

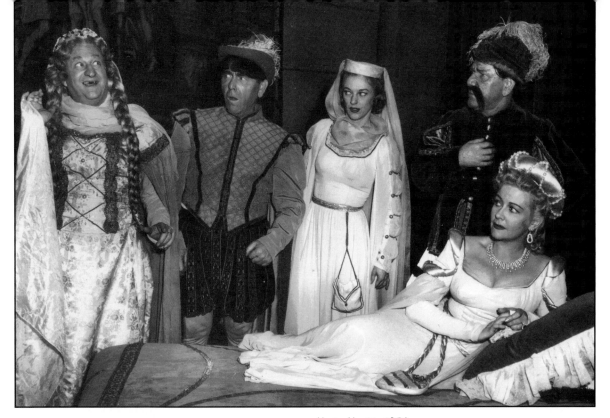

Knutzy Knights, 1954.

Knutzy Knights,

1954. With Jacques O'Mahoney, Christine McIntyre, Philip Van Zandt. Screenplay by Felix Adler. Produced and directed by Jules White.

The opening graphic tells us we're in trouble, plunging right into another regurgitated short: "In days of old—When Knights were Bold. The guys were hot, but the girls were cold." The boys are troubadors cheering up the princess, but when they playact in a skit about Larry (in drag), unable to marry the man she loves, the princess begins crying again. Turns out her father has pledged her hand in marriage to the Black Prince, while she wants to marry Cedric the blacksmith. From there, we slip back into original footage from *Squareheads of the Round Table,* in which the boys try to help Cedric—especially hearing of the prince's plan to kill the king and Cedric once he's married the princess so he can rule the kingdom. The Stooges once again save the day, staving off the blowing of the trumpets that will signal Cedric's beheading. They do this by tossing fruit into the instruments. When Cedric conks the bad guys, the king lets him marry his daughter. Once again the trumpeters blow and the boys are wearing fruit.

SLAP COUNT: 15
CONKING HEADS: 6

"Beneath This Monumental Stone Lies 80 Lbs. of Skin and Bone"; Moe's reads "Mama Loved Papa, Papa Loved Women, Mama Caught Papa with Two Girls in Swimmin' "—the boys brawl with the bad guys and eventually defeat them, winning the hands of the girls. They're serenaded by a god-awful rendition of "You're the flame in my heart that keeps a-burnin'."

SLAP COUNT: 8
EYE POKES: 1

Shot in the Frontier, 1954.

157.
Shot in the Frontier,
1954. Story and screenplay by Felix Adler. Produced and directed by Jules White.

After two straight shorts that were little more than patched-together oldies, this fresh one exhibits the cleverness and depth of plot most common in scripts penned by the comedy vet Adler. It's the Old West and three women wait on a porch for the Stooges, who gallop up on a hunched-over horse. The boys marry Ella, Della, and Stella. The bliss is short-lived because the Noonan Boys are out to kill them. After some clever *High Noon*–like footage of the Noonans looking for the Stooges and the boys looking to escape them, there's a shootout as the boys duck behind headstones at the outlet Diggs, Graves & Berry Undertakers, M. Balmer, Mgr. After the boys chuckle over the headstones they hide behind—Shemp's reads

158.
Scotched in Scotland,
1954. With Philip Van Zandt, Christine McIntyre, Charles Knight. Screenplay by Jack White. Produced and directed by Jules White.

Opens at the Wide Awake Detective School and the desk of O. U. Gonga, Dean (get it?). The boys have a private ceremony, garnering the lowest honors in school history. After some clever punishment delivered to the hand of Larry and nose of Shemp by a staple-wielding Moe, the trio is sent away by the dean, far away, to be detectives. They're sent all the way back to the 1948 short *The Hot Scots,* where most of the footage for this short originated. They arrive in Glenheather Castle. An earl needs them to watch the castle while he goes off to a clan meeting ("Oh, a clan bake," says Shemp). Ghosts are cleaning it out. The rest of the short is an almost incomprehensible mix of old and new footage. And some old gags, like the

Scotched in Scotland, 1954.

flying-parrot-in-the-skull routine. The ending is the same as the original, with a bagpipe-playing skeleton emerging from the liquor cabinet.

SLAP COUNT: 7
CONKING HEADS: 2

159.

Fling in the Ring,

1955. With Richard Wessel, Claire Carleton, Frank Sully. Screenplay by Jack White. Produced and directed by Jules White.

The short is a slight reworking of the inaugural 1947 Shemp effort, *Fright Night,* which featured the boys training Chopper Kane for a bout against Gorilla Watson, then being told to make sure he loses. Most of the footage is from that original short, with some new stuff, such as a shot in which a pug tells them, "Bozz sez Chopper has to lose or you end up in concrete kimonos." When Gorilla punches Moe and breaks his hand on a wall when Moe ducks, the boys are brought to a warehouse to be killed. They wind up in a chase scene that is pretty much verbatim from the original.

Sam White, the brother of Jack and Jules White, said that Jules was given little choice in

Fling in the Ring, 1955.

Fling in the Ring.

160.

Of Cash and Hash,

1955. With Christine McIntyre, Vernon Dent, Frank Lackteen, Kenneth MacDonald. Screenplay by Jack White. Produced and directed by Jules White.

After robbers knock off an armored car, the bad guys engage in a gun battle with the car guards. Stuck right in the middle are the Stooges. That leads to familiar footage of a squad car getting the call to look for robbers and finding the Stooges in a garbage can. Soon they're taking lie detector tests, and you know that we're right back into another 1948 short, this one *Shivering Sherlocks*. With a few scant insert shots, that short is presented almost in its entirety, with the boys operating the Elite Cafe and following one of the armored car thieves to a house where they capture the bad guys when Shemp drops large barrels on them.

SLAP COUNT: 14

reusing the footage. The entire exercise tired him out and frustrated him, and though he gamely hung around until Columbia chairman Harry Cohn died and Cohn's beloved short subjects department got shuttered, Jules was more than ready to hang it up and hunt and fish instead, where a repetitive exercise was palatable.

SLAP COUNT: 43
EYE POKES: 3
PIES THROWN: 2

161.

Gypped in the Penthouse,

1955. With Jean Willes, Emil Sitka. Story and screenplay by Felix Adler. Produced and directed by Jules White.

The sign outside reads "Woman Hater's Club 87." Inside, Shemp bumps into (literally) Larry and

Gypped in the Penthouse, 1955.

"There must be a way to get that ring without getting in trouble with the censors." Suddenly, there's a knock on the door and she reveals it's her husband (Moe). "I thought you were separated?" Shemp says. "We were, he was on a trip. That's separated, isn't it?" she replies. Back at the Woman Hater's Club, they meet up with Moe, who has become a member. They brawl and head for the street, where they bump into the woman and give her the business pretty good.

SLAP COUNT: 12
EYE POKES: 2

they have a belt of Old Panther (still distilled yesterday in good old Rotgut, Kentucky, according to the label). Larry recounts how he became a member, answering an ad for a handsome man (even though his face stops a clock and breaks a mirror). When Larry gives the girl a ring, Moe shows up and also proposes. When they brawl, Larry surprisingly gives Moe better than he gets. Shemp tells his story. After getting scalded in the kitchen of his girlfriend, Shemp wears her robe and serenades from the piano, looking all the world like Liberace right down to the candelabra. Complimented on his ivory tinkling, Shemp brags: "I play that in four sharps. I used to play it in five flats, but I got kicked out of the last one." The same gold-digging woman takes Shemp's ring. It falls into the piano and Shemp becomes intertwined in the strings. When the woman drops the ring down her cleavage, Shemp says:

162.

Bedlam in Paradise,

1955. With Vernon Dent, Philip Van Zandt, Sylvia Lewis.
Story by Zion Myers. Screenplay by Felix Adler.
Produced and directed by Jules White.

Another rip-off from an earlier short, *Heavenly Daze*. This time Shemp is depicted sick in bed with galloping hoof sounds coming from his heart. That means he's nearing the finish line. After Shemp swallows a thermometer, he indeed kicks the bucket but not before telling the boys they'd better behave or he will haunt them. Suddenly, we're being haunted by old footage, in which Shemp is told by his uncle Mortimer that he'll only get to heaven if he can reform his mates. There's insert footage of the devil, who tempts Shemp with a devilishly sexy woman named Helen Blazes, who beckons: "Why don't you come down and see us, we have some hot dances." They break into a full dance sequence, orchestra and everything, before Shemp regains his senses and returns to footage of the older shorts. (One amazing thing about the recycled footage is how the Stooges never really seemed to age, even though they are seven years older.) Shemp thwarts Moe and Larry's attempts to con a rich guy with their invention of a fountain pen that writes under whipped cream. He beats the devil, then wakes up on fire, just the way he did in the original short.

SLAP COUNT: 10
PIES THROWN: 1

Stone Age Romeos, 1955.

163.

Stone Age Romeos,

1955. With Emil Sitka, Virginia Hunter, Nancy Saunders, Dee Green. Story by Zion Myers. Screenplay by Felix Adler. Produced and directed by Jules White.

The sign reads "Museum of Natural History, B. Bopper Curator." The Stooges, who wear beards, listen as the curator appeals to them to find some cavemen. They study the familiar map of Jerkola, with such hot spots as Drop Dead Sea, Hot Sea Tot Sea, and Giva Dam, Canabeer, and Rigor Mortis. The boys are told they'll be paid $50,000, with another $25,000 if they find evidence of cavemen. Suddenly, we're back in another old short. This time it's 1948's *I'm a Monkey's Uncle*, where the boys are indeed cavemen getting ready to court women and battling off their boyfriends. At least in this one they've made a pretty good excuse for the old footage. They wind up showing it on a projector to B. Bopper, who's ecstatic they found the evidence he was looking for. While he goes out to get their money, Larry says, "Bopper will never suspect we made this picture in Hollywood and we were the cavemen." The curator then shoots them in their tails and himself in the foot.

SLAP COUNT: 7
EYE POKES: 2
CONKING HEADS: 1
MEMORABLE LINE: Shown a map and told this is the last known whereabouts of the dinosaur, Larry replies, "Go on, she's on television. I always watch Dinah Shore." A hard slap follows.

Wham Bam Slam!, 1955.

164.

Wham Bam Slam!,

1955. With Matt McHugh, Alyn Lockwood, Doria Revier, Wanda Perry. Story by Clyde Bruckman. Screenplay by Felix Adler. Produced and directed by Jules White.

Still another reworked short. Moe wakes up for breakfast lamenting there seems to be no cure for Shemp. Larry suggests a pal, Claude A. Quacker, who is a health restorer and adviser. After some fun in the kitchen with hotcakes (Shemp gets his wife's powder puff on his plate and gets even sicker when he confuses it with a hotcake), we cut to the 1948 short *Pardon My Clutch*. Shemp is doctored by the amateur, who pulls his tooth and sells them a lemon of a car for $900. There's new footage of Shemp soaking his feet in a barrel of live lobsters, but most of this is dated footage. The car falls apart. New footage has Moe ready to take the money out of Larry's hide because he introduced the friend. But Shemp says he's been cured by all the excitement. The same can't be said of the audience in this rather unexciting effort.

SLAP COUNT: 10
CONKING HEADS: 4

a whole new short, guess again. Instead, this segues into footage from the 1948 *Crime on Their Hands.* In that original, the Stooges were cub reporters trying to locate the gem. Here there's some new footage to make them detectives, with Shemp again swallowing the diamond. Last time, a gorilla was central to the plot, but here Shemp coughs up the gem himself, only to gobble it up again. Larry conks Shemp on the head and Moe begins drilling into his stomach while Larry attempts to saw off his neck.

SLAP COUNT: 9
EYE POKES: 1
CONKING HEADS: 1

Hot Ice, 1955.

Hot Ice,

1955. With Kenneth MacDonald, Christine McIntyre, Barbara Bartay. Story by Elwood Ullman. Screenplay by Jack White. Produced and directed by Jules White.

Starts with a legend, "Scotland Yard—Inspector McCormick," where the boys apply for jobs as "experienced yard men." The footage is straight from the 1948 short *The Hot Scots,* and when the boys get a case after a scrap of paper floats down from McCormick's desk to where they're picking up debris, the task is different from the original. Here they're out to find an American named Dapper, who's got the Punjab diamond. Lest you think this is the Stooges taking old footage to fuel

Blunder Boys,

1955. With Benny Rubin, Angela Stevens, Kenneth MacDonald. Story and screenplay by Felix Adler. Produced and directed by Jules White.

The intro is right out of *Dragnet,* and it's clever. Deadpanned, Moe, talking into the camera, shows his badge and says "Halliday"; Larry follows with his badge, saying "Terraday," with Shemp smiling and saying, "I'm St. Patrick's Day." Over the course of the short, that intro is repeated with Shemp changing it to Groundhog Day, New Year's Day, Christmas Day, and Independence Day. Short shows how they went from being war heroes—Larry, conked on the head, falls into a trance and knocks out a nest of machine guns—

Blunder Boys, 1955.

167.

Husbands Beware,

1956. With Maxine Gates, Lou Leonard, Dee Green, Christine McIntyre. Story by Clyde Bruckman. Screenplay by Felix Adler. Produced and directed by Jules White.

Moe and Larry marry two very large ladies who are Shemp's sisters. When the boys request a smooch, the oversize brides deck their husbands, just to show them who's boss. Into the kitchen they go, told to make a turkey. After some clever culinary bits in which the boys take a turkey and shave off the feathers barber style, the bird is marinated in turpentine and the coffee is laced with soap. "It's too good for those elephants we married," says Larry. The ladies don't appreciate the results. "Trying to poison us, why you no-good assassins," one says as the giants chase the boys out of the house. Next we are melded into the 1947 short *Brideless Groom,* where Shemp is a voice teacher and has seven hours to get married and inherit $500,000. The short is pretty much a verbatim lift, except in the end Moe tells Shemp that: his uncle Caleb isn't dead; he hasn't inherited $500,000; but he's married a hag just like Moe and Larry and now they're even. Shemp shoots at them as the short ends.

SLAP COUNT: 21
CONKING HEADS: 1

to detective wannabes at college. After graduating, they're assigned to solve the case of the Eel, a man who dresses like a woman and smokes cigars of the La Stinkadora brand. The boys botch the case, and in their last *Dragnet*-like intro, they're depicted as ditchdiggers. "The Eel gave us the slip but we got the gate," says Halliday as the short closes with the familiar *Dragnet* ending. Okay, maybe the short wasn't that good. Maybe at this point it's gratitude for seeing one that was original from beginning to end.

SLAP COUNT: 13
EYE POKES: 2

Creeps, 1956.

168.

Creeps,

1956. Story by Felix Adler. Screenplay by Jack White. Produced and directed by Jules White.

The boys are saying good night to their children—who are the Stooges, dressed in kiddie nighttime attire. The tots want a story, with knights, ghosts, and murders. It's an excuse to go back to a fairly straight run of the 1949 short *The Ghost Talks,* in which the spirit of a knight waits for Lady Godiva and urges the Stooges not to move him. When we cut back to the present, the kids aren't satisfied, but the dads get them to slumber—with the aid of hammers.

SLAP COUNT: 9
EYE POKES: 1

169.

Flagpole Jitters,

1956. With David Bond, Vernon Dent, Mary Ainslee. Story by Felix Adler. Screenplay by Jack White. Produced and directed by Jules White.

The boys sleep until a blonde in a wheelchair raps on the pipe and wants breakfast. It's the opening of the 1949 short *Hokus Pokus,* where the boys help the woman get ready to petition for a big check from an insurance adjuster. That time, the woman was conning the money, but here that story line is altered. New footage is inserted with the boys working at the Garden Theater putting up posters billing the great hypnotist Svengarlic. This time the hypnotist is masterminding a daring daylight robbery, and he hypnotizes the boys and sends them up on a flagpole to distract cops. In a mix of mostly old and some new footage, Svengarlic is knocked to the ground by a passerby, and the Stooges hang helplessly from the pole until it breaks. In the original, they thwarted the woman from collecting her insurance check when she sprang to her feet by surprise. Here they knock the robbers into the safe, catching the bandits and getting a reward so Mary can have that operation.

SLAP COUNT: 26
EYE POKES: 1 (another 1 blocked)
CONKING HEADS: 2

For Crimin' Out Loud, 1956.

For Crimin' Out Loud.

170.

For Crimin' Out Loud,

1956. With Christine McIntyre, Ralph Dunn, Emil Sitka. Story by Edward Bernds. Screenplay by Felix Adler. Produced and directed by Jules White.

Opens with the door of the "Miracle Detective Agency—If We Solve Your Crime It's a Miracle." The boys are summoned by a rich guy, and the rest of the short is almost uninterrupted play from the 1949 short *Who Done It?* The boys are chased by a hairy brute, Shemp is poisoned by Christine McIntyre and does some nifty floor work, and the boys solve the crime. In one chase scene, Moe can be seen limping down a hallway. Edward Bernds, who was responsible for the original, said that Moe often had accidents but didn't stop working as a result.

SLAP COUNT: 31
EYE POKES: 2
CONKING HEADS: 5

Rumpus in the Harem,

1956. With Vernon Dent, George Lewis. Story by Felix Adler. Screenplay by Jack White. Produced and directed by Jules White.

Opens in "The Orient—Where Men Are Men and Women Are Glad of It." The boys sleep, but when they wake Shemp, he's left a note. "You guys snore so loud I couldn't sleep so I have gone down to open the restaurant. Will see you later. If you don't get note let me know. I will write you another." Not likely. This is the first of the shorts in which they have good reason to use old footage. Shemp has died, and the boys and White once again are trying to fill their quota and keep Shemp in the rotation until they replace him the following year with Joe Besser, a contract player at Columbia. There's a flimsy story line in which a girl is set to be sold to a sultan unless they come up with money in three days. Then we're back to the 1949 short *Malice in the Palace,* with Hassan Ben Sober and Hafadollah conspiring to steal a diamond from Rootentooten's tomb. The occasional Stooge character actor Joe Palma takes Shemp's place in fresh footage, the little bit there is. Shemp's back is to the camera each time, and Moe and Larry handle most of the new story line. They wander into a harem and frolic a bit before they head out of a window with the gem. It must have been difficult for Moe and Larry to act in a short in which Moe's brother and their partner had just died, having to pretend he was still there. Clearly, to the vaudevillians, "The show must go on" was more than a cliché.

SLAP COUNT: 23
EYE POKES: 2
CONKING HEADS: 7

Hot Stuff,

1956. With Christine McIntyre, Emil Sitka, Philip Van Zandt. Story by Elwood Ullman. Screenplay by Felix Adler. Produced and directed by Jules White.

The second short to mix old footage with new insert shots that use the phony Shemp. Officials of the government of Anemia hold up the *Urania Daily Bladder,* which proclaims that Urania will have air supremacy because of Professor Sneed's super rocket formula. The boys sport beards, as government operatives for Urania's Department of Inferior. As they come in for their orders, Moe and Larry make time with two cuties in the office. Larry goes from smitten to bitten by the target of his affection. Moe gets his hand stapled and is impaled on a letter-holding spike for his trouble. They're told to work undercover to protect Professor Snead. "You will go to his house and pretend you are carpet layers." "I'm not that rugged," says Larry. Anemia? Rug layers? Well, sure, because we're about to go back in time to *Fuelin' Around,* where the Stooges were really rug layers who were mistaken for the prof—at a time when Shemp was alive and well.

From here, we get nearly the entire old short, with a few new flourishes. Once the officials of Anemia locate the real prof, the boys are told they're getting a last meal—"raw potatoes boiled in pure varnish, and head cheese garnished with nails, rusty nails." We can see Shemp, but again from the back as Joe Palma does his best to look like him. The boys knock out the captain of the guards, and we're back into the old short again, as they use their own rocket fuel to escape.

SLAP COUNT: 23
EYE POKES: 2
CONKING HEADS: 7

Scheming Schemers,

1956. With Christine McIntyre, Emil Sitka, Kenneth MacDonald, Dudley Dickerson. Story by Elwood Ullman. Screenplay by Jack White. Produced and directed by Jules White.

Opens on the Day and Nite Plumbers—We Never Sleep. Moe, reading a how-to-be-a-plumber book, answers the phone "Nite and Day Plumbers," switching the name just as he did the first time he delivered it, in the 1949 *Vagabond Loafers,* which was essentially a remake of the Curly classic *A Plumbing We Will Go.* In new footage, Sitka asks them to find an expensive ring he dropped in the bathroom basin, and please be quiet because he's unveiling an expensive Van Brocklin painting downstairs (old short). Moe finds the ring right off, but Larry drops it into the drain. Moe tries to stick him down the pipe. Outside, Shemp beeps the horn and carries in pipes. You don't see his face, because, of course, he died months before. There's a mix of footage, and the

Scheming Schemers, 1956.

insert gags are genuinely funny. They use the Niagara Falls routine. For the third time, the woman turns on the TV, sees footage of the falls, and then has a full force of water crash through the screen, flooding the living room. Kenneth MacDonald and Christine McIntyre steal the painting again, and this time Moe and Larry chase them into a dining room—for a massive pie fight. They catch the thief and Sitka mentions a reward. "Hey, won't Shemp be glad to hear this?" says Moe. "Hey, where is that puddinhead Shemp?" They look upward (a tribute to their fallen Stooge comrade?). We see one final shot of Shemp upstairs, encased in a prison he has made out of pipes. It might have been nice for this to have been Shemp's last screen moment. Yeah, right. Snap out of it. They were determined to use the dead Shemp until they replaced him.

SLAP COUNT: 3
EYE POKES: 2
CONKING HEADS: 2
PIES THROWN: 15

Commotion on the Ocean,

1956. With Gene Roth, Emil Sitka, Harriette Tarler, Charles Wilson. Story and screenplay by Felix Adler. Produced and directed by Jules White.

Hoofs and Goofs, 1957.

Mercifully, the last short in which Shemp is visible. Short begins in the office of J. L. Cameron, managing editor of the *Daily Gazette*. The office is abuzz with news that a spy has stolen atomic documents. The Stooges, who are office cleaners, want to break in as reporters. This flimsy intro bridges into the 1949 short *Dunked in the Deep*, when the Stooges had befriended a spy who hid microfilm in watermelons and got the Stooges to stow away with him on a boat headed for home. They battle the spy, played by Gene Roth, and knock him out. "Oh, boy, we got our scoop, we're reporters from now on," says Moe. "All we gotta do is notify the boss." And, with that, almost a year after he abruptly dropped dead on the ride home from the fights, Shemp is officially retired as a member of the Three Stooges.

SLAP COUNT: 6
CONKING HEADS: 1

Hoofs and Goofs,

1957. With Benny Rubin, Harriette Tarler, Tony the Wonder Horse. Story and screenplay by Jack White. Produced and directed by Jules White.

This features the first star billing for a nonhuman being in a Stooge short, and it is a White-wash in terms of creative credit. (Jules and brother Jack handle all the duties. Jack has been weaving new story lines into the footage from old shorts, but here he comes up with a new one and gets the story credit that usually goes elsewhere.) This short is most memorable for unveiling new Stooge Joe Besser. The pudgy Joe reads a book on reincarnation and laments the death of sister Bertie (a photo shows Moe in a wig). Moe and Larry talk about sending him to an institution, citing the fact he also thinks he's a chicken. Notes Larry: "We need the eggs." (That joke first surfaced in the 1952 short *Listen, Judge.*) Turns out Joe's not crazy because Bertie is now a talking horse who says hello to the boys in a chance meeting on the street. After getting reacquainted with sis, they promptly kidnap her and bring her to the apartment. She doesn't go easy—she swats at Larry and Joe with her tail until Larry ties a brick to it, which only makes their punishment a bit more painful. Once they get the horse into the apartment, the landlord gets suspicious—Bertie smashes the floor, dropping pieces of the ceiling into the landlord's dinner one floor below. At about this time, we get the feeling that Besser will be different from Curly and Shemp. In fact, they are Mike Tyson and Sonny Liston compared to the new Stooge. His total wussiness is revealed when water is dumped on him and he retaliates by landing a girlish slap on Moe and crying out, "Ow, that hurrrrts." The horse gives birth to a foal, and it turns out that Joe has been dreaming and Bertie (Moe in drag) is still alive after all.

SLAP COUNT: 2

176.
Muscle Up a Little Closer,

1957. With Maxine Gates, Harriette Tarler, Ruth Godfrey, Matt Murphy. Written by Felix Adler. Produced and directed by Jules White.

This one is more of a sitcom episode than a Stooge short, and it makes strong use of Besser's unusual comic skills. His girlfriend, an oversize blonde, is distraught because her diamond ring is missing from her locker. They suspect Elmo Drake, the burly trucking foreman who had a passkey to the lockers and who heard her boast about the rock. There are some good gags that take place in the shipping plant, such as when Besser uses rope to wrap a package and winds up sewing it to his shirt. After they've destroyed much of the merchandise, they send Joe to the gym, where his girlfriend, the inappropriately named Tiny, cleans and presses a barbell. She then pins her wussyboy beau to the mat when she passes the weight to him. Elmo grabs Joe in a headlock and Joe comes away with a soap impression the trucking foreman has made with the key. Tiny takes over and brains the foreman, flattening him and coming away with the ring. Tiny carries Joe off in her arms, with plans to marry.

SLAP COUNT: 6

177.

A Merry Mix-Up,

1957. Written by Felix Adler. Produced and directed by Jules White.

Another effort that is more of a sitcom than a Stooge short. Once again it's scripted by Adler, the veteran scribe who is most adept at tailoring material to its cast. Here we've got three sets of Stooges, triplets born a year apart. Moe, Larry, and Joe served in the infantry, coming away with the lowest possible honors. They're described in a voice-over as three bachelors with a weakness for striped ties, pretty girls, and more pretty girls. Louie, Max, and Jack went in the navy and never got out of boot camp but have gotten married. Luke, Morris, and Jeff were in the air corps, where they were kitchen pilots. "They'd pile it here, they'd pile it there, they'd pile it anywhere." The three sets of triplets, who've lost touch with each other, show up at the same restaurant, confounding their girlfriends and creating serious romantic complications for the nine Stooges. They come together just in time to be chased by a cleaver-wielding waiter, who's had enough of their duplicity.

SLAP COUNT: 21
EYE POKES: 3
CONKING HEADS: 1

178.

Space Ship Sappy,

1957. With Doreen Woodbury, Benny Rubin, Marilyn Hanold, Lorraine Crawford, Harriette Tarler, Emil Sitka. Written by Jack White. Produced and directed by Jules White.

Though Moe reads the stock tables, the boys are unemployed and hungry. They answer an ad from a Professor A. Rimple, asking for three sailors. Soon they learn they're sailing into space with the prof and his beautiful blond daughter, earning $300 a month. They go to the moon, by way of Sunev (Venus spelled backward, for the non-dyslexic). Thinking they're doomed, the boys proclaim they're going to die. "I can't die," pleads Besser. "I haven't seen *The Eddy Duchin Story* yet." They land on the planet and encounter tall supermodel-looking cannibals, who chew on the boys' faces, tie them to poles, and attempt to tickle them to death. When a giant lizard comes, the girls flee, and the boys take off in the ship, but head back toward a crash landing when they destroy the "ascend" handle. As they're upside down, heading to their doom, they're suddenly on a podium in a banquet hall, accepting a trophy from Emil Sitka, at the 27th Annual Liars Club Convention. Aside from Eddy Duchin and an Elvis Presley mention, there's not much to recommend this one.

SLAP COUNT: 3
CONKING HEADS: 1

Guns-A-Poppin', 1957.

179.

Guns-A-Poppin',

1957. With Frank Sully, Joe Palma, Vernon Dent. Story by Jack White, Elwood Ullman. Screenplay by Jack White. Produced and directed by Jules White.

We're back to pillaging the oldies, and this time Jules White has gone all the way back to the 1945 vintage Curly short *Idiots DeLuxe*. Call this a combination remake and rip-off of the original, with original footage interspersed with the needed new shots to put Joe Besser into the Curly role. Short opens with Moe defending himself in court against charges that he assaulted his roommates with intent to commit mayhem. An ax handle is evidence. After Moe and the judge compare scars for their respective operations to repair "crushed grapeseeds," Moe goes into a story about how his business was failing and a nervous breakdown resulted. That wasn't helped by Larry and Joe practicing their "The Original Two-Man Quartet" act. After some battling, the trio heads to the country for some peace and quiet in a cabin. "This area's fine for hunting," says Joe. "I saw a sign that said 'Fine for Hunting.'" After the breakfast disappears courtesy of a bear, the story line veers into original territory. The sheriff is after Mad Bill Hiccup, who wanders into their cabin. When the boys catch the bad guy, the sheriff tells them about the $10,000 reward. So pleased are they to save Moe's business with the dough that they hug the sheriff, allowing Hiccup to pick up and go. Moe then tries to behead his buddies. Back to the courtroom, where Moe's acquitted and brains the boys with the ax handle once more.

SLAP COUNT: 1
CONKING HEADS: 1

Horsing Around,

1957. With Emil Sitka, Harriette Tarler, Tony the Wonder Horse. Story and screenplay by Felix Adler. Produced and directed by Jules White.

A sequel to Besser's first short, *Hoofs and Goofs,* in which Joe's sister, Bertie, was reincarnated as a horse. Even though the original ended with its being a dream, she's a horse again. Her mate, the circus horse Schnapps, is going to be destroyed, so says the radio. The Stooges go with their sister to save the horse, with Moe and Larry engaging in a bit of fun horseplay, getting into a horse costume to fill in for an about-to-be-killed Schnapps.

SLAP COUNT: 3
CONKING HEADS: 1

Rusty Romeos,

1957. With Connie Cezan. Story by Felix Adler. Screenplay by Jack White. Produced and directed by Jules White.

This effort, essentially a rip-off/remake of the 1952 short *Corny Casanovas,* is highlighted by the most egregious continuity gaffe featured in the latter shorts that interspersed new and old footage. The boys are crowing about having found the perfect woman—and just as in the original, they're unwittingly fixated on the same dame. There's some new footage here, but they've used the original scene in which each guy visits the same girl and presents her with a ring. There's new footage of Besser giving the girl both a picture and a ring, and that's where the great gaffe comes in. When the boys figure out they're dating the same gold digger, they begin to fight. Joe apparently intends to make the belly bump his signature attack move, but again he's not a spirited pugilist in the Stooge tradition. After Moe knocks down Larry and uses a fireplace tool to fill his belly with soot, Larry strikes back and knocks Moe across the living room. There, in clear sight, is the photo of Besser that the gold digger has placed on the table. Only this time the photo features the distinctively ugly mug of Shemp! In the next shot, Joe's mug is back in the picture. He ends the short by dropping a hundred-dollar bill, which the woman quickly bends to retrieve. Besser machine-guns her posterior with upholstery tacks and paddles her butt with the rifle barrel, calling her a "jezebel." It's a funny word when he says it.

SLAP COUNT: 8
EYE POKES: 2

182.

Outer Space Jitters,

1957. With Emil Sitka, Gene Roth, Philip Van Zandt, Don Blocker. Written by Jack White. Produced and directed by Jules White.

Opens with a legend: "The Planet of Sunev Somewhere in Outer Space (Sunev is Venus spelled backwards)." A rocket ship arrives, carrying the Stooges and Sitka. He's Professor Jones and they're his aides. The Stooges take advantage of the gorgeous females (the atomic electricity that flows through the women's veins makes kissing a problem, but the boys get over it). The professor learns that the aliens have unearthed cavemen they'll use to take over earth. From there, it's a long chase sequence, with the boys figuring out that water short-circuits the aliens.

SLAP COUNT: 7

183.

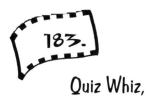

Quiz Whiz,

1958. With Greta Thyssen, Gene Roth, Milton Frome, Emil Sitka, Bill Brauer. Written by Searle Kramer. Produced and directed by Jules White.

Joe wins a $15,000 jackpot, and the boys find he's made a seemingly unwise investment in Consolidated Fujiyama California Smog Bags. After a visit

Quiz Whiz, 1958.

from the IRS (Sitka, asking for a $5,900 share), the boys head off to get their money back. The swindlers send them dressed as kids to be taken care of by a rich guy (actually accomplices who plan to bump off our boys with rat poison). After Joe turns white eating a whole Cuban cigar, and Larry's Lothario-like attempts to make time with a curvaceous blond beauty ends when she brains him with a Louisville Slugger, the Stooges fight back and prevail. They get the check back, Moe tears it in thirds, plus an extra little for the IRS. They're happy, until they realize they've torn up the check and look for glue.

SLAP COUNT: 11
EYE POKES: 1
PIES THROWN: 1 (a cake)
MEMORABLE LINE: Beautiful villainess to children (Stooges): "How would you like to play games?" Larry, in Little Lord Fauntleroy attire: "That's what I was thinking, woof woof. How about post office?" Moll: "That's a kid's game." Larry: "Not the way I play it."

184.

Fifi Blows Her Top,

1958. With Vanda DuPre, Philip Van Zandt, Harriette Tarler, Christine McIntyre. Written by Felix Adler. Produced and directed by Jules White.

Joe frets about his long-lost love Fifi, and the boys begin reminiscing about long-lost loves. That's as good an excuse as any to segue to *Love at First Bite,* the 1950 short. Larry falls in love in Italy as he sloppily eats spaghetti in a restaurant; Moe meets his love after knocking on the door and wrestling with a beautiful blonde in the mess she's made while mopping; Joe talks about his time with Fifi in Paris and how she "used to show me the parisites." This is interspersed with Shemp footage as they fall in love. Besser's scenes are indoors while Shemp's were outdoors, and the contrast in shadows as a dog rubs against Shemp's leg shows the inconsistencies. Besser is then grabbed by MPs for going AWOL and is shipped out. By the time he gets back, Fifi's gone. Turns out, of course, she has moved in just next door and is married. They manage to soak her and give her their pajamas, and get into the familiar routine, hiding her from the jealous husband. Only this time the hubby wants to get rid of her, and she finds out and brains him good.

SLAP COUNT: 6

Pies and Guys, 1958.

185.

Pies and Guys,

1958. With Greta Thyssen, Milton Frome, Gene Roth, Emil Sitka, Harriette Tarler, Helen Dickson. Written by Jack White. Produced and directed by Jules White.

This short is a straight remake of the Curly classic *Hoi Polloi,* with the pie battle from the first remake of that short, 1947's *Half-Wits' Holiday,* thrown in for good measure. This remake of a remake might well be the funniest short Joe Besser made with the Stooges. It's fairly faithful to previous incarnations, the story of two eggheads arguing over whether heredity or environment molds gentlemen. A $1,000 bet is wagered just as the Stooges enter to remove a gas pipe. The bettors then quiz the boys. "If you have one dollar and your father gives you one dollar, how many dollars do you have?" Larry: "That's easy, one dol-

Pies and Guys.

186.

Sweet and Hot,

1958. With Muriel Landers. Story by Jerome S. Gottler. Screenplay by Jerome S. Gottler, Jack White. Produced and directed by Jules White.

A Besser-sized farmgirl belts out an elegant version of "Let's Fall in Love" as she serenades a cow into giving milk. We see a montage of animals, and Larry, dancing. She's Tiny, who, per Larry, "is prettier than a spotted heifer." She's easily as large as one. Larry wants to bring her and Joe back to vaudeville. They're not swayed by the prospect of money and the fame but are hooked when Larry begins describing all the food opportunities in the big city. "When do we eat, I mean leave," says Tiny. First, they need to cure her fear of singing in front of people. Moe is Hugo Gansamacher, M.D., the psychiatrist/psychologist. He gets Tiny to have a cosmic flashback. She's a child, screeching "Three Blind Mice," and her father (Moe) tries to whip her when she won't sing. She's cured and sings, with Joe and Larry doing a tap dance.

SLAP COUNT: 1
CONKING HEADS: 2

lar." "You don't know your arithmetic," he's chided. "You don't know my father," Larry replies. Most of the dialogue and gags are the same as the better-executed original effort. There's even some pie fight footage from the original.

SLAP COUNT: 7
PIES THROWN: 25

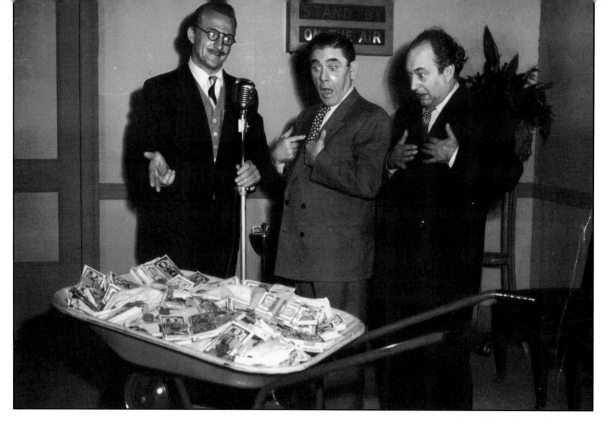

Flying Saucer Daffy, 1958.

187.

Flying Saucer Daffy,

1958. With Gail Bonney, Emil Sitka, Bek Nelson, Diana Darrin. Written by Jack White. Produced and directed by Jules White.

In a takeoff on *Cinderella*, a toothless woman is shown swigging liquor and living in squalor. Moe and Larry are her adored sons, Joe the abused stepchild. Asked to get her a drink, Joe gives her water and she does a spit take, bellowing, "Water! Don't ever do that again." Joe heads off on a vacation and takes a photo of a pie plate that Moe and Larry enter in the Facts and Figures contest to find a flying saucer. They win $10,000. Once they've about emptied the wheelbarrow full of money, they're exposed as frauds. After Stepmom gives Joe some clever double slapping and eye poking, he is kicked out. Joe's visited by some real Martians, who are of the leggy female variety. It's hardly as dramatic as *Close Encounters of the Third Kind,* as we see a pie plate landing and a spandex-clad woman announcing that she's "Electra from Planet Zircon, we want to make friends with you earth people." She gives him a shot of the space-craft and a good-bye kiss. The boys don't believe him and he cashes in the photo himself. He's next seen riding in a ticker-tape parade, the alien lovelies alongside him.

SLAP COUNT: 20
EYE POKES: 3
CONKING HEADS: 1
PIES THROWN: 1

Oil's Well That Ends Well, 1958.

him to plug up the well when they strike oil, with Joe bobbing in the air, screaming, "I'm an unsuccessful cork," just as Curly did in the more successful original.

SLAP COUNT: 18
EYE POKES: 3 (another 2 blocked)

Triple Crossed,

1958. With Angela Stevens, Mary Ainslee, Diana Darrin. Written by Warren Wilson. Produced and directed by Jules White.

Still more pillaged footage from an old short. This time it's *He Cooked His Goose* from 1952, when Larry was a three-timing pet shop owner out to frame Shemp for having a romance that would

Triple Crossed, 1958.

Oil's Well That Ends Well,

1958. Written by Felix Adler. Produced and directed by Jules White.

The boys are unemployed and worried about their father. He's hospitalized and in need of an operation. Dad tells them to go to his mining property and find uranium. What they find is a remake of the 1939 Curly classic *Oily to Bed, Oily to Rise*. It's not an exact remake, but, like Curly, Joe wishes on things and gets them. And they use

free up his girl to marry Larry. It opens with Larry courting a beautiful blonde. When she says, "I have a date with Joe," you can see her mouth saying the word "Shemp." The short uses insert shots each time Besser comes into play, but it follows the original story line faithfully.

SLAP COUNT: 11
EYE POKES: 1
CONKING HEADS: 1

190.

Sappy Bullfighters,

1958. With Greta Thyssen, George Lewis. Written by Jack White. Produced and directed by Jules White.

Opens in Mexico, "where men are men and women are glad of it." Pan to a show marquee in Spanish, where "The Three Stooges" are crossed out. Backstage, they're crying over their bad luck. Greta, a gorgeous blond headliner, gets them a job at the bullring. They mix up suitcases, and her jealous husband thinks she's two-timing with Besser. It's the story line out of the 1942 Curly short *What's the Matador,* where the husband gets revenge by setting loose a real bull in the ring for a battle with Curly, who charges and knocks out the bull. Joe does the same. Here the insert shots of Joe are pathetic. It's tough to put him in Curly situations, because he's no match for Curly Howard. A comparison shows that it couldn't have been a tough decision for Columbia to stop the shorts at this point, because they were obviously just filling out their quota.

SLAP COUNT: 17
EYE POKES: 1

INDEX

ABOUT THE AUTHOR

Anna Fleming

Michael Fleming is a columnist for
Variety who lives in New York State.
The Three Stooges™ is his first book.